The Roots of

The Roots of Perestroika

The Soviet Breakdown in Historical Context

SIDNEY PLOSS

McFarland & Company, Inc., Publishers
Jefferson, North Carolina, and London

LIBRARY OF CONGRESS CATALOGUING-IN-PUBLICATION DATA

Ploss, Sidney I.
    The roots of perestroika : the Soviet breakdown in historical
context / by Sidney Ploss.
        p.   cm.
    Includes bibliographical references and index.

    ISBN 978-0-7864-4486-1
    softcover : 50# alkaline paper ∞

    1. Soviet Union — Politics and government.   2. Soviet
Union — Economic conditions.   3. Soviet Union — Foreign
relations.   4. Perestroika — History.   5. Social change — Soviet
Union — History.   6. Heads of state — Soviet Union — History.
7. Gorbachev, Mikhail Sergeevich, 1931–   — Influence.
8. Gorbachev, Mikhail Sergeevich, 1931–   — Political and social
views.   I. Title.
DK266.3.P465   2010
947.085'4 — dc22   2009037616

British Library cataloguing data are available

Front cover photograph ©2010 Shutterstock

Manufactured in the United States of America

*McFarland & Company, Inc., Publishers
   Box 611, Jefferson, North Carolina 28640
   www.mcfarlandpub.com*

To Monique

"Theory is theory, but practice — real politics — always has the last word."

— Mikhail Gorbachev, *Memoirs*

"In this country a lot depends on the leader's personality, way of thinking, moods, likes and dislikes."

— Anatoly Chernyaev, Gorbachev aide, 1984

"You cannot agree with those who propose to forget history or to use only some parts of it. Now we understand that this approach is unacceptable. Without a thorough examination of the past we will not know the roots of many tendencies that have affected us."

— Mikhail Gorbachev, January 1988

Table of Contents

Preface

The 2008 border war between Russia and Georgia showed the dust still had not settled from the collapse of the Soviet Union in 1991. Dissolution of the USSR was indeed a milestone in world affairs with ongoing repercussions that can be difficult to predict. The Soviet Union was a police state with a vast arsenal of modern weapons and forward bases in its satellite states of eastern Europe. Behind the Kremlin wall secretive leaders vied for decades with Western rivals for global influence. East-West crises over Berlin (1948) and Cuba (1962) might have gotten out of hand, and an exchange of nuclear weapons resulted in a death toll of over 200 million. We shall see that a Soviet defense minister once startled civilian associates with advice to take action that risked the outbreak of war with the United States. The world has become a somewhat safer place since the crumbling of the Soviet empire.

During the late 1980s Soviet president Mikhail Gorbachev democratized his closed political system under the reform program of perestroika or restructuring. He presented the gift of freedom to eastern Europeans and ended the U.S.–Soviet competition for strategic advantage. Boris Yeltsin, first president of the liberalized Russian Federation, replaced the remnants of the Soviet command economy with free markets.

Since then Russian reality has remained complicated. On the one hand, Vladimir Putin after succeeding Yeltsin in 1999 tightened up inside his country. He created a regime that earned unfavorable ratings from foreign watchdog bodies concerning political rights, corruption, favoritism in governmental decisions, protection of property rights and independence of the judiciary. On the other hand, Russians under Putin were freer than they had been in Communist days: 120,000 millionaires and over 50 billionaires emerged; local computer search companies were able to service over 20 million Internet users without political interference; over 700 nongovernmental organizations were functioning and native journalists published op-ed

1

pieces in the Western press that were unfavorable to the Kremlin but suffered no reprisals.

All told, the new Russian system can be categorized as semi-authoritarian and designed largely to check unbridled regional separatism. What drove the Gorbachev reforms, which came as a major surprise to foreign observers? Just a few years before a former U.S. national-security official painted a gloomy picture of the Soviet horizon: "the likelihood of a round of economic-political experiments seems quite remote.... One can foresee a leadership more or less tied to conservative elements, doomed to maneuver within narrow limits, caught up in an economic crisis but unable to adopt policies that would constitute a decisive solution."[1] Shortly after Gorbachev's accession a strategic historian absolutized the Russian tradition of concern for safety of the homeland. He warned that it was most unlikely that any regime in Moscow would liberalize or sharply cut defense spending.[2]

Once these grim forecasts proved to be wrong the thrust of public commentary was that external pressures drove the Kremlin to make sweeping internal changes. U.S. President Ronald Reagan's policy of intensifying the arms race and Pope John Paul II's patronage of the free trade union Solidarity in Poland were credited with triggering the Soviet convulsion. American Secretary of State Condoleeza Rice held that Reagan's success as a presidential candidate "made it possible to spend the Soviet Government into a rapid collapse." U.S. Vice President Richard B. Cheney hailed Reagan and John Paul for having cast off "the stagnation of imperial dictatorship." A Washington think-tank fellow alleged that "it simply took the optimism of a Ronald Reagan to reverse the Communists' notion that capitalism would die of its own contradictions."

The reader will learn that Kremlin leaders viewed Reagan as a "clown." Gorbachev thought he was dangerous and incapable of understanding Soviet motivations. Only after Reagan's visit to Moscow in June 1988 did Gorbachev tell the Politburo that the U.S. President had become a realist who had tardily changed his mistaken opinions. Former high-ranking Soviet officials have further scoffed at the idea that Reagan's missile-defense vision (Star Wars) was the catalyst for Gorbachev's revitalization initiatives. They believe that Reagan's mirage failed to arouse any serious interest in Moscow ruling circles.[3]

The most plausible case for external influence on Soviet official thinking is made by Jiri Pehe writing about the 1968 political liberalization in Communist Czechoslovakia: "Ideas generated during the Prague Spring were a source of inspiration for Mikhail Gorbachev's glasnost and perestroika in the mid–1980s. Like the Czechoslovakian leaders of 1968, Mr. Gorbachev believed that a degree of political and economic democracy could be combined with communist rule."

What follows is a study of Russian and Soviet experiences that framed the conduct of Gorbachev's perestroika. That reform program originated in ideas that developed prior to and under Soviet rule. The dynamic Soviet leader knew of these historical moments and thoughts for several reasons: his people's strong oral tradition; party documents outlining and condemning policy deviations; Karl Marx's writings on human alienation; verbatim records of debates at Bolshevik party congresses during the Lenin era; authorized translations of Eurocommunist studies of the Soviet past; and personal interviews with Stalin-era officials. Besides, Gorbachev was an eyewitness to Chairman Nikita Khrushchev's anti–Stalin campaigns and those indictments of arbitrary rule would be at the heart of perestroika. What Gorbachev failed to realize was that old anti–Russian national movements would revive once he allowed pluralism to flourish on the Soviet scene.

A few words about how this study is organized. Those seeking the sources of German National Socialism (Nazism) do not begin with the events immediately preceding the advent to power of Adolf Hitler in 1933. They first look back 60 or 70 years to the influential writings of German nationalist and racialist theorists. The centerpiece of perestroika was the rekindling of liberal democratic ideas from the late tsarist period. Once Gorbachev broke with the shadowy elite politics of Sovietism, competing policy agendas and diverse constituencies arose for attacking major issues of socioeconomic, nationality and foreign affairs. The clash of rival platforms and personal ambitions led to cratering of the Soviet regime. This inquiry, accordingly, begins with a review of the harbingers of a modern body politic in Imperial Russia. Unlike rigidly ideological studies, our narrative attaches importance to the hand that Old Russia dealt to Soviet leaders: geographic vulnerability, ethnic diversity, general poverty and arbitrary governance. Then emergence of lesser Gorbachevs through the course of Soviet history is surveyed. Final chapters address the unfolding of perestroika with the aid of recent documentation that was unavailable to earlier investigators. An Epilogue summarizes main points and comments on analyses of Soviet affairs performed in the Western world.

Bibliophiles may be interested in the primary sources on Soviet leadership evolution under Stalin (1923–1938), Khrushchev (1954–1964) and Gorbachev (1985–1991) that have lately been published in the Russian Federation: *Stenogrammy zasedaniy Politbyuro TsK RKP (b)-VKP (b) 1923–1928 gg. V trekh tomalh* (Moscow: Rosspen, 2007), abbreviated: *SZP*; *Prezidium TsK KPSS 1954–1064 Chernovye protokolnye zapisi zasedani Stenogrammy postanovleniya* (Moscow: Rosspen, 2004–2008); and *V Politbyuro TsK KPSS. Po zapisyam Anatoliya Chernyayeva, Vadima Medvedeva, Georgiya Shakhnazarova (1985–1991). Sost. A. Chernyayeva (ruk. Proyekta), A. Veber, V. Medvedeva. Izdaniye 2-e, ispravlenoye i dopolnennoye* (Moscow: Gorbachev-Fond, 2008), abbreviated: *VPB*. These materials enable a better understanding of Kremlin thinking insofar as they are minutes or notes taken at decision-making sessions under Stalin, Khrushchev and Gorbachev. Unfortunately, these records fail to cast light on vital developments such as policy talks prior to the 1934 assassination of Politburo member Sergei Kirov, which set in motion the greatest Stalinist purges, and the May 1960 Kremlin shakeup of the party command, which occurred on the heels of the shootdown of a U.S. spy plane over the Soviet Union. Other informative party and secret police documents are on the website of the late Aleksandr Yakovlev's International Democracy Foundation: www.idf.ru.

Groundbreaking work in archives was done by historians Yuri Aksenov, Nikolai Barsukov, Oleg Khlevniuk, Leonid Naumov, Aleksei Osipov, Rudolf Pikhoya, Anatoly Ponomarev, Boris Starkov, Dmitri Volkogonov, Aleksandr Yakovlev, Yuri Zhukov and Yelena Zubkova. The works of Pikhoya and Zhukov showcase an assortment of Politburo documents from Stalin to Gorbachev. Oral history was the specialty of dissident scholars Anton Antonov-Ovseyenko and Roy Medvedev, whose findings were illuminating. M. E. Glavatsky of the A. M. Gorky Urals State University is to be commended for having led a number of Russian scholars who compiled the collection of Soviet documents from 1917 around which British scholars Edward Acton and Tom Stableford built rich volumes. The memoirs of former Soviet officials deserve scrutiny in the absence of full records of the policymaking Politburo. This is true of the reminiscences of Aleksei Adzhubey, Abel Aganbegyan, Georgi Arbatov, Fyodr Burlatsky, Anatoly Chernyaev, Anatoly Dobrynin, Mikhail Gorbachev, Nikita Khrushchev, Yegor Ligachev, Anastas Mikoyan, Vladimir Novikov, Yevgeny Primakov, Pyotr Rodionov, Georgi Shakhnazarov Dmitri Shepilov, Oleg Troyanovsky, Gennadi Voronov and Boris Yeltsin. The Ellman-Kontorovich interviews with former Soviet officials and scholars offer some cogent opinions on the Soviet economic crash.

CHAPTER 1

A False Dawn of Freedom

The balance between Russian history and Marxist theory in the making of Soviet politics has prompted intense debate. Professor John Lewis Gaddis is one of the believers in the primacy of ideology as shaper of Kremlin behavior. Gaddis, however, does recognize that during the 1960s the age-old hostility between Russia and China overshadowed the commitment of Khrushchev and Chinese leader Mao Zedong to a common doctrine.[1] There is also much to argue that Russian traditions influenced the first Soviet leaders. A tsarist bureaucrat might easily have recognized the new Bolshevik regime as a variation on the native theme of bureaucratic centralism. Since the late 1920s Stalin promoted the glorification of Tsars whose state-building actions predated his own. Each was bound by the constraints of world politics, ethnicity and regionalism. All that followed would also be subject to the historical law that events are often stronger than the plans of men.

At the start of the twentieth century the direction that Russia would take was a matter of concern to the international diplomatic, financial and military worlds.[2] The Russian Empire stretched over one-sixth of the globe's surface, from the Baltic and Black seas in the west to the Pacific port of Vladivostok in the east. Russia was the most populous country in Europe, its 1897 census reporting 125,700,000 inhabitants. The population of towns numbered only 16,289,00 or about 13 percent of the total population. Two-thirds of the people were Slavic: Great Russians, 44 percent; Ukrainians, 18 percent; and Belorussians, 5 percent.

The nationality border areas were crucially important at the start and finish of the Soviet experiment. Imperial Russian centralization inflamed national feelings in the western provinces, Baltics and Caucasus. Georgians were in the front ranks of those who craved independence. Their most prominent leaders were the aristocrats led by Prince Machabelli, Social

Democrats, Federalists and Nationalists, whose most illustrious figures were Irakly Tseretelli and the brothers Leo and George Kereselidze. Of the other non–Slavic ethnic groups of the empire, Muslims constituted 11 percent; Poles, 6 percent; and Jews, 4 percent. Muslims were concentrated in the Volga valley, Caucasus and Central Asia. Many were loyal subjects of the Tsar thanks to the presence of Russian troops and exercise of the tactics of divide-and-keep-conquered.

Roman Catholic Poles staged uprisings in the 1830s and 1860s, and Warsaw was a hotbed of terrorism. Jews needed special permission to reside outside the Pale of Settlement in western Russia and no more than 6,500 lived in Moscow. Anti-Jewish mob violence (pogroms) was rife into the 20th century. In 1911 a Blood Libel trial was held in Kiev and while a jury acquitted the defendant of ritually murdering a Christian boy, Jew-hatred was pervasive and remained so. Oppression or poverty caused millions of Poles and Jews to emigrate to North America.

The German colonists of Inner Russia numbered 2 million and had the highest birth rate in Europe. Some had begun to settle in the Baltics prior to World War I. The German landowning aristocracy was only about 7 percent of the population of the Baltic provinces and ruled with little Russian interference. Its members were eager to build a counterweight to the growing national activity of Letts and Estonians.

In general it was to the benefit of revolutionaries that the Russian Empire resembled more a prison house of the peoples than melting pot. Poles, Jews, Balts and Georgians were especially prominent in revolutionary circles. Under Stalin only the Georgians as compatriots of the Leader would prosper and the others would be subject to suspicion as likely collaborators of hostile foreign states or movements.

Geography seriously impacted the attitudes and character of the Great Russians. One chaotic age followed another on the vast Eurasian steppe until the Rus state was formed in 862. It was named after the Normans or Vikings of Scandinavia who were the original settlers. It cannot be repeated too often that security was usually uppermost in Russian thought. The national community early sensed that absolute monarchy was best suited to fend off the nomadic tribes which drifted into the steppe. Later it was pressure from Lithuania, Poland and Sweden that imposed on the Russians the creation of modern military forces. The share of the state budget spent on military needs ranged from 85 percent in the 17th century to 60 to 70 percent during the 18th century to 50 percent under Nicholas I in the 19th century.

The immensity of their living space made endurance a necessity for the Russians. Climatic conditions were also important in molding national character. The breadbasket of Ukraine in the south was one of the few regions with favorable conditions for agriculture. Elsewhere only one or two months a year could be devoted to field work because of rainy or cold weather, and in some dry spots poor harvests were experienced in 75 of every 100 years. Until the peasants were freed from serfdom in 1861 the dangers of the steppe prevented most from fleeing oppressive landlords and tax collectors. In sum, a culture of fear and tenacity were products of the Russian's environment that his masters long exploited.

The legendary cruelty of Russian rulers is attributed to the dominance of Mongol invaders for over 200 years of the medieval era. An example of royal severity was Tsar Ivan the Terrible's massacre of 60,000 citizens of Novgorod in 1570 for having resisted the town's annexation to Muscovy. Peter the Great flogged, tortured and beheaded many religious dissenters. Although the scale of royal brutality diminished over time, Queen Victoria dubbed Russian Emperor Alexander III (1881–1894) "barbaric, Asiatic and tyrannical." Still popular among his compatriots is the aphorism of Alexander III that "Russia's best friends are its army and navy." His son Nicholas II (1894–1918) had no better reputation in the outer world.

Religion and alcohol offered comfort to the oppressed lower classes. Whatever their moral scruples, ordinary Russians were devoted to the rituals of the Greek Orthodox ("Right thinking") Church. The Church was an instrument of the supreme monarchy, which paid the salaries of village priests and expected them to teach literacy and Holy Writ, as well as act as police informers. Unlike the fanatical Christian sects, which embraced one-tenth of the population, Orthodoxy was unable to curb the wholesale drunkenness that afflicted its peasant devotees. Vodka was used to bribe peasants who ran village affairs and served as judges in district courts. Some intellectuals were dubious of the ethical standards of their lower-class neighbors. The 19th-century historian Nikolai Karamzin when asked to describe the common folk responded "Voryut" or "They steal." In the last years of tsarism the parish clergy urged glasnost* to win recognition of their poverty. Bishops frowned on the grumbling and often were religious bigots and uncritical regime loyalists. In return, the most extreme revolutionists who took power exacted a great toll in clerical lives and treasure.

The Russian terms "perestroika" and "glasnost" are central to the topic of this work and are not italicized in the text.

Against this harsh background, the social profile of Russia in 1900 differed sharply from that of western Europe. The gentry, professional and business classes made up about 7 percent of the nation. Peasants and industrial workers accounted for 93 percent. Only one in five Russians was literate and 1 percent had a higher education. Disparities in wealth were huge. The Court nobles, a few of them who owned large estates, and big businessmen were affluent. Wealthiest was young Prince Felix Yusupov, who possessed 17 estates, five factories, a coal mine in Ukraine, eight rental properties and five palaces. His income in 1914 reached 1,260,000 rubles. A slightly larger middle class was more or less comfortable.

The landowning nobility prided itself in playing "the leading role" in society. They numbered only 20,000 but since the peasants were freed from serfdom held the most fertile soil and rented land to them. The offerings to peasants declined as noble proprietors began to stay in their manors and farm more arable. This resulted from less opportunities to make a career in state service and professionalization of the bureaucracy. Overall, the gentry estates were progressing with the introduction of new farming methods, foreign machinery and development of commercial concerns. But the peasants were becoming more alienated from the gentlemen due to the land-hunger (*malozemele*) while gentlemen saw the villagers as simple-minded children, whom they addressed as such.

The multitudes of peasants and workers were dirt poor. Heavy taxes on peasants and the low wages of workers meant that their diet and housing were inadequate. The standards of popular hygiene were low: rural families often vacated their wooden huts every few winters and moved into the forests where they waited for freezing winds to destroy the vermin-infested dwellings. Workers were crammed into shabby tenements, barracks and cellars. Ironically, Aleksandr Kerensky, popular democratic premier in 1917, privately scorned Russian commoners as "dark people" (*chorn*) just before he was overthrown that autumn. One judgment on peasant Russia was reached at the British Embassy in St. Petersburg: villagers were divided between loyalty to the Tsar and a deeper desire for land and freedom from exploitation, according to historian Michael Hughes.

Tsar Nicholas II and Tsarina Alexandra Fedorovna capped the social-political pyramid. In theory and practice His Majesty's authority was absolute. He alone could issue a Supreme Command that overrode the law. A minister whom the Crown appointed might interpret a law in any way by means of a circular. The Tsar's governors were empowered to veto the decisions of *zemstva* or provincial self-government bodies or refer disputes to the Interior Minister. A step lower in the governing hierarchy were the local land captains, who exercised discretionary power over the peasantry. The Corps of Gendarmes or secret police were equally free of legal restraints. Special tribunals tried political offenders and police officers could send them to a distant town for an indefinite term of years. Working in favor of the sovereign until a 1905 massacre of protesting workers was a folk saying that "the Tsar is good but the nobles bad."

As a personality Nicholas was charming, moderately intelligent, and a good public speaker. But he was distrustful, suspicious and fatalistic. Aleksandr Tikhomirov, a high official in the Education Ministry, thought that Nicholas was "a very strange man" who "seemed intentionally to have appointed as ministers the worst and most insignificant men as if fearing they would diminish his authority."[3] One prelate wrote in a letter intercepted by the police that the Tsar was an untalented mediocrity.[4] Foreign representatives too had grave doubts about Nicholas. A British diplomat privately scoffed at the Tsar as weak, stubborn and with little savvy.[5] Well-known to courtiers was the Russian emperor's Anglophobic and anti–Semitic remark "An Englishman is a *zhid* (kike)." The left-wing militant Leon Trotsky poured scorn on Nicholas in his book *1905*: "Dull-witted and scared, an all-powerful nonentity, the prey of prejudices worthy of an Eskimo, the royal blood in his veins poisoned by all the vices of many generations, Nicholas Romanov, like many others of his profession, combines filthy sensuality with pathetic cruelty. By tearing every sacred veil from his person on January 9 [1905, the date of slaying of protesting workers in the capital], the revolution finally corrupted him. The times when he was content to remain in the shadows, using [palace commandant] Trepov as his secret service agent in pogrom affairs have gone."

The Tsar's despotic German wife incited him to distrust sensible royals. Suspicious of the moderates who induced Nicholas to grant a consultative assembly in 1906, Alexandra warned him against "those terrible political parties, which dream only of seizing power or of subjecting the government to their will." She felt the same about candidates for the posts of government ministers when Nicholas consulted her about their fitness to serve. Together they shared a conception of Russia which Nicholas dubbed "a landed estate of which the proprietor is the Tsar, the administrator is the nobility, and the workers are the peasantry." After the imaginative premier Pyotr Stolypin was assassinated in 1911 the government fell into the hands of nonentities who were Crown favorites. The most notorious was Ivan Logginovich Goremykin, reared during the iron rule of Nicholas I and named premier in 1914, aged 76. A caricaturist's delight because of his mutton-chops facial hair, Goremykin was observed to nap and read French novels during the work day.

In spite of the backwardness, Imperial Russia was heading toward modernity. A stream of European capital enabled it to rank fifth among the world's manufacturing nations. Oil production and the gold reserve were the largest in Europe. Manganese was needed for steel production and up to 1914 50 percent of the world production of manganese came from Russia, which supplied three-quarters of Germany's requirements of the ore. German heavy industry had penetrated the mineral deposits of Krivoi Rog and Chiaturi in Ukraine and Caucasus. The German Thyssen concern was part owner of the Chiaturi manganese mines. German banks financed these plans through ties with Russian banks, since big profits could be made out of Russia's need for armaments. Later a German aim in World War I would be to open, expand and modernize the Georgian Black Sea port of Poti. Overall, Russian industrial growth was at an impressive annual rate of 6 percent. Since the famine of 1891–1892, which claimed over ten million lives, Russia was self-sufficient in basic foodstuffs. It was the world's fourth leading grain exporter thanks to 30,000 private estates that were in many cases efficiently run by German stewards.

It was the vast grain exports that paid for the importation of machinery for the start-up of Russian industrialization. The marketed grain was supplied by the large estates and taxation of the peasant communes. "We will starve but export!" was the famous remark of Finance Minister Ivan Vyshnegradsky. About 8 million are indeed estimated to have died of hunger and relatable causes in 1901–1911. General Staff Colonel Prince Bagration wrote in 1901 that only one in three Russian army recruits was physically fit for service and 40 percent had never tasted meat before entering the army. The words of Vyshnegradsky might have been uttered by a Stalin fundamentalist during the 1930s, when the new party-run collective farms pumped grain out of the villages for very little payment so that it could be shipped abroad to secure heavy industrial goods.

Stalin's apologists have argued that the dictator and his barbaric methods were necessary for the modernization of Russia. Still, on the eve of World War I a commission of the French Republic's Senate visited Russia to ascertain its credit worthiness and the depth of risk for external investors. The commission reported that Russia's development strategy was sound enough to expect that by mid-twentieth century the country would be leader in the world economic system.

A number of factors drove the Tsar to adventures in Great Power diplomacy. These included quest for national grandeur and love of military pomp, as well as need of capital for internal improvements. Nicholas disposed of Europe's largest standing army of 1.5 million, twice that of the German and 300,000 more than the German and Austrian together. It was expected that in 1917 the Russian army would reach its maximum peacetime strength of 2.2 million. But the high command, equipment, medical services and hygiene were far below modern standards. The tsarist forces met with crushing defeats at the hands of Japan in a 1904–1905 war over control of Manchuria, a region of China with rich natural resources and equal in size to the area of Germany and France. Kaiser William II in 1905 gave Russia a choice of keeping its existing alliance with republican France or signing a new pact with him. Economics counted for more than ideology in making the choice. St. Petersburg needed a sizable loan for domestic projects and that kept the Russian monarch loyal to his French partner.

Despite the setback in Asia, Russia stayed in the jockeying of rival imperialisms. An Anglo-Russian convention in August 1907 recognized a division of zones of influence in Persia, Afghanistan and Tibet. A Russo-German agreement of 1910 provided for cooperation on railroad building near the Russian-Turkish border. But the risk of conflict with Germany and Austria was escalating. The Germans in 1909 took advantage of tsarist unpreparedness for general war and humiliated Russia by insisting that it bow to an Austrian demand that the Slav statelet of Serbia renounce any claim to compensation for Austria's annexation of the Balkan provinces of Bosnia and Hercegovina. During the Balkan Wars of 1912 and 1913 Russia had again to climb down. With Serbia it conceded to Austrian pressure and demobilized rather than press a Serbian military advance to the Turks' Adriatic coast in Albania. Russia likewise yielded to the other Powers and told its Montenegran friends to give up a prized Albanian town they had wrested from the Turks.

During these years progress was made in nudging Russia away from the infamous status of police state. The gentry-led and underfunded *zemstva* or assemblies in 34 provinces grew to over 10,000 deputies in 1908, and their staffs rose to 70,000. By then most of the *zemstva* had passed resolutions critical of "the bureaucratic order" that monitored them and insisted on regular *zemstvo* participation in law-making. Appeals for glasnost was a staple on the agenda of self-government bureaus. Dmitri Shipov, head of the Moscow *zemstvo* from 1895 to 1902, argued openly for both civil liberties and freedom of publicity in financial matters. Count V. A. Bobrinsky drew official censure for advocating publicity about crop failures and the inability of officials to arrange famine relief. This pressure mounted until in 1904 a national *zemstvo* meeting voted for the immediate introduction of freedom of speech and press, and the introduction of a strong national assembly. This agitation had the effect of reducing government financial secrecy and narrowed the vaguely defined powers of governors.

The political diehards fought devolution of power and their stubbornness swelled the ranks of dissenters. To ensure social discipline little official notice was taken of the delinquencies of bureaucrats (*chinovniki*). British journalist Donald Mackenzie Wallace relates that *zemstvo* assemblies once exercised the right of publicity but lost it to the bureaucracy. Independent and vigorous action became impossible.[6] Yet, official control of political thought was far less than airtight. Underground publications were printed abroad and smuggled into Russia by a coalition of constitutionalists and socialists known since 1902 as the Union of Liberation.

The privileged class was unaware of a crisis brewing in the lower depths. As the population increased, village protests over *malozemele* rose and from 1883 to 1903 the army was used to suppress 1,500 civil disturbances. Among industrial workers, massive strikes occurred in July 1903 around the Black Sea and Caucasus. Around 200 workers were killed in the cited suppression of worker protestors in the capital in January 1905. After this "Bloody Sunday," gentry moderates vented their anger: Nine of 15 *zemstva* that were in session called for a national assembly with legislative powers, in effect urging a limitation of the tsar's authority. The Palace replied with a stiff manifesto attacking the constitutionalists as "those who propose to sever the natural connections with the past, destroy the existing state order and found the administration of the country on principles alien to the fatherland." The manifesto exhorted to combat with "the internal and external enemies of the nation." Defiantly, a *Zemstvo* Congress in April 1905 resolved that a national assembly should become a constituent assembly with its main task the creation of a state legal order with broad representation and secret ballot.

What is most dramatic is usually most important. In 1905–1906 peasants gutted almost 3,000 manors (15 percent of the total), hoping to drive the gentry off their land and into the towns. Troops were summoned at least 2,700 times to quell rural disturbances. The Japanese defeat of a Russian naval squadron in the Tsushima Strait in May 1905 led to unrest in the Black Sea Fleet. One of the battleship crews mutinied over the severity of its officers and rioting that spread to the port city of Odessa led to a massacre of civilians. This smashing of rebellion steeled the will of the tsar to assert that he forbade the adoption of universal suffrage and a standing legislature. A *zemstvo* delegation that recently met with him had implored him to take those steps.

Regime brutality provoked terrorist acts by the Anarchists and Combat Detachment of the Socialist-Revolutionary Party (PSR or SRs). Yet in 1902 the SRs produced a pamphlet, "Our Task" (*Nasha Zadacha*), which revealed the multifaceted nature of terrorism:

> One of the powerful means of struggle, dictated by our revolutionary past and present, is political Terrorism, consisting of the annihilation of the most injurious and influential personages of Russian autocracy.... Systematic Terrorism, in conjunction with other forms of open mass struggle (industrial riots and agrarian risings, demonstrations, etc.), which receive from Terrorism an enormous, decisive significance, will lead to the disorganization of the enemy. Terrorist activity will cease only with the victory over autocracy and the complete attainment of political liberty. Besides its chief significance as a means of disorganizing, Terrorist activity will serve at the same time as a means of propaganda and agitation, a form of open struggle taking place before the eyes of the whole people, undermining the prestige of Government authority, and calling into life new revolutionary forces, while the oral and literary propaganda is being continued without interruption. Lastly, the Terrorist activity serves for the whole secret revolutionary party as a means of self-defense and of protecting the organization against the injurious elements of spies and treachery.

The subsequent victims of terrorism included Interior Minister V. K. Pleve; Moscow governor general Grand Duke Sergei Aleksandrovich; and Father Georgi Gapon, creator of the Assembly of Russian Factory Workers, who was suspected of ties to the secret police. One of the most illustrious SR terrorists was Maria Spiridonova, who murdered a governor and survived rape by a guard of Cossacks, only to die at the hands of the Soviet secret police.

British ambassador Charles Hardinge sensed trouble on the eve of the 1905 revolution. In a dispatch that February he was contemptuous of the tsar's ministers as drifting and feuding. Hardinge thought the autocracy had to be reformed but Imperial rigidity and bureaucratic corruption were huge roadblocks to the onset of parliamentary government.[7]

The world's first nationwide general strike occurred in Russia in autumn 1905. At the insistence of fearful monarchists, Nicholas promised in his October Manifesto to grant civil liberties and that no law would go into effect without the approval of a popularly elected legislature. A day later, anti–Jewish and antistudent pogroms began. The revolutionaries claimed that up to 4,000 were killed and 100,000 injured in 100 towns. At the same time, peasants in the central region began to demolish landowners' houses and property. In the Baltics, Estonian and Latvian peasants threatened the German ruling class. Interior Minister Durnovo issued instructions to troops to exterminate rioters and burn their dwellings in the event of resistance. Moscow radicals were distrustful of the authorities and stayed at the barricades until over 1,000 of them were killed. In St. Petersburg a council formed to direct the strikes, the Soviet of Workers' Deputies, also fought on. It was named after the first such body that was created in the textile center of Ivanovo-Voznesensk.

The ultimate leader of the St. Petersburg Soviet was an event-making individual and one of the most colorful political figures of the 20th century. Leon Trotsky was born in 1879 as Leib Bronshtein, the son of a rich Jewish farmer in Ukraine.[8] Young Trotsky attended high schools and became renowned as brilliant and self-centered. At age 18 he joined the commune of a local Czech socialist and the abolition of private property became his cherished life-long goal. He was arrested and deported to Siberia with his radical wife for spreading the ideas of Marxism among dockworkers in Odessa. The alias "Trotsky" dated from this period and was taken from a jail guard.

Some of the biting articles Trotsky wrote for the provincial and foreign press were reprinted in the newspaper of Russian Social-Democrats abroad. The editors of *Iskra* (The Spark) called their new contributor "Pen." He escaped from Siberia in 1902 and that October arrived in London and met Lenin, who correctly sized him up as someone "of exceptional abilities, staunch, energetic, who will go further." Trotsky was invited to join the editorial board of *Iskra*, lectured in European capitals and met socialist leaders. All this set Trotsky apart from rough militants of the socialist underground inside Russia. The personal jealousies that underlay future power conflicts between Trotskyites and Stalinists were nurtured in these years.

Trotsky broke with Lenin at a 1903 congress of Russian Social-Democrats in Brussels and London. Representing Siberian exiles, Trotsky staked out an independent position between the Jewish Workers' Union (Bund), which sought party federalism, and Lenin, advocate of a centralized movement of full-time revolutionaries. A walkout of the Bund and others from the congress over personnel matters split the Social-Democrats into Leninist *bolsheviki* (majoritarians) and *mensheviki* (minoritarians), whom Trotsky joined.

Known to European socialists as "the warring brothers," Bolsheviks and Mensheviks had a raft of differences. The historical importance of the

Mensheviks is that reform Communists were to inherit from them a belief in the worth of democratic and humane sentiments. The more radical Bolsheviks were less afraid of the volatile peasantry and more wary of liberals ready to compromise with the tsarist regime. At first, Lenin urged a "democratic dictatorship of the proletariat and peasantry," without immediately abolishing private property. Having overthrown absolute monarchy, Russians would enjoy political and civil rights, free compulsory schooling and separation of church and state.

The authoritarian personality of Lenin indicates that his democratic credentials were minimal. In any event, Bolsheviks approved and Mensheviks balked at robberies and embezzlements to refill party coffers. After the Bolsheviks took power in 1917 it was the Mensheviks who fought primarily for democratic rights while the Bolsheviks pushed for immediate socialization under a dictatorship of soviets, which had to be under their control. Generally speaking, the Mensheviks were representative of western Europe while the Bolsheviks mirrored the semi–Asiatic character of Russia.

Trotsky laced into Lenin's obsession with police spies, and famously wrote in 1904 that the Bolshevik leader's autocratic style "lead, as we shall yet see, to this: the party organization is substituted for the party, the Central Committee is substituted for the party organization, and finally the 'dictator' is substituted for the Central Committee." The feud peaked when Trotsky told another Menshevik that Lenin was "a professional exploiter of any backwardness in the Russian labor movement" and "The entire structure of Lenin is at present based on lies and falsification and carries within it the poisonous seeds of its own destruction." Little did Trotsky imagine that eventually he would assist Lenin in establishing a state that featured the vices he initially detested in Bolshevik thinking.

What later united Lenin and Trotsky was shared belief in the theory of "permanent" or "uninterrupted" revolution. It was axiomatic for Marxist thinkers that workers would help the propertied classes (bourgeoisie) to take power from absolute monarchies such as Kaiser Germany or tsarist Russia. After civil liberties were introduced, proletarians would learn the arts of management and government from liberal rulers over a long period of time. Trotsky in 1905 developed the bold theory of permanent revolution with assistance from the Russian-born German socialist Aleksandr Helphand, who wrote under the pseudonym Parvus. They argued that Russian workers had to initiate the drive for state power and keep it since the bourgeoisie in Russia was too devoted to its property rights and bar socialists from governance.

Trotsky stated the new idea of telescoping the liberal and socialist revolutions in his 1906 book *Results and Prospects*: "In our view, the Russian revolution will create conditions in which power can pass into the hands of the workers — and in the event of the revolution it must do so — *before* the politicians of bourgeois liberalism get the chance to display to the full their talent for governing." Trotsky ridiculed Russian Marxists who disagreed as comrades "who replace independent analysis of social relations by deductions from texts, selected to serve every occasion in life." Lenin enriched the concept of permanent revolution with a 1915 vision of Russian workers sparking a general European uprising and pioneering socialism across the continent. World War I was raging and a few thousand Russian and German radicals agreed to target monarchists and liberals as joint foes of the world proletariat.

Illegally returning to Russia in February 1905 Trotsky wrote leaflets to foster worker strikes and army mutinies. He became known for a speech at St. Petersburg University which rejected the tsar's October Manifesto as duplicitous, tore up a copy and tossed it aside. Trotsky soon led the capital Soviet and was arrested in December 1905 after telling the public to refuse to pay taxes until the government fulfilled its political promises. Sentenced to a term of lifetime exile in Siberia, Trotsky escaped and made his way to Europe and New York. He wrote for the émigré press until the overthrow of tsardom in March 1917 allowed him to return home.

Meanwhile, Russian left and right extremists were locked in conflict. Anarchists and SRs in 1906–1907 used bombs or revolvers to kill or injure an estimated 4,500 officials. In October 1907 the arrest of a potential suicide bomber figured in the letter that an American diplomat sent home from St. Petersburg.[9] When the army returned from its Asian war the regime cracked down on protesters. One reckoning is that from October 1905 to April 1906 34,000 rioters were shot and 14,000 insurgents killed. At least 1,000 were executed after sentencing by field courts-martial, most of them Balts, Georgians and Poles. Around 70,000 were imprisoned. Cossacks whipped and torched during punitive expeditions to restive villages. The police winked at reactionaries who incited anti–Jewish pogroms during which many died and were injured for belonging to an ethnic group heavily represented in left-wing circles. The repressions and pogroms stained the reputation of Nicholas II among foreign statesmen. U.S. President Theodore Roosevelt called the diminutive tsar a "preposterous little creature" and British politician James Ramsay MacDonald inveighed against Nicholas as "a common murderer" who was "bloodstained."

Still, the Romanov dynasty remained powerful. Most villagers remained loyal to elders in the peasant commune, an ancient institution that was a microcosm of the Russian political universe. Historian Orlando Figes has observed about Imperial Russia that its villages were strife-ridden entities presided over by elders who ruled with a heavy hand. *Khozyain* was the peasant term for Head of the Household and later Soviet citizens would refer to Stalin as such. The interaction of village elders and assembly might find the elder saying "Well, Orthodox, have you decided so?" and the people might shout back "Ladno! Ladno!" or "Agreed! Agreed!"

Survival of the commune until Soviet farmland was collectivized in the 1930s merits a closer look at this venerable institution. The headman periodically redistributed fertile soil in scattered strips according to the changing size of household members. Farming standards were poor as wooden tools prevailed and shallow plowing increased the likelihood of drought. After 1905 Premier Stolypin launched a reform of the commune aimed at transforming it into a system of family farms with enclosed land. That was supposed to make the countryside a stronghold of political conservatism and higher farming standards.

But only about one-tenth of the peasant households had left the communes before the outbreak of World War I. It is still obscure if the revolutionist and police agent who murdered Stolypin in 1911 was carrying out the orders of Crown reactionaries, as alleged by Baron Nicholas Wrangel and novelist Solzhenitsyn.

After the turmoil of 1905–1906 certain regions were kept under a kind of martial law known as "Safeguard." Elsewhere a loosening of police controls in many towns helped to stabilize the country. The parliament (State Duma) was consultative but attracted wide interest and visiting scholars from America and Britain met illiterate peasants who were knowledgeable about Duma debates.

New political parties voiced a broad spectrum of opinion. Right-wingers were dominant over constitutionalists and revolutionaries. Unfriendly to both moderate bureaucrats and reformist gentry, the stark conservatives agreed to change only if it meant reviving the 16th-century consultative assembly known as the *Zemski Sobor* (Assembly of the Land). Vladimir M. Purishkevich and Dr. A. I. Dubrovin formed the Union of Russian People. A squabble between the two led Purishkevich to create his own hard-right League of Michael the Archangel. A Russian Monarchist Party was led by journalist V. A. Gringmut; and the Union of Russian Men headed by the Sheremetyev brothers, whom Metropolitan Vladimir of Moscow supported. The Police Department estimated that in 1905–1906 the Union of the Russian People had 360,000 members who with almost 50,000 activists of other monarchist groups were known as the "Black Hundreds." which later rampaged through streets much like stormtroopers in Nazi Germany. The right-wingers in 1906–1907 received government subsidies of three million rubles, or $1.5 million, but failed to gain leading state posts or affect policy.

Ultranationalists, however, long echoed the 1906 manifesto of the Black Hundreds for elections to the First State Duma; it lamented "the ongoing spontaneous hostility of Jewry to Christianity and to non–Jewish nationalities, and the Jews' striving for world domination."[10] The rancor of the Black Hundreds would echo in the pronouncements of the "Rodina" (Homeland) club during the 1960s and "Pamyat" (Memory) Society of the 1980s.

Softer conservatives were attracted to the Union of October 17, which took its name from the Tsar's Manifesto promising the observance of human rights. The Octobrist party grew out of a September 1905 *Zemstvo* Congress and claimed 20,000 members among landowners, businessmen and officials. As cautious reformers they opposed universal suffrage and autonomy of the non–Russians inside a federative state. Octobrists wanted a law-based state with independent judges. Like Stolypin, members hoped to build a new class of independent farmers respectful of private property rights. The Octobrist leader Aleksandr Guchkov was a friend of Stolypin, born into a wealthy merchants family in Moscow and fought in the Boer War on the anti–British side. He was a duelist too and for one such episode was sentenced to detention in a fortress but spent only a week there.

Under more restrictive voting rules of 1907, the Octobrists became the government's party. They no longer backed the confiscation of some privately owned land and concessions to the Jews. When state policy turned still more reactionary in 1911 Guchkov stepped down from the post of Duma speaker. His replacement was Mikhail Rodzyanko, a landowner from Ukraine who as Octobrist head tried to bring a sense of urgency to slack government departments after the lost opening battles of World War I.

Just as fearful of mob rule was the Constitutional Democratic Party, or Party of the People's Freedom (Kadets). It was formed on the initiative of *zemstvo* constitutionalists and town professionals. Over half belonged to the nobility, and professors accounted for almost half the Central Committee. The goals of these 100,000 or so moderates were a redistribution of landowners' estates, progressive income tax, eight-hour day and employer-paid health insurance for laborers, factory inspectors to include worker candidates, and self-rule for Poland and Finland. A rift soon opened between nobles and liberals ready to expropriate the large landed estates. Count Saltykov, addressing the first Duma, rallied the nobles: "Let your motto and your slogan be: not a square inch of our land, not a handful of earth from our fields, not a blade of grass from our meadows, not the smallest twig on a single tree from our forests!"

A Kadet icon was founding father Pavel Dolgorukov. He was born with a twin brother in 1866 to a wealthy noble family in St. Petersburg. The family moved to Moscow, center of Russianism (*russkost*), a trend of thought opposed to the westernization period of national history. Dolgorukov was a civil servant and businessman who organized a vast lumber trade on his estates. A liberal conservative in the eyes of his twin, he helped to found a pacifist lobby and campaigned for restoring independence to Poland. Having left Russia with the Whites' defeat in 1920, Dolgorukov secretly crossed the Soviet border in 1924. He was released, but a second illicit trip in 1926 ended in tragedy. Dolgorukov was arrested and shot along with 19 other prisoners, clearly in retaliation for the assassination of Pyotr Voikov, Soviet envoy to Warsaw. Stalin publicly mocked a protest of British Laborites against the execution of Dolgorukov.

In the camp of half-reformers was the Progressive Party, whose nucleus was the Moscow business elite. The Progressives lobbied for Russian control of the Turkish Straits, where much of the Empire's foreign trade passed. Their leader in the Duma was landowner Ivan Yefremov and one of the liveliest dailies was the party organ *Utro Rossii* (Morning of Russia). On the middle ground too was a Democratic Reforms Party founded by Professor Maxim Kovalevsky, Moscow law historian. Like kadet leaders he hoped that after the 1914–1918 war Allied politicians would press the tsar to establish parliamentary rule in his domain. This expectation helps to account for the Russian Liberals' unstinting support of the Allies in spite of heavy Russian losses at wartime fronts.

The left-wing parties of the early 1900s curried favor with discontented peasants and workers. By far most popular was the Socialist-Revolutionary, which sprung from the Populist movement of the 1870s. The SRs urged the nationalization of all private and state lands with transfer of ownership to the peasant communes. They favored national self-determination for the largest non–Russian minorities, and this gave them partisans among intellectuals in the Caucasus and Baltics. SR rolls included many university students and rural school teachers; peasants were absent from the leadership.

The party was nearly destroyed in 1908 by exposure of activist Evno Azef as both terrorist and police agent. The SR leader was Viktor Chernov, grandson of a peasant and former law student at Moscow University. He founded the Agrarian-Socialist League, which in 1902 merged with the SRs following a peasant revolt in southern Russia. Mocked by foes as "Blackman," his name in English, Chernov authored the SR farm program, which Lenin later adopted.

The Bolshevik party had little more than 15,000 members in 1917 but that was enough for Lenin to grab the remnants of state power. He was born Vladimir Ilyich Ulyanov in 1870 in the provincial capital Simbirsk and the alias may have derived from the Lena River in Siberia.[11] His sister Anna got an order from Stalin to search records and discovered that her brother was of mixed ancestry: on the maternal side were Swedes, Jews and Germans; on the father's side, a grandmother was a Kalmyk, which accounts for the pronounced Mongol features of Lenin in some photographs. (These findings were never reported openly in the Soviet Union, where it was necessary to avoid adding grist for the mills of Communist-hating anti–Semites.) The family was well-off; father Ilya was a schools director and the mother, too, was educated. Young Vladimir was a superior pupil whose elder brother, Aleksandr, was executed in 1887 for complicity in a plot to kill the tsar. Lenin enrolled at Kazan University and was expelled for taking part in a protest demonstration. While in Kazan he learned of the workings of the secret terrorist society People's Will, which was organized along military lines. After four years of inactivity and the family's social ostracism because of Aleksandr, Lenin took correspondence courses at St. Petersburg University and for a time was a defense attorney.

In 1893 Lenin joined a group of Marxist intellectuals in the capital that had contacts with workers. What attracted Lenin to Marxism was its class-war analysis of society and objective to destroy the existing order. His thoughts of proletarian dictatorship are inscrutable but it is clear that he loathed other intellectuals for their supposed indecisiveness. With the future Menshevik leader Yuli Martov, Lenin created in 1895 a worker study group called "Union for the Struggle for the Liberation of the Working Class." Martov and Lenin were a union of opposites, the former devoted to freedom and individualism, and the latter to personalized leadership and collectivism. Lenin was arrested in 1897 and banished to Siberia.

After release in 1900 Lenin spent nearly 17 years in European exile. Funds were supplied by his mother, rich patrons and robberies by undergrounders. None of the donors — writer Maxim Gorky, opera singer Fyodor Chaliapin and Moscow textiles magnate Savva Morozov — could have dreamt of the scale of repressions that Lenin was to demand after he reached the seat of power and met with armed resistance. Speaking of Gorky, our focus on politics should not belittle the importance of humanistic literature in shaping the thought of the educated public in the pre-revolutionary era. A few poets would admire the 1917 Bolsheviks for their uncompromising stance. But later many like Boris Pasternak said that they regretted their failure to convince new Soviet intellectuals that the Communist party was enveloped in pagan power politics that robbed the people's soul of vital nourishment.

During the 1905 Revolution Lenin took advantage of a political amnesty and returned to Russia. Uniquely among political leaders, he instructed workers in the tactics of street fighting. The October Manifesto with its talk of civil liberties moved Lenin to demand "pursuit of the retreating enemy" and "wipe the throne of the bloody tsar from the face of the earth."

After the failed rising Lenin left Russia for Europe. Émigré disputes raged over issues such as participation in Duma elections and whether socialism ought to be a religion. Most of Lenin's comrades left him and he stigmatized them as "pseudo-revolutionary, unreliable, un–Marxist elements." In turn they attacked him for "a regime of dictatorship in the party," "party tsarism" and "the monarchic structure of the party." A new crop of Bolsheviks wished to reconcile with the Mensheviks, whose leader Martov in 1908 condemned Lenin's faction as a "bandit gang."

Inside Russia, Martov had the support of the vast majority of an estimated 10,000 Social-Democrats. When Bolsheviks and Mensheviks finally split in 1912 both claimed to be worker parties though intellectuals led each side. The rivals grew distinctive insofar as the Bolsheviks were mostly younger, Great Russian, former peasants living in towns, and richer. The Mensheviks were largely skilled workers, Georgians and Jews.

After splitting with the Mensheviks Lenin brought into his Central Committee someone as untiring as himself, Iosif Vissarionovich Dzhugashvili, who took the alias "Stalin" or "man of steel" because of a strong will.[12] He was born in 1878, a fact initially revealed in 1990, when church records were examined. Until then Stalin's birth date was thought to have been 1879 because of an error of aides who filled out questionnaires for him in 1921–1922. The birth was in a shack of poor peasants who became town-dwellers in Gori, Georgia, which lay in the Caucasus mountains between Europe and Asia. (Georgia's name origin was from the Greek word for agriculturalist since early visitors were favorably impressed by local vineyards.) A well-traveled British diplomat usefully reminds that Stalin came from a region of violent tribes where blood-feuds were usual and trust of neighbors almost nonexistent.[13] Vissarion, Stalin's father, was a Georgian shoemaker and alcoholic who abused his Ossetian wife and their son.

After the father left the household Iosif's mother strove to raise her son to become a village priest. She failed to gain his respect and he was absent from her funeral in 1935. At the Gori church school young Stalin appears to have been unruly, instigating fights and tormenting teachers, for which he suffered more beatings. He spent five years (1894–1899) at Tiflis seminary, which historian Alfred Rieber describes as repressive and with a record of many student expulsions for antigovernment activities. It was at the seminary that Soso made the transition from village-centered populism to urban Marxism.

Was Stalin really a Marxist? Writings that focus on his ethnicity and scholastic debates about the true meaning of Marxism raise this question. In addition, Stalin's mass murders of fellow party members during the 1930s signified departure from the precedent set by Lenin, his established Marxist forerunner. Still, the medieval Crusaders were both ardent Christians and serial killers. Stalin was indeed a Marxist if we look at the kinds of class enemies that he identified from youth to old age. These included first and foremost peasants, followed by clergymen, landowners, private businessmen and liberal intellectuals. Like his role model, Lenin, Stalin thought all of them to have mind-sets supportive of the tsarist police state and exploitative capitalism. The party intellectual Dmitri Shepilov relates in a memoir that after World War II Stalin lectured him for over two hours on what he said was the life or death issue of writing a political economy textbook so as to convey faith in the communist vision of the future.

As for practical tasks on the road to communism, Stalin knew that politics was not the long, straight sidewalk of the Nevsky Prospekt in St. Petersburg. It was a zigzag route that demanded of rock-solid Bolsheviks great flexibility and tenacity. Stalin's master plans can be reduced to two: the creation of farm collectives in the early 1930s and the no less violent drive of 1935–1938 to destroy suspected renegades.

In 1898 Stalin joined the Marxist organization *mesame-dasi* (the third generation). He was elected to the Tiflis committee of the Russian Socialist Democratic Worker Party in 1901 and described in police reports as an agitator who "conducts himself in a highly cautious manner." He moved to the oil town of Batumi near the Turkish border to spread Social-Democratic ideas among unruly workers. Back in Tiflis he met the legendary Kamo, who taught him how to stage bank robberies to help fund the movement. Stalin's Batumi career ended with arrest and imprisonment, after which he proceeded to Baku and worked as a labor organizer.

As a committee man Stalin attended the Bolshevik conference in Finland in December 1905 and first met Lenin. The Georgian was bound to be displeased with the conference rejecting conspiratorial methods of the Bolshevik underground and endorsing party elections with glasnost. During this interlude of Menshevik sway, Stalin was expelled from the party in 1908 for violating a resolution barring holdups like one he recently carried out on a steamship line. Thus, by age 30 Stalin was a brigand in the eyes of authorities and fellow Social-Democrats.

It is unlikely that Stalin viewed Lenin as a father figure. The young Stalin, it seems, was impressed by Lenin's bold and firm leadership. By 1909 Stalin was self-confident enough to have shrugged off one of Lenin's quarrels with party men as a "tempest in a teapot" and called for "smoothing over the sharp edges of Bolshevism." That was not held against him and after one more of seven arrests and five escapes from jails or exile Stalin in 1912 visited Lenin in Poland. Under the tutelage of the Old Man he wrote the essay *Marxism and the National Question*. Arguing with the Jewish Bund and Georgian Mensheviks, Stalin rejected federalism and upheld the preservation of centralized rule in a new Russia. But he conceded for each big ethnic group the right of self-determination to the point of secession — if the rights of other peoples were not infringed upon.

Marxist scholar Fred Williams has proposed that in the writing of this essay Bolshevik theorist Nikolai Bukharin coached Stalin with German language sources and Lenin inserted the caveat "Not the national but the agrarian problem decides the fate of progress in Russia." Stalin's murky theoretical effort and Caucasus ties qualified him as Bolshevik specialist on the nationality question. But he later took special pride in work as a practitioner rather than theorist.

A case has been made that Stalin's involvement with ethnic relations led him further to share Lenin's hatred of Western governments. In their public pronouncements both attacked Imperialism for enslaving colonial and semicolonial lands such as tsarist Russia. Both held that starving proletarians in Europe were fated to be good partners of the future revolutionary Russia. By 1920, however, the setbacks of foreign Communist parties would lead Stalin to doubt the imminence of world revolution. Privately he shrugged off the new Communist International as a retail goods shop (*lavochka*).

After recruiting Stalin into his Central Committee, Lenin in 1912 named him an editor of *Pravda*, the new Bolshevik newspaper in St. Petersburg. The Georgian again proved to be his own man, fraternizing with Mensheviks, and building a coterie that included fellow editor Vyacheslav Molotov. Their association was to last 40 years or until Stalin turned on Molotov for a still obscure reason. In 1913 the Russian strike movement heated anew and Stalin was arrested and exiled to Siberia, where he spent four years in low spirits but continued to read serious political books. Historian Yuri Yemelyanov suggests that the frequent isolations of Stalin might have deepened his mistrustful nature. He remarks that prisoners were often baffled that the police knew so much about the Bolshevik underground. They suspected comrades still free and those arrested who under torture or offered money may have agreed to act as informers.

In sum, Stalin before 1917 was an earthy rebel endowed with talent for organization. He was inferior to Lenin or Trotsky as conceptualist and forecaster, later rectifying this deficiency by forging a personality cult that vastly exaggerated his above-average intelligence. Stalin readily accepted the Leninist understanding of world politics as a class-based struggle for power. The pathologies of Stalinism loomed on the horizon and at this stage few had heard of this shadowy militant.

One of the scourges of tsardom were the Anarchists, who worked for the eradication of state institutions and private property. As early as 1890 Anarchist cells mingled with bandit gangs. In 1905–1907 they had only 5,500 or so followers but their violence made national life quite uncertain. Historian Anna Geifman reckons that most of the 17,000 casualties of terrorist acts between 1901 and 1916 were intended and accidental victims of Anarchist attacks. The hotbeds of Anarchism were Riga, Vilna and Warsaw, where some terrorists were former Socialist-Revolutionaries and Social-Democrats. Anarchist gangs were reckless and known as Black Bannerites, Black Ravens, Hawks, Black Terror and Bloody Hand. A theorist of these utopians was Prince Pyotr Kropotkin, who returned to Russia from exile in London after the March 1917 Revolution. Soon after Lenin took power Anarchists blew up a building housing the Bolshevik Moscow Committee, which incited the Soviet secret police to occupy an Anarchist base in the town of Kraskovo.

The more culturally advanced borderlands had equivalents of the center and left parties. This was in part a reaction to the official campaign of Russification. In 1899 the tsar refused to receive a 500-man Finnish delegation that came to St. Petersburg to present to him a "Great Address" opposed to an Imperial manifesto applying Russian laws to their Grand Duchy. A 1901 law abolished Finland's army and extended conscription to the Finnish provinces. That was done against the will of premier Sergei Witte, who lost a dispute with Finland's governor-general, N. I. Bobrikov, and Interior Minister D. S. Sipyagin.

Nationalist movements stirred too in Ukraine, Poland, the Baltics, Georgia and Muslim provinces. Officials replied to the ferment by stoking hatreds between rival ethnic groups such as Christian Armenians and Muslim Tatars in the Caucasus. The political arms of those minorities were the Armenian Revolutionary Federation (*Dashnyaktsutyun*) and the Muslim Unity Party (*Ittifak*), which allied with the Kadets.

Jews were the most politicized ethnic group. Their Marxist Bund was stronger than either the Bolsheviks or Mensheviks. It was founded in 1897 in Vilna and urged self-government for all Russian provinces. What fired up the Bund and gave it a popular hero was a military tribunal sentencing member Gersh Lekert to be hanged for the May 1902 shooting and wounding of Vilna Governor-General Viktor von Val. The Bund reached a strength of 34,000 in 1906, when the rival Workers of Zion (*Paoli-Zion*) party had 25,000 members. With financial aid from abroad, the Bund had a popular daily newspaper and weeklies in Yiddish and Russian. The Zionist and socialist Jewish parties disbanded after revolutionaries were defeated in 1907. Morale sank with the discovery that Israel Kaplinsky, a founder of the underground Bund press and member of the leadership, was an agent of the secret police.

The Bund revived after the overthrow of tsarism and in late 1917 surged to around 40,000 members, most of whom supported the Mensheviks. Bundists were divided in the 1918–1921 Civil War and the party was dissolved anew. Although some former Bundists were admitted to the Bolshevik party and rose to high posts in the secret police, the Bund was never forgiven its national exclusivism. A secret police report of August 1934 pegged to the upcoming congress of Soviet Writers denounced the writer I. D. Kharik for "idealization of the Bund."[14]

Many surviving Bundists were arrested and perished during the Stalin purges. One victim was Mikhail Liber (Goldman), who as a Menshevik served on the executive committee of the Petrograd soviet in 1917 and on its behalf negotiated with Stalin during the July Crisis. The secret police had arrested Liber several times after 1923 and he was executed in 1937.

The Duma was fading as the Romanov dynasty celebrated its tercentenary in 1913. Kadets had won elections to the First Duma in 1906 but the government disapproved of their reformist agenda and dissolved the assembly. The Second Duma was shut down on the pretext that Social-Democrats were plotting to kill the tsar. A new voting law narrowing the franchise was enacted in June 1907 and the conservative gentry gained control of the Duma. The Fourth Duma in 1913 passed bills granting social benefits to workers but kept on the books the indignity of flogging for peasants disrespectful of authority.

An informal political process existed within the Russian government. High officials preparing new laws consulted provincial nobles, who were deemed experts on local or agrarian issues. In exchange for such backing the officials arranged interviews for the gentry with capital grandees or audiences with the tsar. The lobbying of interest groups was usual after 1905, and a conservative society known as the United Nobility was able to thwart an effort to bring Kadets into the government. How many were engaged in this politicking? Aside from a fraction of the 20,000 landed nobles, the top tier of bureaucratic and military elites in 1900 numbered less than 2,000.

Linking these influentials were personal friendships, old school ties and membership in exclusive social clubs. Scholar Roberta T. Manning has identified the lobbies of tsarist Russia as *zemstva*, city dumas and noble organizations, merchantry and wealthy peasants. Her judgment is that in the early 1900s "high government officials routinely sought support for their pet projects among local gentry and other elite groups ... as the state bureaucracy became more socially diversified, and thus more internally divided, such outside support became a vital factor in policy-making decisions."

Ultimately, palace cliques sought to gain the ear of the tsar. In 1899 Nicholas sided with Finance Minister Witte and rejected a proposal by Interior Minister Goremykin to introduce *zemstva* in more provinces. Witte opposed the idea as liable to raise a threat to industrial interests from those of agriculture. Witte as premier in 1903 clashed with Interior Minister Pleve. The Police Department saw germs of revolution in Witte's line of heavily taxing the rural classes to promote the growth of industry. An upshot was that many peasants were impoverished and forced to seek work in the towns. Pleve's men whispered that Witte's clique was appointing Socialists to professorships in academies it controlled. The Peasant Bank that Witte protected was also known to be successfully increasing the number of small landholders and irking landowners, whose estates would in time be bought by the peasants and find themselves uprooted. Nicholas II heeded the alarms of Pleve and withdrew his support from Witte.

In 1904, the emperor had to ponder whether to back jingoist state ministers advising a forward policy in the Far East. A hard-nosed stance was taken and war with Japan resulted in heavy casualties and domestic upheaval. Prince P. D. Svyatopolk-Mirsky, the Interior Minister, wanted a "policy of trust" to gain Liberal support for the throne. That November a memorandum from the Interior Ministry to the tsar advised legality and press freedoms, but former ministers and grand dukes successfully objected.

Just five years later Nicholas mediated a dispute over whether the armed forces should be under the control of the government cabinet and Duma or the Crown. He upheld the traditionalists and one consequence of the verdict was to keep overaged staff officers in their chairs. The policy disputes were accompanied by court intrigues that undermined one premier after another. Witte was the object of the cabals of General Trepov, commandant of the Tsarskoye Selo palace near the capital. Right-wingers led by Prince V. P. Meshchersky schemed against premier Stolypin as a threat to the authority of the tsar. Prime Minister V. N. Kokovtsov is reputed to have fallen in January 1914 due to reactionary plotting. As noted, the power of the tsar was still vast, but he was vulnerable to the suggestions of hardliners that reformers were building independent power bases to diminish his standing.

New revolutionary outbreaks threatened in 1912 after police shot down striking workers in the Lena goldfields. As many as 700,000 workers across the country grew idle and in 1914 the number rose to 1.5 million. That summer workers in the capital skirmished with troops and put up barricades. Nicholas was preoccupied with the foreign policy issue of whether to confront Austria and Germany over their intention to crush Serbia for having allegedly sponsored the murder of Austrian heir-apparent Franz Ferdinand. Russian nationalists begged the tsar to protect Serbia while a pro–German faction urged neutrality. One of the "internal Germans" was former Interior Minister P. N. Durnovo, who in a memorandum advised the tsar to avoid foreign imbroglios lest revolution erupt anew. Other Germanophiles included courtiers Prince V. P. Meshchersky and Count V. B. Frederiks; Interior Minister N. A. Maklakov; diplomats Baron R. R. Rozen and P. S. Botkin; State Councilors Count Witte and Count D. A. Olsufev; and State Duma deputy N. Ye. Markov II.

The absolutist pro–Germans met with resistance from diplomats among whom were many Anglophiles. Foreign Minister S. D. Sazonov was a partisan of small Slav peoples and suspected Berlin's ambition to detach Poland, Lithuania and Ukraine from Russia. In concert with top generals he pleaded with Nicholas for full mobilization against Austria to avoid the destruction of Russian influence in the Balkans and dependence upon the will of the Kaiser. Some contend that it was the tsar's approval of a mobilization of troops directed against Austria that evoked German countermeasures and the start of World War I. But historians Luigi Albertini and Fritz Fischer have documented that in the great crisis of July 1914 German elites were confident of the Reich's military superiority and determined to force a conflict with the Russia colossus, which they saw as a menace to European civilization.

Tsarist generals won laurels as their troops advanced into Polish Galicia against the weak resistance of Austro-Hungarian forces. Russification started with decrees that Galician schoolchildren be taught in Russian and Catholics converted to Orthodoxy. German incitements to revolution boded ill for the Jews, and Cossack whips drove many from their homes into Austria-Hungary or Russia. In 1915 Russia needed Western loans and laws were passed abolishing the Jewish Pale of Settlement. This was followed by measures enabling greater access for Jews to educational institutions, repealing of limitations on Jews in the choice of a profession and lifting a ban on the Yiddish press.

The chivalrous Nicholas gladly satisfied Allied requests for the launching of costly Russian offensives to relieve German pressure on the Western Front. An invasion of East Prussia in summer 1914 resulted in the Battle of Tannenberg, during which over 30,000 Russian soldiers were killed; Russian prisoners numbered 125,000; and the Germans took 500 guns. British General Sir William Ironside later remarked that Tannenberg was "the greatest defeat suffered by any of the combatants during the war." The first ten months of fighting did bring awful news to palaces and huts: 3,800,000 Russian soldiers were killed, wounded or taken prisoner. The public got an inkling of the shocking truth that during 1914 6,500,000 men were mustered into the Imperial army but only 4,000,600 rifles were available. Some units went into battle with many soldiers lacking weapons. Shortages of ammunition and clothing were chronic.

The fear factor on the Eastern Front was significant. During the war 70 percent of the casualties were the result of artillery fire. Austro-German forces attacking in Galicia in May 1915 had 334 heavy guns to four Russian, over 1,200 field guns to 675 and 96 trench mortars to none. A million Russian soldiers surrendered in the retreat from Poland, and by September front-line forces were reduced to one-third of the 1914 level.

Once private initiative was unleashed it had a salutary effect on the war effort. The War Industry Committees that Octobrist leader Guchkov started were able to convert many small factories to the production of munitions. Historian Dmitri Volodikhin suspects that Guchkov in late 1916 or early 1917 plotted with military and industrial figures to overthrow the government in response to its decline of orders for armaments. A Red Cross organization was mercifully begun by *zemstva* under the direction of Prince Georgi Lvov and it both increased army supplies and helped the wounded.

Britain's prestige in Russia collapsed in 1915 as many blamed London for failing to provide enough material support to an ally. Especially important was the failure of British forces to break through the Turkish Straits and open a supply route to Russian Black Sea ports. British diplomats in Petrograd were anxious that political instability could affect Russia's ability to stay in the war.

One rumbling was a June 1915 Kadet demand for the formation of a new government likely to enjoy public support. Defeatism spread with Nicholas' August decision to leave the capital to take command of the field army. The tsarina and her spiritual adviser Grigori Rasputin undertook wholesale personnel changes that hurled the regime into further disrepute. In and out went a series of premiers and ministers of interior, foreign affairs, war, transport and agriculture. Nicholas was persuaded to dissolve the Duma and that caused labor unrest and rumors of treason in high places.

When French Minister of Armaments Albert Thomas visited Russia in April–May 1916 he saw a power vacuum and commented that the premiership of grandee Boris Shtyurmer was a fiasco. British ambassador George Buchanan viewed Shtyurmer as vacant, inept and corrupt.[15] The Germanic ancestry of Shtyurmer raised popular suspicion of treasonable intent.

To rescue beleaguered Italy, General Aleksei Brusilov in June 1916 attacked the Austrians in Galicia and Russian casualties soared to 550,000. Foreign Minister Sazonov was ousted in September on grounds that his pro–Allied views had stymied the launching of a needed crackdown on dissidents. At the Duma, Kadet leader Milyukov in November denounced government missteps as either folly or treason. The heavily censored speech was hand-copied and distributed throughout the country in tens of copies. A secret police commentary was that "the general public is interested in political intrigues, dissatisfied with the dull reports of the newspapers and craving all sorts of lithographed and handwritten news."

Right-wingers offered to the tsar a preview of imminent horrors if he failed to appoint a dictator. Their November 1916 memorandum described Russian society as politically immature and unprepared for the onset of a Western-style constitutional regime. If that road was ever taken, the conservative parties would be defeated and chaos would break loose. The monarchy would fall and the peasant-bandit (*muzhik-razboynik*) would destroy private property. After an orgy of slaughter, autocracy would be restored and a new monarch would emerge.

Disgust with the war spread among the frontline troops. News of bread shortages, refugee influx and crime waves back home incited many to desert. Thousands of Kazakhs were killed in a revolt in Central Asia over a planned mobilization of native labor and the expected arrival of more Slavic settlers. Worker discontent caused a rise in the number of Bolsheviks in Petrograd from perhaps 500 to 2,000 in 1916.

The tipping point came in March 1917 with shortages of food and fuel in the capital because of railroad mismanagement. The insurrection of a reserve battalion of the Preobrazhensky Guards validated the old saying that the fate of Russia could be decided by a single battalion. Striking workers joined the mutinous soldiers and civil authority disintegrated in an orgy of burning, looting and lynching of policemen. One incident of pervasive class hatred was reported in the London *Times* (March 17, 1917): "Baron Stackelberg fired on the soldiers from his window yesterday. He was dragged out of his home, taken to the quayside, and there summarily executed." The top brass had no stomach to suppress the rioters and coaxed Nicholas to abdicate. Amidst popular rejoicing Duma members formed a Provisional Government with agreement of the reborn Soviet. Burying the hatchet, Liberals and Socialists in a unified voice agreed to hold early elections for a constitutional convention. The Soviet's appeal for an early peace "without annexations or indemnities" failed to meet with a positive response from the Germans and the Allies continued to exert financial pressure on Russia to stay in the war.

Dissolution of the Empire caught Lenin by surprise. In Swiss exile he had been thumping for Imperial Russia's defeat in World War I. He developed a theory that world socialist revolution might begin in Russia rather than modern Europe, as Marxists generally believed. Lenin saw Russia as the most unstable of the belligerent states. Acting on this belief, Lenin in 1917 was able to imagine that a Bolshevik seizure of state power could turn the war into European civil strife of mutinous soldiers against fighting governments. Stalin was to champion this view at the Bolshevik party congress in August 1917 while Lenin was in hiding from Russian revolutionary authorities. The mixed motives of Lenin may have included cold analysis and thirst for power, as were most of his original interpretations of the logic of history.

As early as March 1915 Parvus Helphand advised the German foreign ministry to mobilize Russian socialist exiles in Europe around Lenin and return them to Russia. There a mass political and peace strike might overthrow the tsar and install a government ready to take Russia out of the war. The Germans did send Lenin into Russia, fed millions of gold marks into his propaganda mill and rejoiced at his eventual overturn of the bourgeois-liberal government that succeeded tsarism. Today few recognize the name Parvus Helphand but his influence on world history was of incalculable magnitude.

Lenin's return to Russia in April 1917 stirred up a furor among Bolshevik activists. At the time one of the few Bolsheviks who shared his vision of immediate socialist revolution was young Molotov. His seniors — Stalin, Lev Kamenev and Matvei Muranov — returned from Siberian exile and at the helm of *Pravda* laid down a line of military defense and social peace. Lenin swung his followers over to a radical program calling for

- Russia to break with the Allies and withdraw from hostilities;
- granting state power to the soviets as prelude to a revolutionary dictatorship;
- nationalization of land and its distribution to peasants;
- confiscation of banks and their control by revolutionary authorities;
- worker control of production and distribution of goods;
- abolition of the standing army and bureaucrats;
- and creation of a revolutionary International for struggle with world Imperialism.

This agenda was like that of the 1870 Paris Commune and framed to make the Bolsheviks competitive with their Anarchist rivals. Decades later student dissidents in Stalinist prison camps would acclaim this platform as True Work of Lenin and claim to have founded such a progressive organization. Opposition to Lenin's radicalism was overcome, but the memoirs of Menshevik leader Tsereteli inform that moderate Bolsheviks secretly cooperated with the Provisional Government in the hope that their party would become a legitimate parliamentary opposition.

Lenin correctly sensed that Kadets and Mensheviks would reaffirm Russia's partnership with the anti–German alliance. But Liberals and Socialists split over war aims and the street howled down Foreign Minister Milyukov when he upheld the tsarist claim to the Turkish Straits. As early as May 1917 British ambassador Buchanan was concerned that lawlessness was spreading from Petrograd to provincial towns.[16] Menshevik Tsereteli is convincing that in July lower-ranking Bolsheviks organized a big demonstration in Petrograd and in Lenin's absence reported to his lieutenants that the masses wanted to pressure the Soviet Executive Committee into taking power. Lenin was dubious of the venture and went into hiding as government forces cracked down. The refusal of Socialist-Revolutionaries and Mensheviks in the Soviet to play a leading role inside the Provisional Government weakened their influence over the street. This lack of "will to power" separated the revolutionary democrats from dictatorial Bolsheviks and predestined the further course of events.

The task of strengthening ties between the Provisional Government and Soviet fell upon the theatrical Aleksandr Kerensky. He was a renowned lawyer and Socialist-Revolutionary appointed prime minister in July 1917. One savvy observer's contemporary view of Kerensky is in the diary of Yuri Got'e, historian of Russian agriculture and local government:

> Kerensky is a sincere and strong individual, but I consider him to be Russia's greatest evil genius. In the February and March days, who organized the Soviet of Workers' Deputies and the other organs of disintegration? Who provoked the shift of the revolution in the direction of the "dictatorship of the proletariat"? Kerensky, [Menshevik Nikolai] Chkheidze, [Menshevik Matvei] Skobelev, and company; that is, the extreme left members of the Duma. It is of no importance that Kerensky entered the Provisional Government "at his own risk" — in doing so, astride two stools he had bound together by a slender thread, he held things together with one hand and with the other he broke them apart. Kerensky is the most gifted of those evil geniuses, and he later came to his senses and began to think of himself as a man of the state and perhaps even a statesman. But all the same, in creating the Soviet of Workers' Deputies in the first days he did more for Russia's destruction than [he has done] for her fortification ever since. Therefore his responsibility is greater than anyone else's.[17]

Kadet Fyodor Kokoshkin met Kerensky in August 1917 and wrote that the premier gave an impression of "extreme uncertainty and instability in his mood and behavior on vital issues. He is in the psychological state of Nicholas II: mistrustful and indecisive, seeming not to have his own line of conduct."[18] The same could hardly be said of Lenin at the time, and some intellectuals admired the decisiveness of the Bolsheviks in comparison to the hesitation of their foes.

In their quest for power the Bolsheviks alleged that the propertied class was inciting economic chaos to set the stage for counterrevolution. Actually, new military reverses for which Kerensky was responsible helped to trigger new disorders. A wave of violent strikes erupted and managers were carried out of their offices in wheelbarrows. General Lavr Kornilov, commander-in-chief, warned that a Bolshevik coup was imminent and ordered troops to impose martial law in the capital. Kerensky ordered that weapons be distributed in factories to forestall a putsch and the planning for it came to naught. Armed workers flocked into the Bolshevik militia and Lenin gained a majority inside the Soviet.

A pair of Lenin's oldest colleagues opposed his plan for insurrection. Grigori Zinoviev and Kamenev were fearful of resistance in the provinces since party membership in October 1917 stood at only 350,000, or a fraction of 1 percent of the population. After Lenin gained the upper hand, Trotsky, as director of military affairs at the Soviet, organized a small number of armed Bolsheviks to occupy government headquarters on November 7 and arrest cabinet members. Kerensky escaped the capital but failed to rally troops for an effective counterstroke. Only in Moscow was there staunch resistance to the assertion of Bolshevik authority.

American John Reed witnessed Lenin addressing the Soviet Congress on November 8. Reed later described Lenin as dressed shabbily and unimpressive to have been so admired by the lower classes as he was.[19] A smart challenge was raised to Lenin's rosy view of the prospects for worker risings in Europe and peace with Germany. Boris Avilov had left the Bolsheviks over Lenin's ideas and formed a small group of Social-Democrat Internationalists. He soberly told the Soviet Congress:

> The governments of the Allied powers will refuse to enter into relations with the new government [of Lenin] and will not under any circumstances agree to its proposal for peace negotiations. The new government will be isolated and its proposals will be left hanging in the air. It is almost impossible to count on the support of the proletariat and democratic camp in the enemy and Allied countries. In the main they are still very far from revolutionary struggle.... The representatives of the left wing of German Social-Democracy have stated most definitely that one should not expect a revolution in Germany before the end of the war. As a result of the isolation which is being prepared for Russia, it is inevitable that either the Russian army will be routed by the German army and a peace will then be concluded by the Austro-German and Anglo-French coalitions at the expense of Russia, or there will be a separate peace between Russia and Germany. In either case the peace terms will be most onerous for Russia. And, unless we capitulate without resistance to the will of the German victors, the peace will not come soon.[20]

Some Bolsheviks warned Lenin that his refusal to share power with moderate socialists boded ill for civil peace. They resigned from official posts with a prophetic declaration: "We stand for the formation of a socialist government consisting of all parties in the soviets. We believe that otherwise the preservation of a strictly Bolshevik government will be possible only with resort to political terror." Undaunted, Lenin remarked to Trotsky that revolutionary terror had become inevitable. Together they outlawed the Kadet party, announced press censorship and dispersed the Constituent Assembly after the Socialist-Revolutionaries had won a crushing victory in a long-awaited free election. The historian Dmitri Volkogoov comments in his Lenin biography that now the Bolshevik leader revealed himself as a utopian fanatic, but his innermost thoughts about power and policy must of course remain unknown.

The civil war came after a separate peace between Russia and Germany. From 1918 to 1921 millions were killed, died of hunger or disease or emigrated. Leninists prevailed in a struggle that forever diminished the value of human life in Russia. The anti–Communists lost largely because of the heavy ideological baggage they lugged from tsarism. Some White Guard leaders such as General Aleksei Budberg were honest enough to admit to their diaries that a backlash was prompted by their troops' acts of rape, flogging, robbery, torture and indiscriminate killing. Meanwhile the Bolsheviks won support from many who had engaged in the massive looting of land and private property that was known to the Communal peasantry as "Black Re-partition" (*chorny peredel*). The Leninists also won over many elites in the nationality border areas with promises of autonomy in a universalist state of "Sovdepia," as the first Bolshevik-run state was often known.

Although the Bolsheviks were victorious in the civil war it soon became clear that their militarized version of socialism was a far cry from the humanistic society that their leftist foes had looked forward to. Ahead was a lengthy internal struggle over the method of government that pitted revolutionary despots in the Kremlin against democratic socialists inside and beyond the Bolshevik party membership. A fitting bookend of this saga was an expression of regret over the Bolsheviks' dispersing of the Constituent Assembly that was uttered at a 1990 session of the Russian Federation's Congress of People's Deputies. This action effectively delegitimized over 70 years of Kremlin rule and was foreshadowed by a slew of historical inquests that Gorbachev instigated as the heart of his perestroika campaign.

CHAPTER 2

Lenin and Stalin:
Terror and Fissures

The Stalin phenomenon remains a topic of concern for Russian and foreign students of Soviet affairs. In the year 2008 an international conference was to be held in Moscow on the theme "History of Stalinism: Results and Problems of Inquiry." The major topics to be examined were institutions and methods of the dictatorship, political economy, social-cultural features, nationality policy and the ethnic factor, international relations and World War II and survivals in present-day attitudes. The general public's curiosity about Stalinism is apparent from a series of talks on the liberal radio station "Echo of Moscow" that aired in 2008–2009. The conversations with specialists delved into facets of Stalinism such as the New Economic Policy (1921–1928), pubic opinion, living conditions, nationalities, 1937–1938 purges, Red Army and farm collectivization, official anti–Semitism and impact on eastern Europe.

Like so much else in Russia, politics was the catalyst of these developments. Moscow journalist Nikolai Svanidze spoke after the 2008 conference and warned that many Stalinists remained in the country, whose leaders failed to appreciate the danger of a return to Stalinist totalitarianism. At the conference itself the Russian Federation's Minister of Education and Science Andrei Fursenko was criticized for approving a school history text that made him look like a "conductor of the new policy of rehabilitating Stalin."

In the West the relationship between Lenin and Stalin had earlier divided analysts. Some argued the continuity of their basic ideas and dismissed the policy differences separating them as reflective of mere personal frictions. Others held that Lenin and Stalin had fundamental disagreements over where to take the Soviet experiment. If the second view is more accurate, critical alternatives presented themselves to the Bolsheviks during the post-revolutionary era.[1]

Whichever interpretation is sounder the issues and attitudes that crystallized in Soviet leadership under Lenin and Stalin would prove to be durable. A section of the governing class followed Stalin and embraced the Russian tradition of despotism and centralization. They were deeply suspicious of the West and eager to build Fortress Russia while others favored a less regulated socialism with diversity of opinion inside the ruling party. This anti–Stalin element was torn between those wedded to a forward revolutionary line and others who allowed for an essentially cooperative posture in foreign relations. Without knowledge of the Westernizing heritage it is inconceivable that moderation would have arisen and ultimately led to the onset of liberal democracy.

The original Soviet leaders were united in creating basic pillars of their new regime. One mainstay was a system of censorship that was officially said to have been temporary or due to end after the consolidation of Bolshevik power. Lenin's November 1917 press decree ordered the closing of 575 printing shops and over 2,000 newspapers and journals. At the same time, Lenin embraced glasnost insofar as he published secret tsarist treaties with the Allies in order to discredit imperialism, and incite world revolution. The civil war necessitated military censorship, which the Revolutionary Military Council imposed in 1918. Under Stalin censorship was exercised by GLAVLIT or Main Administration for Keeping Military and State Secrets in the Press. GLAVLIT was attached to the government cabinet or Council of People's Commissars. The operations of GLAVLIT were monitored by the Agitation and Propaganda (Agitprop) Department of party headquarters and the secret police. In March 1927 press secrecy was extended to information about harvest prospects, including unfavorable weather forecasts. A ban was put on news about grain exports, secret police structure and activities, the Kremlin, train wrecks, suicides and insanity, whereabouts of senior officials and financial matters.[2]

By 1940 GLAVLIT had over 4,500 censors on the central and local levels. Stalin and his successor Khrushchev occasionally were the judges of literary works, as was Mikhail Suslov, a federal party secretary, who served both leaders as chief censor. Suslov met with writer Vasily Grossman in 1962 for almost three hours and approved of the KGB seizing the manuscript *Life and Fate* as harmful to the authorities. Only 25 years later did Soviet censorship end with Gorbachev's drive for glasnost.

The second pillar of the Soviet regime was the secret political police. It was founded in December 1917 as the All-Russian Extraordinary Commission for Combating Counter-Revolution, Speculation and Sabotage

(Cheka). This body was put under the direction of Polish revolutionary "Iron" Feliks Dzerzhinsky, who recruited an ethnically diverse leadership to be merciless toward Russian intellectuals and clergy. The Cheka organized a "Red Terror" in response to an attempt on Lenin's life in August 1918 and is believed to have shot at least 10,000 hostages linked to the old regime. Menshevik leader Martov later protested that the Cheka shot four Romanov grand dukes, one of whom was an eminent historian. It was largely the Cheka murders during the Russian civil war that led western statesmen to view the Bolsheviks as evil and antipathetic. The so-called "organs," however, were an indispensable instrument of governance, engaging in domestic spying, protecting leaders, collecting foreign intelligence and organizing special operations abroad.

Despite frequent name-changes (GPU, OGPU, NKVD, NKGB, MGB, MVD and KGB) ordinary citizens always regarded the Chekists as dangerous and to be avoided if possible. Whatever his mixed motives, Khrushchev deserves credit for the wholesale eradication of infamous secret police generals in the post–Stalin era and imposition of a ban on Chekists continuing to fabricate antiregime plots.

Lenin followed in the footsteps of Imperial German Chancellor Bismarck, who cynically used the federal idea to attract the south German states to his Prussian powerbase. The varied Soviet republics were promised home rule in a January 1918 Declaration of the All-Russia Soviet Congress. This laid down basic principles that included "allowing the workers and peasants of each nation to make a decision independently at their own plenipotentiary Soviet congresses as to whether they wish to participate, and on what terms, in the federal government and other Soviet federal institutions."

Just three months later, Stalin as commissar for nationalities openly recognized how important it was for Soviet leaders to control the borderlands. (Ukraine supplied one-third of Russia's agricultural production and 70 percent of its coal and ores.) Stalin told *Pravda* that federalism was only a step toward a socialist unitary state. He outlined the future Russian Federation as embracing Poland, Ukraine, Finland, Crimea, Trans-Caucasus (perhaps divided into the subentities Georgia, Armenia, and Azeri-Tataria), Turkistan, Kirghizia, Tatarstan-Bashkiria and Siberia. Stalin envisaged a strong state cabinet at the center with regional autonomy for cultural and linguistic affairs. Above all, the decisions of central party bodies were supreme.

By autumn 1920 Stalin assailed ethnic separatists whom he said risked

becoming vassals of hostile western powers. Poles and Finns in the run-up
to formation of the USSR in 1922 managed to gain foreign assistance and
ward off Red Army attacks that elsewhere enforced the tough Leninist line
on the nationalities. But the Soviet unitary state became a reality only in
the late 1920s. Tatars in particular resisted Moscow control during the writing of the 1924 USSR Constitution. Their delegates to the Constitutional
Commission argued for abolition of both the huge Russian Republic and
elevation of its inner republics to the status of federal entities. Tatar national
Communist Mirsaid Sultangaliev fought for an independent Tatar Communist party and was arrested on Stalin's orders. This national-liberation
struggle burned itself into the memory of Soviet Muslims, who down to the
perestroika years covertly honored Sultangaliev and other martyrs of their
lost cause.

Lenin and his longtime confidants dominated the power structure to
set general policy. The Bolshevik patriarch ruled through a party Central
Committee of 15 to 20 members and this established a precedent for inter-
regnums and the resolution of disputed issues during periods of one-man
rule. The Central Committee elected a Politburo of five to act as a super-
government, routinely deciding major questions and conflicts. The original Big Five were Lenin, Trotsky (military and naval affairs commissar),
Nikolai Krestinsky (finance commissar), Kamenev (Moscow Soviet chairman) and Stalin (nationalities commissar). A party Organizational Bureau
of five was to appoint senior personnel; and a three-man Secretariat run party
administration. The Council of People's Commissars or state cabinet was
headed by Lenin to do legislative work. Lenin was able to deal with an
immense number of topics by severely limiting discussion at executive meetings and assigning lieutenants to form commissions on problems that
required study. A Labor and Defense Council was the interdepartmental
coordinating body for state-run heavy industry.

Only Stalin was a member of all three party bodies, and at the Orgburo he was able to select regional party secretaries who formed the dele-
gations to party congresses that elected the Central Committee, or party
parliament, through which Lenin ruled. As workhorse, Stalin added to his
portfolio the commissariats for nationalities and state control, known as the
Worker and Peasant Inspectorate (*Rabkrin*).

During the civil war a mixture of Marxist values and breakdown of
social ties led to unpopular grain requisitioning in villages and meager barter
payment of factory wages. Boris Bazhanov, an aide to Stalin who later
defected, reports hearing from Lenin's personal secretaries that their chief

initially believed that the public would embrace noncapitalism but finally had to concede that decades were required to promote socialist values. Vast peasant uprisings and worker strikes forced Lenin in 1921 to shelve his Marxist recipes and allow some private enterprise. This led some party militants to feel betrayed that the "heroic period" of the revolution was unfairly terminated. Although Trotsky in a moment of pragmatism had vainly pioneered Lenin's New Economic Policy (NEP) he quickly returned to leftist positions and engaged in a debate over economics that lasted several years. The clash pitted Trotsky against Stalin, who championed moderation until events forced his hand.

In 1922 Stalin was posted to the new office of party general secretary and converted the tiny party headquarters into a switchboard of power. The appointment was made almost certainly with the approval of Lenin, who wanted a lid put on factional strife among the Bolsheviks. Stalin's assignment enabled him to take charge of the single-candidate lists that local party conferences used for their electoral meetings. The limited education of many party militants and suspicion of outsiders determined that personnel appointments of the General Secretariat would be made largely on the basis of political criteria, not ability.

That procedure never really changed over the years. As early as 1923 around 30 percent of the regional party secretaries were nominees of the central party staff. The avoidance of genuine elections in lower party circles helped the center to suppress local and nationality interests. On the state side, the once-popular soviets were reduced to a decorative vestige. With his 1936 constitution Stalin put a cross over nationwide soviet congresses, which Gorbachev revived.

The top Bolsheviks were youthful, iconoclastic and cosmopolitan. Of the many professional revolutionaries, one-fifth were the offspring of tsarist bureaucrats, officers or nobles; one-fifth came from the intellectual class; 3–4 percent from the clergy; 5–10 percent from merchants and businessmen; and 15 percent from shopkeepers and service industries. The majority of Politburo and Secretariat members were from the old intelligentsia. Almost two-thirds of the Central Committee and Politburo members lacked specialized education — many had been expelled from colleges for political disloyalty. A complete higher education was attained by 6.6 percent of Politburo members, 15 percent of Central Committee members and 11.2 percent of higher officials. By age, the majority were 35–37. Russians accounted for 60–70 percent; Jews held 13–14 percent of the top posts, with almost double that ratio in the Politburo and Secretariat. Armenians and Georgians comprised 4–5 percent and twice that number at the top. Balts were close behind at 4–6 percent with Germans and Poles at 4–5 percent, and Muslims at 2–3 percent.[3]

The scholar Robert Daniels has described as the "conscience of the revolution" the post–1917 factions of Workers' Opposition, Democratic Centralists and Workers' Group. Essentially, the Workers' Opposition wanted the Bolsheviks to keep hands off the work of Soviet trade unions and the appointments to bureaucratic posts, which it thought should be a union prerogative. Basic slogans of perestroika are to be found in Alexandra Kollontai's 1921 pamphlet espousing views of the Workers' Opposition. Kollontai said her group fought for "reconstruction and development of the creative forces of the country" on the basis of "return to democracy, freedom of opinion, and criticism inside the party."

Lenin was so incensed that he urged the Central Committee to expel from the party Worker Opposition leader Aleksandr Shlyapnikov and fell a single vote short of doing so. Glasnost figured too in the 1921 theses of the Democratic Centralists, who were for "guaranteeing in fact to all tendencies within the party the right of free and complete expression in the press, at party assemblies, and in the responsible organs of the party and soviet apparatus." An outgrowth of these factions was Gabriel Myasnikov's Workers' Group in the Ural city of Perm. Myasnikov was a bench worker expelled from the party for demanding freedom of speech "from monarchists to anarchists." He was arrested in 1923 during a wave of wildcat strikes, escaped from the USSR in 1927, returned in 1946 and disappeared.

Differences over the relationship between party officials and state experts can be traced back to 1922, when Lenin worried about the anti–Bolshevism of technical specialists. Trotsky objected to party overreaching and requested a clear-cut separation of politicians and specialists. Lenin overrode Trotsky for raising a threat to party supremacy.[4] A short time later practice taught Lenin the virtue of tyros listening to experts. But Stalin insisted that "we cannot surrender the economy to the specialists." The issue recurred at the 1923 party congress, a defender of the specialists complaining that incompetents were often assigned to managerial posts on the basis of party loyalty. A circular was sent to party secretaries ordering them to allow experts freely to solve technical problems.

Before long party bosses were again criticized for their failure to consult experts before taking economic decisions. These complaints too were ignored because of the fear of undermining party authority. It became customary for someone once recruited for political work to later head a factory, local government office, party district committee, cultural establishment or diplomatic bureau. A strictly professional career was long rare and was true in less than half the careers of Soviet state ministers. Only in the final years of the regime were most diplomats genuine career officers.

Non-Russians among Soviet officialdom were long aware that Lenin was more attuned than Stalin to their sensitivities. As apostle of world revolution Lenin knew that peoples in colonial areas wanted to know how the Kremlin handled its Muslims or Mongols. In September 1922 Lenin had to resolve a controversy involving Georgian comrades who resented Stalin's plan to declare outlying Communist-led republics "autonomous" regions of Russia rather than sovereign states. Stalin wrote to Lenin deploring "complete chaos and the absence of any order" in relations between the center and periphery. He held that economic activity in Russia was paralyzed by conflicts that he blamed on "the younger generation of communists in the regions" who "refuse to see the independence game as a game. It insists on taking words about independence at face value, and demands that we implement the constitutions of the independent republics to the letter." Stalin advised that "the periphery should defer unconditionally to the center on all fundamentals."[5]

This viewpoint was at the core of a draft law on formation of the Soviet Union that Stalin had drafted. What will remain problematic is Stalin's main motive for wanting to incorporate other republics into Russia. It could have been to bring into the orbit of his Nationalities Commissariat Ukraine, Belorusia and Transcaucasia.

Lenin's appreciation of the link between policy and personality stands out from his December 1922 letter to the Politburo arguing for tactful handling of the Georgians. "Stalin's haste and his infatuation with pure administration," Lenin said, "together with his spite against the notorious so-called 'nationalist-socialism' played a fatal role here. In politics spite generally plays the basest of roles." Lenin alluded to Stalin as "the Georgian" who "carelessly flings about accusations of 'nationalist-socialism' whereas he himself is a real and true 'nationalist-socialist,' and even a vulgar Great Russian bully." In turn Stalin fired back with a missive to the Politburo accusing Lenin of "national liberalism." Lenin's victory was hollow: the new constitution granted borderland republics only cultural and linguistic rights, along with formal sovereignty within a super-sovereign Union state.[6] In September 1924 Georgian nationalists staged an armed uprising that the Moscow-controlled Cheka suppressed with heavy loss of life.

Neither doctrine nor precedent gave a clue to solving the riddle of political succession. Lenin failed to see anyone worthy of inheriting his mantle and on the eve of his last stroke he wrote a December 1922 letter to the Politburo endorsing a collective leadership to rule in his absence. The popularity of Trotsky as leader of the Red Army in the civil war should have made him the top candidate for succession but Lenin warned that he was too inclined to the use of coercive measures (*administrirovaniye*).

Stalin was viewed more harshly as someone who "has concentrated an enormous power in his hands, and I am not sure that he always knows how to use that power with sufficient caution." Soon Lenin heard that one of Stalin's clique had struck a Georgian deviator. In a letter to the Politburo he rounded on "Stalin's haste and coercive impulse" and insisted that Stalin be held "politically responsible for this whole truly Great Russian nationalist campaign" to bridle the Georgians.[7]

Almost a decade later, former Soviet official Sergei Dmitriyevsky imagined Lenin's mixed feelings about Stalin. The general secretary was certainly filled with lust for power, innately a despot of the Asian type and if he became Soviet dictator would confront both internal social classes and the Western powers. But perhaps a cruel leader was needed to overcome Russian backwardness. While this rough sketch underrated Stalin's patience in questing for domination of men and affairs, it was accurate about essentials.

Whatever his doubts Lenin soon overcame them and wrote a postscript to his musings about leaderology. In January 1923 he dictated a letter to the party congress vilifying Stalin's crudeness toward his wife Krupskaya over sick-room management. Lenin advised that "Stalin is too rude and this fault of his, which is tolerable within our intimate group and in view of the connections between us, becomes unbearable from one who holds the post of general secretary. I therefore suggest that the comrades should discuss the question of dismissing Comrade Stalin from this post and appointing for it another person who, in all respects is only distinguished from Stalin by one quality, i. e., that of being more tolerant, loyal, civil, and considerate toward the comrades, less moody, etc."[8]

One of Lenin's personal secretaries was entrusted with the safekeeping of his Testament and thoughtlessly gave it to Stalin, who ordered that it be burned. Krupskaya, however, possessed copies of the document and it became available to party bigwigs, who filed away its contents. Until Lenin's death in January 1924 Stalin spied on him and made him a virtual prisoner at a government estate outside Moscow.

Opportunism was a striking feature of interregnum politics. Ironically the iron-fisted war commissar Trotsky campaigned for inner-party freedom. One substantive aim was to shift the Kremlin power balance away from the Stalinist machine. The second was to use party forums to promote a leftist attack on urban poverty and unemployment through planned renewal of industry at the expense of peasants. Trotsky sent a letter to the Central Committee in October 1923 belittling mid-level Stalinists as "a very broad stratum of party workers" who "completely renounce their own party opinion, at least the open expression of it, as though assuming that the secretarial hierarchy is the apparatus which creates party opinion and party decisions. Beneath this stratum, abstaining from their own opinion, there lies the broad mass of the party, before whom every decision stands in the form of a summons or command."[9]

Trotsky learned from stormy meetings in universities that dilating on this theme would gain him support among younger party members. He even won over briefly a 29-year-old party organizer in south Russia, Nikita Khrushchev, who has explained, "In 1923, when I was a student at the workers' school, I was guilty of certain waverings in a Trotskyist direction." During the 1937 purges Khrushchev told Stalin about this misstep and the latter along with Molotov agreed that Khrushchev should reveal that to a party conference vetting members for their loyalty.[10]

Stalin remained a fearful and secretive undergrounder. He was convinced that the public might lose whatever confidence it had in the party if its leaders were seen to disagree about policy among themselves. He told the October 1923 Central Committee meeting, "It is necessary to ensure a procedure whereby all future disagreements be resolved inside the collegium [Politburo] and not be dragged into the open." Historian Konstantin Pisarenko registers that the party Secretariat tightened up on attendance at such gatherings and barred from at least one representatives of the Society of Old Bolsheviks and Komsomol Young Communist League, which harbored Trotskyites.

Nevertheless, a Politburo decision in December 1923 announced a sham perestroika to take the wind out of Trotsky's sails. A promise was made to reintroduce into the party multiple-candidate elections of officials, broad discussion of policy issues and sharing of information between the center and regions. A Stalinist later regretted the resolution authorizing the reforms as "a mistaken concession to Trotsky." Yet at the time Stalin was able to remove oppositionists from party posts and higher schools amidst official calls for the strict observance of Leninist iron discipline.

Using glasnost as a sword. Stalin revealed to the political class in January 1924 the secret clause in Lenin's 1921 Resolution "On Party Unity" that enabled the Central Committee to expel from the party violators of discipline. Within a few months, tens of thousands of bench workers were recruited into the party and obediently voted against "Trotskizm." Yesterday's hero was so weakened that he soon had to attend a party congress as nonvoting delegate. Trotsky was relieved of his duties as war commissar and sidelined to work on electrification and foreign concessions.[11]

An offshoot of the struggle for power was a manipulation of history that became a hallmark of Stalinism. Party theorist Bukharin in December 1923 fired a broadside at Trotsky for opposing Lenin during post–1917 disputes and attributing the errors to Trotsky's Menshevik background. Trotsky's *Lessons of October* inveighed against Stalin on grounds that in early 1917 he "tried to push democratic revolution as far as possible to the left ... to 'exert pressure' on the ruling bourgeoisie, a 'pressure' so calculated as to remain within the framework of the bourgeois democratic regime." Trotsky cited Lenin's October 1917 letter critical of Stalin's present-day allies Zinoviev and Kamenev for opposing the armed insurrection. He accused the 1917 partners of "passive fatalism," "irresolution and even incapacity for action," "a fatalistic, temporizing, social-democratic, Menshevik attitude to revolution."

The General Secretariat led by Stalin collected and stored documents about party history. It was divided into departments and commissions that were responsible for the oversight of press and rural work (Molotov); army political education and surveillance, Komsomol and cooperatives (Andreyev); personnel management, statistics, finances and security services (Kaganovich); Agitprop, women's affairs, party history and contact with the Moscow party branch (Zelensky). Under Kaganovich was a system of informants for the "secret observation of political attitudes." To direct this network the Secretariat included a bureau and it regularly organized conferences of department heads. This machinery was effectively a party within the party crafted to do the bidding of Stalin.

Stalin had a premonition that Lenin's death in January 1924 might energize the anti-regime underground. OGPU created a panic in Moscow with mass arrests in April and 1,000 were seized in one night in Petrograd, where the prisons were full. At the party congress in May the ruling triumvirate stood shoulder to shoulder. Zinoviev and Kamenev assured party barons that Lenin's fears about Stalin were unfounded. The Lenin Testament was consigned to the archives and private possession of a copy made from a smuggled source could result in a prison term. Now Stalin replaced Lenin as keynote speaker at the party congress and monopolized that spotlight until failing stamina compelled him to play a lesser role in 1952.

At this stage of his career Stalin used doctrinal hair-splitting to undermine natural rivals. He rebuked Kamenev in a speech to party-school students for having said that Soviet Russia was led by NEP-men (*nepmanovskoy*) instead of a state whose leaders were conducting the New Economic Policy (*nepovskoy*). Zinoviev was chided for alleging a prevailing dictatorship of the Bolshevik party whereas a class dictatorship was said to exist and the party supposedly merely guided ruling soviets. Stalin warned that such imprecision might breed confusion and had to be nipped in the bud.

Kamenev as battle-hardened veteran of party warfare recognized the importance of Stalin's rebuke. From a Caucasus spa he sent a coded message to Zinoviev asking him to bring up Stalin's criticism at the Politburo. Kamenev also sent a note to Stalin for transmission to the Central Committee asking why a polemical thrust was made on the basis of one word in a political text. Kamenev proposed that Stalin publish an explanation that a typographical error was made in *Pravda* and there was no reason to believe that contempt for theory was implied.

Stalin replied that he had failed to insinuate a Kamenev error or intended to start a polemic. Kamenev found Stalin's explanation unconvincing and inserted into *Pravda* a notice faulting the newspaper for the mistake. Readers, however, took Kamenev's notice as a symptom of discord in the collective leadership. In August Kamenev got the satisfaction of a comrades court assembling and reprimanding Stalin for falsely accusing him of theoretical heedlessness.

By then Stalin's attention was riveted on the turmoil in his native Georgia. As noted, an anti–Bolshevik revolt broke out there in summer 1924 and it is believed that 3,000 died in the fighting and 7,000–10,000 were executed during the rising or soon afterward. One of the hangmen was the Georgian OGPU officer Lavrenty Beria, whom Stalin later promoted to head the nationwide political police.

A dispute over glasnost erupted after Trotsky's secretary, M. S. Glazman, shot himself in September 1924. Glazman had been expelled from the party on the basis of false information about his personal life. But the Politburo told *Pravda* editors to conceal the fact that party officials made a mistake in handling the case. Trotsky protested the cover-up as liable to prompt more tragedies. Significantly, in 1924 Stalin was empowered to classify party documents and to compile lists of those eligible to read them, which gave an impression of the party's division into glamorous political actors and dull spectators.

With resurgence of the class-hatred theme in leadership speeches,

Dzerzhinsky sent a letter to the Politburo in October 1924 proposing that OGPU control all criminal investigations. He advised too that OGPU be authorized to try "bandits," which meant revival of the tsarist practice of vesting judicial authority in the Gendarmerie. A Central Committee or Politburo commission weighed the proposal. Justice Commissar N. V. Krylenko dissented, arguing that it would mean approving OGPU's existing abuses of power. Foreign Commissar G. V. Chicherin agreed that "further enlargement of the extra-judicial powers of the OGPU would be dangerous." Stalin sided with Dzerzhinsky and a Special Council (*Osoboye Soveshchaniye*) of secret police officers was created which later passed judgment on countless Soviet citizens suspected of disloyalty.[12] A party decree adopted in 1926 and found in archives by veteran *apparatchik* Leon Onikov authorized the OGPU Collegium to punish any who violated secrecy by disclosing, losing or carelessly handling classified documents.

In 1925 debate sharpened over the rival interests of town and countryside. Bukharin as editor of *Pravda* defended the worker-peasant bond (*smychka*) that Lenin embraced as long-term policy. Bukharin sniped at Leningrad boss Zinoviev during an April 1925 conference of Moscow party activists. Some "comrades" failed to "understand that our industry depends on the peasant market." To increase farm output Bukharin urged increased sales of textiles, cotton and farm equipment at rural marketplaces. He complained that "the peasant is afraid to buy an iron roof for fear that he will be declared a kulak," or village profiteer. "Only idiots," Bukharin stated, "can say that the poor must always be with us. We must now implement a policy which will result in the disappearance of poverty."[13] Bukharin, however, was unable to influence the industrialists, who kept raising the prices of their goods while farm prices were much lower — a crisis which in time led grain farmers to go on a sales strike that jeopardized the urban food supply.

Stalin had a feeling that Bukharin was a wobbly ally. In a letter to intimate Kliment Voroshilov, who replaced Trotsky as war commissar, Stalin referred to Bukharin as "the weak link" of his centrist faction. The mixed emotions about Stalin inside Zinoviev's leftist clique are clear from a private statement of P. A. Zalutsky, secretary of the Leningrad regional party committee: "Stalin is of course a big man with a big mind, and he's a good organizer. But his mind is not analytical, it's schematic. He delves into old issues in order to see present-day things clearly. But he has no vision of the future and is not accustomed to that sort of thing." This opinion tallies with Trotsky's view of Stalin as vulgar empiricist and is probably valid.

Zinoviev in autumn 1925 published the article "Philosophy of the Era." It urged steps toward achieving the goal of social equality and checking pro-kulak bias in ruling circles. Krupskaya had told Zinoviev that Lenin's choice to replace Stalin was Jan Rudzutak, Latvian trade unionist and head of the party's Turkestan Bureau who was also a Politburo candidate. At the Central Committee Zinoviev nominated Rudzutak for the post of general secretary. But the nominee had a reputation for indecision and the gambit failed.

In October 1925 Zinoviev accused Stalin of bureaucratic degeneration, underrating village class struggle and misleading party opinion about the prospects for building socialism. The Opposition soon fought to raise wages and unemployment benefits, invest more in industry and invite thousands to participate in party conferences. The leftist agenda was so explosive that Dzerzhinsky as chairman of the Supreme Economic Council sent a shrill heads-up to Stalin: "What is now at stake is not only the existence of our faction but a direct threat to the party's existence and that of the Soviet government."[14]

Discord over power and policy ran too deep for the leaders to script the party congress that opened in December 1925. The battle was three-cornered, between Left (Zinoviev and Kamenev), Center (Stalin and Molotov) and Right (Bukharin and Rykov). On the eve of the conclave Stalin ousted the head of the Central Statistical Agency for an alarming report that kulaks had risen to comprise 14 percent of the population and held in their grip 61 percent of the marketable grain. The Left held a private meeting of Old Bolsheviks and proposed that Dzerzhinsky replace Stalin as general secretary. Stalin's Georgian friend Sergo Ordzhonikidze blocked the move and it is noteworthy that Trotsky at the time stood aloof from politicking or was simply ignored.

At the congress Stalin and Bukharin cautiously upheld the *smychka* and Socialism in One Country. Zinoviev reached out to the workers for support and proposed that villagers be more heavily taxed to finance an expansion of industry and factory jobs. Kamenev insisted that the Stalinist machine be made accountable:

> We are against a position where the Secretariat, which in reality deals with both policy and organization, stands above other political bodies. We are in favor of our highest bodies being internally organized in such a way that we have a genuinely sovereign Politburo, bringing together all our party's political figures, and that the Secretariat is subordinate to it, concerned with the technical implementation of its resolutions. (Noise from the hall). We

cannot consider it normal and think it harmful for the party if the situation continues whereby the Secretariat embraces both policy and organization and in effect determines policy beforehand.

Kamenev derided Stalin as unfit to win the cooperation of old guarders; "It is because I have said it more than once to comrade Stalin and to a group of Leninist comrades that I am saying it again now: I have come to the conclusion that comrade Stalin cannot fulfill the role of unifier of the Bolshevik staff." The delegates chanted in praise of Stalin and alleged that his critics valued only power.

Voroshilov conveyed the humble image of Stalin that the general secretary found it expedient to project: "Comrade Stalin, obviously, by nature or fate has been judged to formulate questions somewhat more successfully than any other member of the Politburo. Comrade Stalin is — I affirm this — the chief member [glavnym chlenom] of the Politburo. But he never lays claim to primacy. In solving problems he takes a more active part and his proposals are adopted more often than others. And the proposals are adopted unanimously." Stalin forcefully demanded of party soldiers that they avoid earnest talk: "Do not forget," he told the congress, "that any exchange of words at the top is a minus for us in the country; our differences may reduce our influence." Stalin harped too on the encirclement of Soviet Russia by hostile capitalist states and this was later explained to be more than a geographical concept.[15]

Now Stalin lifted more clients to gain a solid working majority in the leadership. Molotov, Voroshilov and simple worker M. I. Kalinin were named Politburo members. Kamenev for his plain talk was demoted to Politburo candidacy. Leningrad was brought to heel after Molotov went there and pressured party cells in factories to adopt resolutions disavowing Zinoviev. New party committees were formed in districts and these approved of delegates to a conference that installed a new regional committee subservient to the Politburo. Zinoviev's replacement was Sergei Kirov, veteran leader of Baku, a handsome commoner and skilled orator.

The independents Trotsky, Zinoviev and Kamenev formed a "United Opposition" to rid the system of NEP and Stalin. This new bloc debuted at a June 1926 Politburo meeting. Trotsky attacked Uglanov, Stalinist party head of Moscow, for discrediting party dissidents as "the non-agreed" (nesoglaschiki). "Worker democracy," Trotsky stated, "signifies freedom of all party members to openly discuss the most important questions of party life, freedom of discussion on those questions as well as the elective nature of leading posts and collegiums from top to bottom." Trotsky identified as the source of factionalism the workers' failure to see that economic policy was benefitting them. Zinoviev denounced what he called "Stalin's autocracy."[16]

In July one of Zinoviev's young followers made a case for introduction of a multiparty system. Writing in the journal *Bolshevik* (No. 14, 1926) Ya. I. Ossovsky argued that party unity was unattainable and it was advisable to allow the creation of Bolshevik factions and legalization of the Menshevik and Socialist-Revolutionary parties, which he thought unlikely to seek dominance. The Central Control Commission ordered that Ossovsky be expelled from the party. The Politburo agreed and in August 1926 voted to lift Ossovsky's party card; Trotsky and Kamenev voted against the move.[17]

That summer Kamenev handed over to Mikoyan direction of the Internal and Foreign Trade Commissariat. Mikoyan's memoirs inform that Kamenev told him that a legal opposition was essential to vocalize real proletarian tendencies. What Kamenev probably meant was laws to ensure the observance of human rights and curbing of bureaucratic privileges. Mikoyan as a Stalin loyalist no doubt reported this information to the general secretary. In party forums, Kamenev and friends repudiated Ossovsky, which gave Stalin further reason to distrust the Opposition's avowals of party loyalty.

It was Bolshevik tradition to resolve policy differences in struggle rather than by compromise. But the Politburo in October 1926 discussed terms for an intraparty truce. Stalinists held that the Opposition was insincere, in fact building a second party with diverse bureaus in big cities and fomenting an anti–Soviet uprising with illicit leaflets, Zinoviev balked at a demand that his faction repent. An Opposition statement complained that party members were expelled for distributing copies of the Lenin Testament, which had become an outlawed document. Deadlock ensued, though *Pravda* on October 26 announced that the essential minimum for ensuring party unity was reached.[18] In retrospect, it seems that Stalin gained ground from the circulation of these Politburo minutes to the lower echelons. He put on record allegations of his rivals' duplicity and made plausible their ultimate pillaring as double-dealers (*dvurushniki*).

Occasionally a reproachful voice got through to the Kremlin. A metalworker in the provinces with some political education wrote to Molotov grousing about hard times:

> You might say that all this is petty trivia and that it's far more important to understand Engels' theses on the possibility of social revolution in one country, whether in 1905 Lenin had Russia in mind when he wrote on the same topic and who understands him better, Trotsky or Kamenev, Zinoviev or you and Stalin. Yes, it is important no doubt, but to us our stomachs are

also important, and while you sit there arguing, my family could starve to death. And I'll be left naked and sick from overwork. We should be saying to you, "Clear out or get down to work and stop making so much hot air about who wrote what and who understands it best!" You remind me of all those medieval religious debates. We can't make heads or tail of it, but just want to work and have full stomachs.[19]

The age-old Russian vice of anti–Semitism was a factor that helped to defeat the United Opposition. Its leaders had Jewish antecedents and Stalin off-stage referred to Trotsky as "Leib Davidovich." Some party candidate members met in the Siberian town of Chita during 1926 and one remarked that "Trotsky cannot be a Communist, his very nationality shows that he needs to engage in speculation [of material goods]." The derogatory label of *nepachi*, or NEP profiteers, was hung on Zinoviev and Trotsky, whom no full-blooded Russian worker or peasant would follow. Central Committee member Yuri Larin led a Moscow seminar on anti–Semitism and recorded workers' questions: "Why does 76 percent of the Opposition consist of Jews? How do the Jews manage to hold all the good jobs? Why do the Jews not want to do heavy work? Why are so many Jews in the universities? Don't they forge their documents? Won't Jews be traitors in wartime? Don't they avoid military service? Isn't the reason for anti–Semitism the Jews themselves, their psychology, ethics and traditions?"[20] Stalin damned anti–Semitism in a meeting with visiting American workers, but a divergence of word and deed was one of his most notable personal traits.

As the party moved toward its December 1927 congress a tumultuous meeting of the Politburo and Presidium of the Central Control Commission convened that September. A crossfire over history was really about leadership skills. Stalin and Trotsky presented two sharply conflicting versions of their work during the civil war. Trotsky claimed that with Lenin he twice removed Stalin from military command on grounds of misjudgment. Stalin countered that Trotsky was pulled back from the front for three years and basic military issues decided without Trotsky and even contrary to his opinions. Stalin replied to Trotsky: "You are talking untruths because you are a pitiful coward, afraid of the truth." Trotsky scoffed, "Rubbish!" and cited the Lenin Testament to the effect that Stalin was untrustworthy A few days later Trotsky and Zinoviev wrote a letter to those at the plenum. Stalin's expertise on foreign policy was questioned and he was accused of being too conciliatory towards the Western Powers, whose capabilities in countries such as China he was said to have overrated.[21]

In November 1927 Trotsky and Zinoviev were expelled from the party for leading a Moscow street demonstration to celebrate the tenth anniversary of the Bolshevik takeover. A symbolic gesture made at the party congress that opened a few weeks later was ironic insofar as Aleksei Rykov, Lenin's successor as premier and future purge victim, presented an iron broom to Stalin with an appeal for him to sweep away regime enemies. Rykov was a firm believer in the NEP and *smychka*, which he perhaps thought Stalin would continue to uphold.

A legacy of the United Opposition to Soviet reformers was a Draft Platform of Bolshevik-Leninists sent to the 1927 party congress. A clause on behalf of limited terms of party office read: "The senior members of regional [party] committees, [soviet] executive committees, trade-union committees, etc. are virtually irremovable (for three, five or more years).... There must be a maximum time limit set for secretarial and other such jobs." Khrushchev would stir up a hornet's nest when he borrowed too from the United Opposition's platform an appeal for volunteer party officials. The Draft Platform said that the party machine "should not be composed entirely of salaried staff and should be regularly replenished from among the workers.... A significant amount of party work can and must be done voluntarily by party members after their productive or other work."[22] Both in 1927 and 1961 party mandarins rejected these steps to bring fresh blood into the party structure.

Trotsky later explained his loss of the contest for Lenin's mantle in "How Did Stalin Defeat the Opposition?" (1935) and *The Revolution Betrayed* (1936). He focused on historic conditions, refusing to consider politics a logical argument or chess match. To Trotsky politics was a struggle of interests and forces rather than arguments. Nor was the quality of leadership decisive. Above all, Trotsky held that since 1917 the revolutionary initiative, spirit of self-sacrifice and pride of Russian workers was replaced by violence, cowardice and careerism. He pointed out too the militarization of Soviet politics after the five-million-man Red Army was demobilized after the civil war. Thousands of former commanders took leading posts in local soviets, economics and education, introducing a military regime and shoving the masses away from participation in leadership of the country.

The defeats of Communist parties in Europe and Asia, Trotsky said, killed the faith of Soviet masses in world revolution and permitted the new bureaucracy to rise as the sole light of salvation. Trotsky sums up the false essentials of Stalin's platform during the 1920s: "For the sake of an international revolution, the Opposition proposes to drag us into a revolutionary war. Enough of shake-ups! We have earned the right to rest. We will build the socialist society at home. Rely upon us, your leaders!" This gospel of repose served to consolidate party operatives, military and state officials, according to Trotsky.

Trotsky was hardly blind to the technology of politics and power. He concedes that Stalin had assets such as the prestige of an Old Bolshevik, strong character, and close ties with a political machine that proved to be the source of his influence. Stalin's vision, however, was depicted as narrow and his policy upon great questions added up to a series of contradictory zigzags. "The theory of each successive turn has been created after the fact," Trotsky observed, "and with small regard for what they were teaching yesterday." Trotsky opined that the new ruling group welcomed Stalin as reliable arbiter of its inner affairs. Accidental factors were important: Lenin's sickness and death hastened the outcome of the succession struggle. Yet in 1922 Lenin was alarmed over bureaucratism and preparing a fight against the Stalin clique. If Lenin lived, the pressure of bureaucratic power would have developed more slowly. Still, the pre–1917 Bolshevism of vibrant idealists disappeared with the revival of market economics and onset of Stalinist rule.

At the same time, Trotsky was baffled over the Stalin victory: "It remains of course incomprehensible — at least with a rational approach to history — how and why a faction the least rich of all in ideas, and the most burdened with mistakes, should have gained the upper hand over all other groups. And concentrated an unlimited power in its hands." Trotsky guessed that the secret of Stalin's success was that the Soviet bureaucracy closed its eyes to its leaders' mistakes provided they showed an unconditional fidelity in the defense of its privileges.

In Trotsky's words, which are applicable to later chapters of Soviet history:

> The USSR is at present still a very poor country, where a private room, sufficient food and clothing are within the reach of only a tiny minority of the population — in such a country millions of bureaucrats, great and small, make every effort to ensure before anything their own well-being! Hence the great egoism and the great conservatism of the bureaucracy, its fright in the face of the discontent of the masses, its hatred of criticism, its angry persistence in stifling all free thought, and finally, its hypocritical and religious kneeling before the "leader" who embodies its unlimited domination and its privileges.

As late as the exiling of Trotsky to Central Asia in January 1928 Stalin remained committed to market-driven economics. Only 8 percent of peas-

ant families belonged to collective farms and Agriculture Commissar
Yakovlev cautioned that although the villages could be modernized only on
a socialized basis, "this obviously cannot be done in one, two or three years,
and maybe not in one decade." "The collective farms and communes,"
Yakovlev predicted, "are now and for a long time undoubtedly remain, only
small islands in a sea of individual peasant holdings." Addressing the Central Committee in April 1927 Stalin was irked at the thought of crash industrialization. He joked that to attempt to build the Dnieperstroy
hydro-electric station would be for Soviet authorities to act like a foolish
peasant who bought a gramophone instead of a cow.

The British economist Alec Nove advanced the fatalistic view that rapid
Soviet industrialization was necessary and in the absence of alternative
sources of capital had to be done at the expense of the peasants. Russian
socialist historian Roy Medvedev is convinced that if NEP was continued
both agriculture and industry would have developed more efficiently, and
the Red Army would have been numerically stronger; Medvedev's assump-
tions are more persuasive than Nove's. A reappraisal of NEP was undertaken
as the result of a grain shortfall due to farmers' refusing to market their sur-
pluses unless prices were increased. Bureaucratic ineptitude was a primary
cause of the new food crisis. Bukharin explained to the July 1928 Plenum
that poor planning and incorrect pricing led to the crisis of grain collec-
tions.

The scholar Jerzy F. Karcz has written a persuasive analysis, *The Economics of Communist Agriculture*. He observes that toward the end of NEP
the Kremlin pursued faulty price and fiscal policies. A grain reserve was not
built up in the good years and additional state investment of 131.5 million
rubles in 1927–1929 would have brought the grain market into balance.
Karcz's view is more compelling than another that the party's ideological
distrust of the market and richer peasants led it to set prices too low to keep
the villages producing.[23]

Russian historian Vladimir Lavrov has presented a variant of this interpretation of Stalin's decision to terminate NEP. He believes that Stalin did
so to prevent the fullest development of capitalism and ensure that the Bolshevik party and its general secretary remain in power. Bukharin, Lavrov
reasons, failed to understand this, and neither did Gorbachev realize that
his perestroika would lead to pluralism of ownership and finally political
pluralism.[24] We have seen that Stalin in this time frame was viewed in party
circles as shortsighted and as such, it can be assumed, not inclined to worry
about the remote chance of free enterprise blossoming in the Soviet Union.

Stalin put into play a theory fraught with danger in his keynote to the July 1928 Plenum. He tied to internal progress a growth of the antiregime sentiment of capitalist elements and their intensified waging of class war. The independent moderate Bukharin might have had this new concept in mind when he told Kamenev at roughly the same time that Stalin was "an unprincipled intriguer who subordinates everything to the preservation of his power. He changes his theories according to whom he needs to get rid of at any given moment."[25] Stalin had secret OGPU reports that kulaks in central Russia were striving to form peasant unions to take control of local government bodies. The allegation helped to convince Stalin that arrests of richer peasants would ensure political stability.

Bukharin was a critic of centralized planning and spoke for the priority of consumer-goods industry.[26] As Stalin's ally in 1925–1927 he became convinced that if the Georgian gained the power of political initiative he would create an inhumane autocracy. Bukharin tardily warned the Politburo in February 1929, "We are against one-man decisions of questions of party leadership. We are against control by a collective being replaced by control by a person, even though an authoritative one."[27]

Stalin was aware that his antipeasant sentiment unnerved party circles. Historian Nonna Tarkhova has examined OGPU records and found that peasant uprisings jumped from 711 in 1928, when state grain seizures began, to 1,307 in 1929, or the start of farm collectivization. As late as the April 1929 Plenum Stalin assured that farming collectives would be created on a gradual basis. Only after months of organizational pressure was Stalin able to secure Bukharin's ouster from the Politburo in November 1929. At that point in time Stalin broke with the Leninist practice of ruling through the Central Committee and chose to rely instead on his Politburo majority.

CHAPTER 3

Stalin: Onset of
Court Politics

With the defeat of Bukharin and his pro-peasant faction, the ruling setup changed. The Central Committee shrank in importance and Stalin as Leader (*vozhd*) mediated the conflicts between alliances that his men wove at the Politburo. The general secretary was publicly lionized on an epic scale, making him almost free from plots; even malcontents feared that the system might collapse with Stalin's demise. But the shock of farm collectivization was so great that some high officials talked of the chances for a palace revolt. The security police dragged their feet in stifling dissidents while Stalin pretended to listen to voices of reason. Ultimately, the *vozhd* unleashed a wave of terror that freed him of ever needing to negotiate with bigwigs — a circumstance that made Stalin unique among post–Lenin rulers of the Soviet Union. Nevertheless, the Western values of liberal democracy survived and were expressed "below" in the last decade of Stalinist rule.

Before the Politburo met to deliberate over a showdown with private farmers, Stalin made a speech favoring a great leap toward socialism in the countryside. In December 1929 he announced that peasants were striving for complete liquidation of the kulaks and entering collective farms in whole villages, counties and provinces. The proportion of collectives rose from 1.7 percent to 3.9 percent in 1929; to 23.6 percent in 1930. Villagers attacked the thousands of Communist factory workers sent to the countryside to dragoon them into collective farms. The dread OGPU recorded 1,400 peasant uprisings in January 1930, 1,048 in February and 6,528 in March. Stalin retreated and blamed the excesses on party soldiers who had become "dizzy with success." In April 1930 the Kremlin directed an easing of pressure on the rural class. Behind-the-scenes planning went forward to resume the collectivization at year's end. The target for 1931 would be socialization of 80 percent of the farms in basic grain areas.[1]

In the meantime, Stalin got OGPU to silence the technical experts who decried the use of draconian methods to feed the towns and force heavy industry. Dozens of specialists were arrested and falsely charged with belonging to sabotage groups. OGPU wrung confessions out of the leaders of an imaginary Industrial Party, Union Bureau of Mensheviks and Peasants Toiling Party. Show trials were staged that were in effect dress rehearsals f or the world-startling Moscow trials of Old Bolsheviks in 1936–1938. The specialist victims in 1930 included eminent statistician V. G. Groman, whom Molotov told the Politburo had failed to realize that free markets and trade were unacceptable in Soviet conditions. Groman died in prison and many like-minded figures perished with him. These men were forerunners of the *tovarniki* or marketeers of the Gorbachev era, who feted them as martyrs.

The Socialist Offensive in the countryside had dire consequences. Seizure of seed grain and a food blockade to crush resistance in Ukraine, the Volga region and North Caucasus led to severe famine in 1932–1933. Seven to ten million died in crowd violence, deportations and famine.[2] Russian archival materials suggest that thousands died in horrific lumber camps that were created beyond the Urals for the detention of exiled kulak families. The country's livestock herds were halved and an exodus of peasant males to factories and construction sites left much of the burden of farm work on women and children. Sixty years later a former Stalin aide remembered the end of NEP. In Kiev he saw the disappearance of private businessmen and emptying of their useful shops. The long-favored potato dumplings and girls who sold them were sadly gone and little else seemed to have been left in the battered city. The awful wound of farm collectivization was never closed.[3]

Palace coups and assassinations ran like a thread all through the history of Russia. Evidently with this in mind Stalin drew far-reaching conclusions from police reports of dissension inside the party. Sergei Syrtsov was a Bolshevik since 1913, active in Petrograd in 1917 and during the civil war fought against White Cossacks in the Don region. In 1930 he was named premier of the Russian Republic and a Politburo candidate. Syrtsov was thought so dependable that in September 1930 the Politburo assigned him to head a special commission to supply food to Moscow. With Vissarion Lominadze, Transcaucasus party head, Syrtsov formed a discussion group opposed to the upheaval in agrarian affairs. In October 1930 Stalin read a denunciation of Syrtsov from B. G. Reznikov, secretary of a party cell in the Literary Department at the Red Professors Institute. His report alleged that Syrtsov accused Stalin of conducting an adventuristic policy and urged that struggle be waged against it. Associates were alleged to have called Stalin "the fatal man" and "disturbed." Another Oppositionist was said to have remarked that persons able to change the regime were in the party, OGPU and army, with OGPU the most powerful organization. He was alleged to have added "We are indeed people who want to save the revolution and return to the proletariat its own party." This was sufficient for OGPU officers to conclude that an "underground factional center" existed, and arrests were made.

The Politburo and Presidium of the Central Control Commission met on November 4, 1930, to discuss "the factional work of comrades Syrtsov, Lominadze and others." Under grilling Lominadze admitted that he had spoken of a certain empiricism of the Stalin leadership, or undue reliance on experience as distinct from theory. Stalin attacked Lominadze for insincerity and emitting Menshevik slander that the Stalingrad tractor plant was a Potemkin village. Stalin implausibly charged that Bukharin from outside the Politburo was cultivating terrorists, and briefly identified party members "Smirnov-Orlov" as suspects. Stalin held too that Bukharin's wife, party member Larina, remarked to someone that Bukharin told her he was still an Oppositionist despite a statement of repentance for political deviation.

At this same session Molotov denounced state planners such as the imprisoned V. G. Groman for flirting with the idea of utilizing market techniques. OGPU chief Vyacheslav Menzhinsky labeled the Syrtsov group "a faction of principled liars." An informer supposedly overheard private talk to the effect that "the Politburo is a fiction, in fact everything is decided by a small band that meets in the Kremlin in a private apartment." Subsequently Lominadze wrote a statement to the Control Commission admitting that he was critical of the Stalin personality cult, disagreed with Stalin's formula about the USSR building Socialism and thought the *vozhd* to be lacking in foresight.[4]

The circulation of minutes of an inquisitorial leadership conclave was obviously intended to warn party officials to beware of seditious talk and trust in their interlocutors. Stalin's vindictive sanctions went much further. Initially Syrtsov and Lominadze were expelled from the Central Committee and sent to lower-standing economic work. Lominadze made a humiliating speech of self-criticism at the 1934 party congress. He condemned the liberalizing ideas of restoring party dialogue and allowing free peasant societies. The penitent committed suicide in 1935 and Syrtsov was executed two years later.[5]

Nevertheless, pressures continued to build for a relaxation of the dictatorship. Living conditions were execrated in leaflets that maverick Communists spread in streets, factories and public housing. Some hero workers were murdered to protest rising inequalities. Impoverished peasants were angered by the words of Agriculture Commissar Yakovlev: "People are eating too much in the collective farms. The harvest is distributed to everyone. Even those who don't work — old people, the weak and sick — receive grain. We must introduce piecework. Grain is only for work that is done, according to a quota laid down by the state."

OGPU troops stamped out uprisings in rural areas of Georgia and Azerbaijan. Kaganovich went to the south Russian city of Krasnodar to learn why Cossacks of the Kuban region would not work the land as collective farmers and many were soon deported to Siberia. The creative intelligentsia was distressed over tighter censorship and writer Olesha remarked that colleagues were "making a list of crimes and good deeds" of officials.

Stalin was vilified in the 1932 letter of Martemyan Ryutin that was hand-circulated. Ryutin was a district leader in Moscow who had been expelled from the party for refusing to recant opposition to collective farming. In his letter signed "Union of Marxist-Leninists" Ryutin called Stalin "limited and crafty, ambitious and spiteful, treacherous and envious, hypocritical and insolent, boastful and stubborn." Ryutin urged the disbanding of collective farms, lowering the tempo of industrialization, return of expelled Oppositionists to the party and the removal of Stalin. Ryutin was arrested in October 1932, a few months after a strike at textile mills in the Ivanovo region. Oral tradition has it that Stalin failed to gain a Politburo majority for the passing of a death sentence against Ryutin.[6]

Politburo member and Leningrad party boss Kirov is reputed to have opposed shooting Ryutin, saying something like, "We mustn't do this. Ryutin is not a hopeless case, he's merely gone astray.... Who the hell knows how many hands wrote that letter.... We'll be misunderstood."[7] Ryutin was sentenced to ten years imprisonment and along with 30 others branded "traitors to the party and the working class" for "trying to create by underground means, under the fraudulent cover of the banner of Marxism-Leninism, a bourgeois-kulak organization for the restoration of capitalism and especially the kulaks in the USSR."[8]

Stalin resumed his hounding of critics at a November 1932 meeting of the Politburo and Presidium of the Central Control Commission. Anti-Stalin talk was attributed to Central Committee member Aleksandr Smirnov, former Agriculture Commissar, and onetime state officials Nikolai Eismont (supply) and Vladimir Tolmachev (construction). OGPU's Secret Political

Department reported that Eismont confessed to having blamed Stalin for peasant risings and wanting him replaced by Smirnov or Defense Commissar Voroshilov. Eismont supposedly remarked that if Lenin was alive he would make a sharp turn away from current regime policy. Terrorist conversations were alleged to have occurred between the arrested son of a former party liberal and a young technologist, with Stalin an intended victim. But the initial punishment of these suspected renegades was mild. Smirnov was sent to economic work in Central Asia and then to Moscow's Light Industry Commissariat. He was not expelled from the party until 1934 and shot only in 1938. Eismont in 1933 got off with a three-year prison term and was released in 1935, only to die in an aviation accident a few months later. Tolmachev was given a three-year prison sentence in 1933, re-arrested and shot in 1937.[9]

As in the fight with Trotsky, Stalin during the political crises of the famine year 1932 rallied his troops around the banner of material privilege. The party salary cap that Lenin had introduced was discarded and special shops and canteens opened for apparatchiks. In 1933 new winds started to blow from unexpected quarters. The eminent Menshevik scholar Boris Nicolaevsky while living in western Europe interviewed many active and former Soviet officials. He heard that Leningrad party head Kirov was developing a plan for regime liberalization. It envisioned the reconciliation of party and peasantry, and mutual amnesty between rival party clans. Kirov allowed old Oppositionists to reside in Leningrad and to collaborate on literary projects, which earned him the favor of Gorky, dean of Soviet writers, who approved of efforts to persuade Stalin to relent. A party circular in May 1933 warned OGPU officers and prosecutors against "reckless, unjustified convictions."

All the political signs did not point in the same direction. Stalin was still brandishing his power. In June 1933 the Central Committee adopted a resolution to expel from the party Shlyapnikov, a leader of the 1920–1921 Workers' Opposition, whom Lenin had failed to banish for lack of a single vote.[10] Other influences presumably allowed onetime Trotskyites and Bukharinists to re-enter the party and work in central media. The low price to be paid was recantation of old views at the party congress due in January 1934.[11]

Kirov was brought into the central party Secretariat at the congress but remained at his post in Leningrad. He may have feared to come to Moscow to be near the moody and unpredictable Stalin, who reputedly told colleagues that he heard from Kirov that some party veterans wanted him,

Kirov, to replace Stalin.[12] Khrushchev supports this version of events in his *Memoirs*, citing party investigators to the effect that Old Bolshevik B. P. Sheboldayev, party leader of the North Caucasus, told Kirov during the 1934 congress that old-timers wished to remove Stalin and replace him with Kirov. Reportedly, Kirov informed Stalin about this conversation and the latter expressed gratitude and assured he would not forget the favor.[13]

In the eyes of most Soviet citizens, Stalin remained absolute ruler. He chaired meetings of the Politburo and Secretariat, approving the agendas and draft decisions. Kaganovich presided at the Orgburo and Andrei Zhdanov, a former regional party boss, ran the Secretariat. Foreign Commissar Maxim Litvinov was the only senior government official known to be free of close party oversight. But Stalin apparently worried about an outcry if it were thought that he wanted to evade group supervision. He adopted the modest title of Central Committee "secretary" rather than "general secretary." The personality cult was toned down. In April 1934 the Politburo on Stalin's initiative reprimanded the editors of *Pravda* and *Izveztia* for celebrating the tenth anniversary of his book *Foundations of Leninism*. In May the Politburo heeded Stalin and rescinded a decision of the Transcaucasus party committee to open in Tiflis a Stalin Institute apart from the Marx-Engels-Lenin Institute. In December the Politburo approved Stalin's proposal to avoid press articles or speeches to mark what was then thought to have been the Leader's 55th birthday.[14]

Doubts arose that famous Oppositionists allowed to return from Siberia had really disarmed. In August 1934 the Politburo took a decision on the journal *Bolshevik* slamming editors and removing Zinoviev from their midst. "Trotskyite-Menshevik tenets" had seeped into the journal and included Zinoviev's carping over Stalin's new policy of flirting with European socialists to isolate Nazi Germany. Zinoviev had written that western Social-Democracy was still "very useful for the bourgeoisie, no less so than fascism." Still resentful, Zinoviev was resuming his feud with Stalin and overconfident of immunity from punishment.

A spate of high-profile murders recently occurred in Japan, Austria, France and Germany. The turn of the Soviet Union came on December 1, 1934. The murder of Kirov by a lone gunman inside party headquarters in Leningrad burst like a thunderclap. What baffled Politburo member Mikoyan was Stalin's refusal to punish secret police chief Genrikh Yagoda after his corps of leadership bodyguards failed to prevent the Kirov assassination. No less than four official investigations of the crime were made in the post–Stalin era but each was inconclusive as witnesses kept changing their testimony. In his memoirs Khrushchev affirms that Stalin orchestrated the slaying of Kirov to prepare the grounds for settling scores with party old-timers who had come to despise him. The absence of a strong body-guard detail around Kirov led to early suspicion in Leningrad that senior Chekists facilitated the crime, and Gorbachev later brought this to the atten-tion of Politburo members, who knew that Stalin exercised firm control of the security services.[15]

It took perestroika to invalidate three of the greatest judicial forgeries of modern history. Over 20 former Bolshevik Oppositionists were put in the dock at Moscow show trials. The post–Kirov reprisals began with the sentencing of Zinoviev and Kamenev to five- to ten-year prison terms for moral culpability in the murder. As many as five trials of "Kirov assassins" resulted in 17 death sentences, 76 prison sentences and 988 internal exil-ings.[16] In March 1935 the NKVD's Secret Political Department blew up into a Kamenev-hatched terrorist plot the malicious gossip of Kremlin clean-ing women. NKVD chief Yagoda sent Stalin a memorandum in May advis-ing that 25 persons be shot for belonging to Kamenev-led terrorist groups based inside the Kremlin.

Ukraine leader and Politburo candidate Kosior attacked Zinoviev and Kamenev as direct organizers of the Kirov murder in a speech to the Cen-tral Committee. Khrushchev as party head of Moscow region blamed fallen leaders for poor housing, food and work clothing. His memoirs reveal a recent outbreak of leaflets with Menshevik verbiage and strikes at factories. Khrushchev told the Central Committee in June 1935 that Zinovievists had joined counterrevolutionaries, kulaks, Trotskyites and spies in acts of wreck-ing and poisoning.

An NKVD circular in March 1936 alleged the discovery of a Trotsky-Zinoviev terrorist gang and arrest of over 500 conspirators. That July a party circular reported the discovery of another Trotsky-Zinoviev murder ring. The Military Collegium of the Supreme Court in August heard Zinoviev, Kamenev and 14 others admit to plotting terrorism and sentenced them to death. Stalin, it seems, was delusional enough to have believed the fantasies that NKVD interrogators wrung out of defendants.

A secret message that Stalin sent to lieutenants during the August 1936 trial reasoned that Kamenev must have sent feelers to British, German and American ambassadors in Moscow, informing them of his plan to murder Kremlin leaders. The foreigners, Stalin explained, must have spoken with Kamenev about the future Zinoviev-Trotsky regime. "This was an attempt by Kamenev and his friends," Stalin wrote, "to conclude a bloc with bourgeois governments against the Soviet government." Stalin's press corps, however, failed to anticipate his wishes about commentary on the first Moscow trial, and he was critical in a secret cable to Kaganovich and Molotov. As Stalin saw it, Soviet newspapers had failed to expose the defendants' platform. The focus was mistakenly put on lust for power rather than effort to restore capitalism. Stalin explained that those like himself whom defendants had marked for assassination personified the victories of socialism and not mere authority. To clinch this argument Stalin claimed that Lenin at the 1921 party congress insisted that any party faction refusing to recognize its errors had to end up defending capitalism and fighting against Soviet rule.[17]

Ironically, Stalin kept alive the memory of revolutionary pluralism while striving for full party unity. He granted an interview to the American newspaper publisher Roy Howard in March 1936 and allowed for multicandidate Soviet elections under a new USSR Constitution that was designed to brighten the Kremlin's image in democratic countries. Historian Yuri Zhukov thinks that local bosses resented the idea and lobbied Stalin to forget about it. While the 1937 Rules for USSR Supreme Soviet elections approved of multicandidate election races, the Politburo did reject the novelty, which was introduced under perestroika.

The American Embassy in Moscow tried to fathom the causes of the August 1936 show trial. Washington was told that the proceedings were designed "to correct misimpressions among party members that the newly prepared constitution (adopted in December 1936) would allow debate of Stalin's policies; to destroy the residual influence of former leaders distrusted by him; to attribute failures in the Soviet economy to the machinations of Trotsky and his adherents in international revolutionary groups by branding them as allies of German fascism."[18]

British diplomats in the Soviet capital speculated that the 1936 trial was intended "to divert public attention away from the shortage of food in the shops or to justify increased repression by the secret police."[19] Eventually the rising terror confused British representatives in Moscow. The scholar Michael Hughes examined the cables that Chief of Mission Lord Chilston sent to London and gisted this reporting:

> While the Ambassador firmly discounted the idea that the purges were driven by ideological zeal, he remained uncertain about Stalin's true motives. Like later generations of historians, he could not decide whether "the ruler of the Soviet Union is a cold and calculating tyrant ... or a homicidal maniac whose mania is exploited for their own ends by a band of bloodthirsty

tyrants." Chilston was inclined to accept the former explanation, particularly after the terror began to wind down during the second half of 1938.

Stalin kept doggedly at his witch-hunts. Party bureaucrat Onikov notes that after the initial Moscow show trial Stalin ordered NKVD chief Yagoda to shoot 5,000 former Oppositionists who were in prison camps. In September 1936 Stalin and Zhdanov on vacation together sent a cable to the Politburo nominating party Secretary Nikolai Yezhov to the post of NKVD chief. Stalin entrusted him with destruction of the NKVD upper crust, which had too many of unreliable ancestry. The ethnic breakdown of police cadres was Slavs (Russian, Ukrainian and Byelorussian): 40 percent; Jews: 40 percent; Latvians, Poles and Germans: 17 percent. Over one-fifth were once members of non–Bolshevik leftist parties. Almost half were born into nonworker or peasant families and so did not feel that they owed their privileges entirely to the Bolshevik regime. Only 15 percent had higher and incomplete secondary educations while 35 percent went only to primary schools. Under the aegis of Yezhov around two-thirds of entry-level Chekists would be Slavic and issued from worker and peasant families.

The second show trial in January 1937 convinced Trotsky that Stalin was leading a tyrannical and nationalistic pack hostile to revolutionary values. "The ruling stratum," he commented, "is ridding itself of all who remind it of the revolutionary past, the principles of socialism, freedom, equality, fraternity, the unresolved tasks of world revolution.... In this sense the purge enhances the homogenuity of the ruling stratum and strengthens the position of Stalin." Bukharin and others were hauled into court in March 1938 after spending a year in custody. A resident foreigner spotted Stalin watching the spectacle. He was perched behind the black glass of a small window located under the ceiling of the court room.[20]

During his relentless pursuit of power Stalin irked career soldiers. In 1930 he condemned as "Red militarism" an ambitious scheme for military buildup from the desk of strategist Mikhail Tukhachevsky. Historian Leonid Naumov informs that Stalin in 1931 sent a letter to regional leaders castigating OGPU officers for spreading false rumors that scoffed at the thought of sabotage in the higher defense staff. In 1937–1938 thousands of innocent Red Army leaders were arrested, beaten, tried on camera and executed for treason. The damage was heavy; 154 of 186 divisional commanders were arrested; 220 of 400 brigade commanders, 50 of 57 corps commanders and 25 of 28 corps commissars. Five men took command of the air forces in 1937–1938 and their experience varied from cavalry officers to veterans of combat in Spain. The Operations Directorate was main generator of ideas in the General Staff and from 1934 to 1941 it had seven chiefs.[21] Supreme leadership of the General Staff was unstable, the chiefs from 1937 being ex-tsarist officer Yegorov (shot); ex-tsarist colonel Shaposhnikov (compliant) ; Meretskov (arrested); and Zhukov (undereducated).

Stalin's motives for the military purges are still unclear. Some assume that Tukhachevsky favored Soviet cooperation with France rather than Nazi Germany, which Stalin feared more. NKVD defectors testified that Stalin was sure of a military conspiracy against him. It is conceivable that like Hitler the Soviet dictator wished to exercise closer personal control over commanders who were less strong-minded and intelligent than incumbents from the civil war era.

To safeguard the Red Army's rear in the event of war, massive repressions of distrusted civilians were carried out. The Politburo in July 1937 authorized an operation to round up and exterminate subversive activists among priests, sectarians, former kulaks and White Guardists, professional criminals and onetime members of anti–Soviet parties. It was charged that ex-kulaks and criminals back from exile were "main initiators of all sorts of anti–Soviet crimes and sabotage, both in collective and state farms, on railroads and in some branches of industry." In August 1937 the USSR NKVD assigned to provinces quotas for the arrest of regime enemies.

Yezhov reported to Stalin a month later that 146,225 persons were lately arrested, 31,530 sentenced to death and 13,669 imprisoned. The final tally was 767,397 arrested and 386,798 put to death. A Yezhov-led nationalities operation resulted in 335,000 arrests and 247,00 death warrants. The targets included Poles, Latvians, Estonians, Germans, Bulgarians, Iranians and Greeks. Some victims' names reportedly were picked at random from telephone books on the hunch that their presumed countries of origin were waging undeclared war against the USSR.

Only a few were brave enough to protest these crimes against humanity. A. A. Solts, member of the party since its founding, told Stalin that officials were groundlessly arrested for wrecking. Solts informed a party meeting that Vyshinsky, prosecutor at the Moscow Trials, was falsifying evidence. Solts was arrested and confined in a psychiatric prison, where he died in 1945. A Politburo decision taken during the purges forbade party members from interfering in the work of the NKVD. Some industrialists dragged their feet over firing subordinates and Ordzhonikidze among them committed suicide or was murdered. Kaganovich as railroads commissar was the only person of that rank known to have denounced as many as 24 of his subordinates as enemies of the people and demanded their arrests.[22]

Khrushchev's memoirs suggest that many Soviet citizens believed that the 1937–1938 terror served the public interest: "The mass arrests were not as numerous [at the end of the 1930s], and civil society began to calm down somewhat. Most people thought that we had already destroyed all our internal enemies, that we had achieved that goal. In other words, people thought that the repression had been necessary and that our vigilance had helped to prevent counterrevolutionary attempts to overthrow Soviet power." This helps to explain why Aleksandr Yakovlev, one of the architects of perestroika, devoted so much energy to document his exposes of Stalin brutalities.

There is no credible record of the number of arrests and executions during the height of the Stalinist terror. Old Bolshevik and camp survivor Olga Shatunovskaya told Khrushchev that according to KGB records from 1934 to 1941 about 1 million Soviet citizens were shot and 18.5 million arrested.[23] Viktor Zemskov of the Russian Academy of Sciences' General History Institute puts the number of arrests in 1937–1938 at 2.5 million and executions at 700,000. Zemskov estimates that in 1939 2 million were in prison camps.[24] Naumov presumes that around two-thirds of Soviet elites vanished in 1937–1938 and puts at 90,000 to 100,000 the number of executed Orthodox priests.

Looking back at the great terror of 1937–1938 one might ask what kind of ruling party Stalin then wanted. It was surely not one of populists like many of the Bolsheviks prior to 1917. They were well-represented in the Central Committee formed at the 1934 party congress. About 90 percent of the members and 80 percent of candidates had joined the party before 1917. During the great purge, 70 percent of all were arrested and shot. Leonid Naumov cites an old Chekist to the effect that "Stalin did not like to surround himself with people loyal to revolutionary ideals. He viewed such people as unreliable and dangerous."

After the purges Stalin lost some confidence in his sidekicks Molotov and Kaganovich. The longtime confidantes may have been against the new policy of abandoning the practice of mass party purges. Now Zhdanov was censor-in-chief and his powers second only to Stalin's. Along with being boss of Leningrad since the Kirov murder, he was an accordion and piano-playing crony who played at Stalin's frolics. During 1937 Zhdanov paid visits to a number of local party organizations to whip up spy mania. Aleksandr Yakovlev, in his study, *A Century of Violence in Soviet Russia*, relates that in

1938 Zhdanov vilified innocent leaders of the party's youth auxiliary as traitors, terrorists, spies, fascists, politically rotten enemies of the people and
counterrevolutionary gang.

Beria was born in 1899 and served in the tsarist army during World
War I. In the Russian civil war he was a Bolshevik agent in Azerbaidzhan.
With the OGPU in Soviet Georgia, Beria as noted helped to crush the 1924
nationalist rising. In 1931 he was appointed top Chekist and deputy party
leader in Transcaucasia. Khrushchev's memoirs note that he met Beria in
1932 and found him humble and witty. Beria rose to national fame in July
1935 with a five-hour speech in the Georgian capital that surveyed Bolshevik history in the Caucasus. The speech is reputed to have been based on
a manuscript that Beria confiscated from a local intellectual, revised to exalt
Stalin, and claimed to have authored. His intrigues were legion and included
a false report to Stalin that Politburo wives were illicitly using the free services of a tailoring shop that was managed by Kremlin guards.[25] Protection
rings thrived in the Beria entourage of corrupt police generals and Georgian party bonzes.[26] What ultimately doomed Beria was that the corps of
higher military officers never forgave him the arrests of senior commanders
on bogus charges of conspiracy just prior to and after the Nazi invasion of
the USSR in June 1941.

A close partner of Beria for many years was Georgi Malenkov, born in
1902 into an aristocratic family that originated in Macedonia. The gradu-
ate of a secondary school and technical college, Malenkov astounded western diplomats in Moscow with his ability to converse in Latin. As a young
Communist he did record-keeping work for the Orgburo, found a patron
in Kaganovich and rose to personnel director of the Moscow party branch.
On the eve of the Kirov affair Malenkov switched his allegiance to party
Secretary Yezhov, and as his deputy in 1936 became nationwide chief of party
cadres. He proposed candidates for high party posts to Yezhov, occasionally interviewed a candidate and quizzed him for political literacy. In 1939
Malenkov was reassigned to oversee industry and railroads.[27]

Khrushchev embodied the shrewdness of peasant Russia and vitality
of the Old Bolsheviks. He was born in 1894 into a miner's family in the
village of Kalinovka on the Russian side of the border with Ukraine. As a
child Nikita herded farm animals and learned the trade of machinist to
work in factories of the Donetsk Basin. In 1918 Khrushchev joined the Bolsheviks and served in the Red Army during the Civil War. He later studied at a workers' school, never mastered Russian spelling and dictated the
speeches to be made at party meetings. Khrushchev in 1929 was chosen to

study at the Stalin Industrial Academy in Moscow. There Stalin's second wife was a party organizer and Khrushchev the party secretary. He was sure that she praised his work to Stalin and that ensured upward party mobility for him. Khrushchev adored Stalin in the early 1930s and as a client of Kaganovich rose to the leadership of Moscow. He threw himself into urban renewal projects that included the demolition of historic sites. Khrushchev and NKVD commissar S. F. Redens in July 1937 complied with a Stalin order and volunteered to sentence to death 2,000 kulaks and 6,500 criminals, and to deport from Moscow 5,869 kulaks and 26,936 criminals.

In January 1938, he took up the duties of party secretary of Ukraine, where over a three-year span almost 170,000 were arrested and nearly 1,200 Chekists shot. A Politburo meeting was held in October 1938 to provide ideological rigor and Stalin made the rustic-looking Khrushchev the butt of humor. There was "mirthful animation in the hall" after a Stalin remark that intelligentsia were "people who have left physical labor and live by mental labor," and "comrade Khrushchev thinks that he remains a worker to this time, but he is nevertheless an intellectual. He has ceased to be a worker because he lives by his intellect, does mental labor, has left physical labor and the worker milieu." Khrushchev was granted Politburo membership just after the 1939 party congress.[28]

Hitler invaded the Soviet Union on June 22, 1941, and in less than a week's time the fall of Minsk endangered Moscow. Stalin met with Politburo members and looked as if he expected to be arrested. His reputed comment on the German advance was "Lenin left us with a great empire and we've screwed up." The Red Army suffered huge losses before it stopped the Germans outside Moscow and counterattacked in December 1941 with newly arrived Siberian divisions. A year of very hard fighting was prelude to the world-historic battle of Stalingrad that decided which side was to grasp firmly the strategic initiative.

Anti-Russian nationalism spiraled in the borderlands. The Germans enlisted thousands of collaborators in conquered sections of the Baltics, Ukraine and Belorussia. In December 1941 Hitler authorized the creation of four national legions in his Army Group South: Turkestani, Georgian, Caucasian-Muslim and Armenian. Some 3,000 Tatars joined German units in the Crimea within four weeks. Early next year there were 60,421 auxiliary police units comprised of ethnic minorities. To counter the disaffection, Red Army units of Baltic and Muslim complexion were created in 1941.

Steps were taken to rally the Great Russians around the regime. The

NKVD spread a rumor that after a Soviet victory separate national republics would be merged with the Russian Federation.[29] A number of towns were again called by their original Russian names instead of the names of Soviet leaders Beria, Dzerzhinsky, Kaganovich, Lenin, Molotov, Ordzhonikidze and Voroshilov. A new national anthem that replaced the Internationale in January 1944 hailed Rus, the ancestral home of Great Russians. But neo–Marxist critics requested and deadlocked a May 1944 conference on nationality affairs that was held at party headquarters. Malenkov keynoted the sessions and like many in the New Class of technocrats and apparatchiks sounded like a Russian nationalist eager to bury the anti–Imperial teachings of old-time Communist historians.[30] Zhdanov led the neo–Marxists and challenged Malenkov in this renewal of controversy over how to tackle the national question. Stalin might have intervened and clarified matters but seemed to desire a balance of doctrinal interests and political personalities.

Below the ruling heights reformist ideas were assertive after the Red Army hurled back the Nazis at Stalingrad in February 1943. A secret police report that July was entitled "Anti-Soviet Phenomena and Negative Political Attitudes among Writers and Journalists." "Among a certain part of the writers," it said, "we notice an increase of so-called 'democratic' tendencies, expression of hopes for basic changes of the Soviet system as a result of the war, and in some cases expectation of a restoration of capitalism in the USSR."[31]

An official report on the mood in educated circles of Kharkov noted that a lecturer at the local university resigned from the party "because of disagreements with party policy." In the spirit of Menshevik Social-Democracy he reportedly said,

> We are at the beginning of a major political and ideological shift. The best thoughts and ideas of Western culture — not only in the scientific and technological sphere, but also in the moral and political spheres — are bound to reach us and affect our lives. The cornerstone of this restructuring will be a refusal to introduce any social ideas by violent means, a general penetration of real democracy with its tolerance of all varieties and currents of ideology and worldview, and the triumph of freedom and humanity in the best western European sense of the words.

The same citizen looked forward to less confrontation in relations with the Western democracies and new freedoms of worship and commerce at home: "After all that we've been through, the government must change its policies. Serious changes must take place — and this is already happening — in the political life of the country, such as agreements with capitalist Britain and the U.S.A., dissolution of the Comintern, the separation of educational institutions according to sex, the creation of a state committee for religious affairs, private trade, etc. These changes must go further, especially towards a greater democratization of the country's life."[32]

The desire of creative intellectuals for a right to sincere expression is recorded in an October 1944 letter of V. N. Merkulov, NKVD deputy head, to Zhdanov. The latest works of six famous Soviet writers were decried as "alien to Soviet ideology, [but] have met with a favorable response among students of the Writers' Union Institute, who reject the principles of Socialist Realism and try to formulate 'new theories' of the development of literature and art."[33]

On the Kremlin Olympus NKVD chief and deputy premier Beria was closest to Stalin. A week after the Nazi invasion he along with Molotov and Malenkov formed the State Defense Committee (GKO) headed by Stalin and the locus of wartime policy making. Beria was put in charge of aircraft production and with expedience his compass released from confinement designer Tupolev and 14 associates. Since 1943 Beria supervised the barbaric deportations of North Caucasus tribes and Crimean Tatars to eastern wastelands for alleged collaboration with the Nazi occupiers. Stalin made him the chairman of a GKO bureau to control defense industry, railroad and water transport. Beria's next promotion was to GKO deputy chairman or Stalin's right-hand man. A few months after the war he left the NKVD to work full time on direction of the Soviet atom bomb project. As a full Politburo member he was admitted to the Politburo Foreign Affairs Commission of six top leaders that Stalin led.

Malenkov had his ups and downs in the wartime corridors of power. An August 1943 Politburo decree authorized him to chair meetings of the party Secretariat and Orgburo. He was empowered to summon to sessions local party leaders and take decisions to rectify deficiencies. Malenkov's oversight priorities were economics, culture and the rebuilding of areas liberated from German invaders. The Politburo, however, rejected in January 1944 his draft resolution for an upcoming Central Committee plenum that would have withdrawn party officials from economic management and reserved it for state professionals. That August, Malenkov gained the status of deputy premier and apparently was charged with vetting Soviet citizens for work abroad. Like Beria, he was granted full Politburo membership in 1946.

Khrushchev was political energizer of the generals holding Stalingrad

in 1942 and played that role in the movement of Ukraine partisans working behind Nazi lines. In 1944 he added the Ukraine premiership to his portfolio of republic party leader. Khrushchev initiated a local decision to sack
from all posts the Ukrainian writer and film director Dovzhenko after Moscow accused Dovzhenko of some kind of political mistakes in his story "Victory." Little did Khrushchev suspect that in 1947 he would lose his Ukraine
premiership to Kaganovich for a year because the Center detected nationalistic tendencies in Kiev.

Western scholars differ over who or what started the U.S.–Soviet rivalry
known as the Cold War. Historian Herbert P. Bix conjectures that President Truman's decision to drop the atom bomb on Hiroshima a week earlier than the scheduled Soviet declaration of war on Japan deepened Stalin's
suspicion of the West and helped to open the Cold War. Bix suggests that
use of the atom bomb resulted largely from what he sees as the truculent
anti–Soviet strategy of Truman and Secretary of State James F. Byrnes. In
contrast, John Lewis Gaddis argues that Stalin was accustomed to "redesign-
ing Russia to fit Marxist-Leninist ideology" and his goal in 1945 "was not
to restore a balance of power in Europe, but rather to dominate that continent as thoroughly as Hitler had sought to do so." Gaddis thinks Stalin
envisioned a postwar settlement that encouraged squabbles among capital-
ists that would lead to a new and self-destructive intracapitalist war.[34]

Stalin was more patient than Truman and had reason to pause. All
kinds of dilemmas beset the Kremlin: how far to carry the Sovietization of
east European countries that the Red Army freed of Nazi rule; whether to
stir up communist trouble in western Europe; whether the party controls
of Soviet professionals that were relaxed during the war should be restored
in all their vigor; whom to groom for leadership succession as Stalin entered
his mid-sixties.

Until Stalin made up his mind about what to do about such problems
a variety of policy opinions were heard behind closed doors in Moscow. We
cannot be certain if this ferment was a Kremlin counterpart of high-level
Western debates about Soviet intentions after World War II. But illustrative of high hopes for change among progressives inside the largely conservative Soviet intelligentsia during 1946–1947 were

- A letter sent by a literary editor to party headquarters in Novem-
  ber 1945 asked that writers be allowed to tell the truth about
  Soviet military failures at the start of the Nazi-Soviet war.[35]
- A party-sponsored conference of moviemakers heard a director

argue that Soviet audiences had grown mature enough to watch honest portrayals of everyday life.[36]

- A factory official in the capital wrote to party leaders advising worker participation in management and the right for collective farms to sell their products freely at market prices.[37]

- A lecture that historian E. N. Burdzhalov delivered at the Higher Party School questioned the universal validity of Soviet doctrine that "proletarian dictatorship" (one-party rule with command economy and police terror) was essential for the building of socialism.[38]

- Professor Evgeni Varga, Director of the Institute of World Economics and Politics, implied in his writings that reforms in the capitalist system had staved off a slump, and revolution in western Europe was a remote prospect, which offered a basis for cooperation between the USSR and democratic states.[39]

In sum, if these reformist proposals were acceptable to Stalin there could have been less censorship and command economics inside the USSR, and prolonged coalitions of Communists and doomed rival parties in eastern Europe. The level of East-West suspicion could have been lower than it became during the Cold War, if that conflict were to erupt, as it did in 1947.

Before spring 1946 Malenkov wielded a strong hand. Rumor was that he advised Stalin to pursue a course of moderation rather than statization and old-style imperialism. Malenkov was identified with a policy of private home ownership for officials and communist-nationalist alliances in eastern Europe.[40] The Central Intelligence Agency got wind that Malenkov was for the plundering of industrial equipment in Soviet-occupied Europe but opposed the outright annexation of such areas. Zhdanov was thought to have counseled the stripping of machinery and communizing of occupied territories.[41]

Unexpected developments proved to be important. Igor Gouzenko was a cipher clerk at the Soviet Embassy in Ottawa, Canada, who defected in September 1945 with documents revealing Soviet atomic espionage. Stalin made a speech in February 1946 that skirted the theme of wartime cooperation with the Allies and hinted that Soviet scientists were trying to build an atomic bomb. Kremlin diplomacy pressed for Soviet military bases in Turkey and control of an oil-rich northern province of Iran. (Stalin was following in the footsteps of the last tsar, who visited Potsdam in 1910 and gained German recognition of a Russian zone of influence in northern Persia.) Churchill in a major policy speech regretted a Soviet "Iron Curtain" in east Europe and proposed the creation of an Anglo-American military alliance.

In turn Stalin told *Pravda* that Churchill was a "firebrand of war." U.S. Secretary of the Navy James Forrestal claimed that the Soviet Union was dedicated to the belief that "the capitalistic and communistic concepts cannot live together in the same world." What had looked like a normal rivalry of two Great Powers was beginning to look like a mortal struggle of rival political faiths.

The defection of Gouzenko seems to have undermined Malenkov and still another blow came from hard-line party official Suslov, who near the close of World War II was sent to Lithuania to restore Soviet rule. Early in 1946 he accused Malenkov of harmfully softening the punishment of Baltic nationalists. Suslov complained to the Politburo that at Malenkov's insistence the USSR Supreme Court's Military Collegium often reversed the verdicts of NKVD tribunals that enforced an August 1945 Central Committee decree ordering the show trials of anti–Soviet elements.[42] Stalin spoke at the Politburo in May 1946 and removed Malenkov from that body. A few days later Malenkov was ousted from the Secretariat and in February 1947 named chairman of the Agriculture Bureau in the USSR Government.[43]

Zhdanov's advance at the expense of Malenkov signified a grave setback for humanistic intellectuals. Stalin made a rare appearance at a meeting of the Orgburo in August 1946 that was attended by 25 senior officials. The *vozhd* assailed the Leningrad magazine *Zvezda* for publishing grim accounts of daily life that he viewed as "manure." Satirist Mikhail Zoshchenko in particular was condemned for authoring depressing portrayals of invalids, drunkards and scandals. Zoshchenko later sent a letter to Stalin in which he swore that his future writings would be free of morbidity and anti–Soviet code language.[44]

During the ethnic violence that beset perestroika Soviet scholars traced its origins to party edicts of 1946–1948 that insulted local patriots in the national republics. Writers were accused of idealizing the past of their nations and compelled to recognize the Russians as "older brother."[45] Underlaying the decrees were Zhdanov memorandums hitting at drama theaters in Central Asia and Transcaucasus for focusing on historical themes and old national heroes. Zhdanov's boldest foray was against Khrushchev. In April 1946 a Politburo resolution adopted on Zhdanov's initiative taxed Ukrainian party leaders with the heresy of bourgeois nationalism. Beria is said to have contributed to the worsening of ethnic relations with a 1949 proposal to cleanse Georgia of Turks, Armenians, Greeks and Iranians.[46]

In his campaign to fulfill Stalin's latest order to throttle reformism, Zhdanov tightened party control over the state experts. A February 1947 Politburo decision ruled, "Questions relating to the Foreign Ministry, Foreign Trade Ministry, State Security Ministry, the circulation of money, hard currency, and also important issues relating to the Armed Forces Ministry, will be concentrated in the Politburo."[47] The Politburo quietly reprimanded war hero Marshal Georgi Zhukov for illegally awarding medals to the entertainers of Soviet troops in East Germany. In time Zhukov would secretly be charged with personal theft of booty in the Soviet occupation zone.[48] In February 1947 the Central Committee plenum dropped from its list of candidate members Ivan Maisky, wartime envoy to Great Britain and as such linked to the policy of East-West cooperation.

That September Zhdanov keynoted a conference in Poland that created the Cominform (Communist Information Bureau) to tighten Soviet control of foreign parties. Broadsides were fired at the "imperialist and anti-democratic camp," and a resolution pegged to Zhdanov's speech warned of "nervous and unstable elements" ready to bend to Western pressure. Malenkov spoke on Soviet internal affairs at the meeting and characteristically urged ruling Communist parties to avoid the practice of party officials substituting for state and economic experts.

It is hard to underrate the importance of Zhdanov's speech at the founding session of the Cominform. The harsh rhetoric of Stalin's deputy further hardened Western attitudes toward the Soviet Union. The distinguished British scholar George Bolsover spoke on the topic of Kremlin intentions at the Royal Institute of International Affairs in November 1947. He warned against the view of Soviet ideology as mere instrument for keeping power at home and extending it abroad. That view was said to be harmful as it suggested the possibility of solving world problems by Washington and Moscow cutting deals. Bolsover affirmed that dialectical and historical materialism were at the core of Marxism-Leninism and keys to unlocking the secrets behind Moscow's policies.

But Edward Crankshaw, who served at the British Embassy in Moscow during the war, interpreted Stalin's abstruse postwar writings as suggesting the relativity of Marxism. In his literary commentaries Crankshaw underscored Soviet vulnerabilities on the home front. Against the background of Stalinist subjugation of eastern Europe and Moscow's robust espionage program, the American president was likely to throw his sizable weight

behind the conservative school of foreign policy planning. The groundswell
of fear of Soviet subversion among Americans at the time makes it hard to
believe that renewed courtship of Stalin on the Yalta model would have been
politically viable.

What Zhdanov usually sidestepped in his orations was the theme of
domestic renewal. Since the February 1947 Plenum it was known that plans
were afoot for a nationwide party congress and delegates would discuss a
new party Program and Rules. The proposals sent from local cells to Moscow included a limitation of terms of office for lower party and soviet
officials, and to hold multicandidate Soviet elections from bottom to top.[49]
The political censorship also grew stricter during Zhdanov's sway. In 1938
the Center ruled that it had to clear for publication all writings about Lenin.
His driver, S. Gil, after the war wrote the brochure *Six Years with Lenin* and
an August 1947 decree of the party Secretariat ordered that publishers and
Agitprop officials erred by allowing the work to be released without the Secretariat's approval.[50]

Stalin's fear of admiration for Western democracy inside the Soviet
Union is a revelation of the Shepilov memoir. In September 1947 Zhdanov
was still dressed as a wartime general and had a long talk with Shepilov. He
forecast that Western imperialists would soon launch an ideological offensive against the USSR, which had to keep its powder dry. Many Soviet citizens, Zhdanov said, were abroad during the war and misled by the
appearance of foreign prosperity and now wanted good housing, food and
clothing. Zhdanov notified that Stalin lately emphasized the primacy of
politics and wanted a fight against the inroads of apoliticism.

It has never been officially explained why Stalin harshly criticized
Zhdanov at a Politburo meeting in July 1948 and removed him from the
party Secretariat. Some have speculated that Zhdanov like the Yugoslav
heretics favored a policy of revolutionary action to undermine Western interests. In any event, Zhdanov died at a health resort on August 31 and the
cause was announced as cardiac disease. Stalin put a premium on familiar-
ity and recalled Malenkov to run the Secretariat. Malenkov's oversight duties
were the central party departments for agriculture and propaganda. To consolidate power, Malenkov with Beria's help assembled incriminating material to the effect that Zhdanov's entire clan was unreliable. Malenkov went
to Leningrad with a Politburo decree charging with antiparty actions a number of high officials with career ties to the city. Regional separatism and theft
of state assets were the main accusations in the Politburo document. The
accused were later tried and shot with around 2,000 others arrested in con-

nection with the case. The most prominent of former Leningraders elimi-
nated was Politburo member and central Planner Nikolai Voznesensky.
Rumor was that Voznesensky favored enlargement of the peasants' household plots and the use of family-type work units on collective farms. There
is diverse speculation that his fall was the result of an investment controversy or misleading method of measuring economic performance that made
him look good.[51]

Well into the Gorbachev era a respected figure for party bureaucrats
was the doctrinaire Suslov. In July 1949 he was chosen to spearhead the
campaign against Soviet Jewish intellectuals suspected of allegiance to the
new state of Israel. Suslov was named Agitprop chief and *Pravda* chief editor. His speech at a Cominform meeting in Budapest attacked independ-
ence-minded Yugoslav Communists as "schismatic agents" of western
intelligence services. That was prelude to a series of show trials of high
officials in eastern Europe that lasted until the close of 1952, when the terror inside the USSR escalated.

A confrontation with the Western powers seemed to be brewing in
August 1949 as the military professional Marshal Vasilevsky took charge at
the Defense Ministry from the civilian politico Bulganin, and Stalin assumed
oversight of the armed forces. Amidst a raging hate–America campaign,
Malenkov annoyed Stalin with a belief that it was possible to avoid war
with the United States. The leader removed from the draft of a major speech
that Malenkov intended to deliver on November 6, 1949, a passage to the
effect that "We are ready to welcome any [U.S.] policy which envisages in
any form and really departs from the line of military adventure." Malenkov
also drafted the conciliatory words, "The Soviet people will not spare effort
to labor to strengthen and expand in all ways the partisans of peace, democracy and socialism." Stalin added "and foil the criminal designs of the aggres-
sor." He inserted a paragraph accusing Germany of causing two world wars
and viewing as guarantor of peace in Europe the newly created Soviet satellite German Democratic Republic and the USSR.[52]

Stalin's long vacations in the postwar period led him to regularize Politburo meetings and keep underlings on a short leash. Historian Oleg
Khlevniuk has studied the protocols of relevant Politburo meetings and read
that some members (Molotov, Mikoyan, Kaganovich, Malenkov, Beria, Bulganin and Khrushchev) met during Stalin's absences from Moscow in
1950–1953. They discussed issues and prepared resolutions, always sending
decisions to Stalin for approval or talking with him over the phone.
Khlevniuk cites a witness that in the rooms where the meetings took place

there was a phone booth behind the chairman where communication with Stalin and aides was maintained.

Beria and Malenkov gained from a February 1951 Politburo resolution that entitled them as deputy premiers to direct the inner state cabinet and decide urgent policy issues. Unlike the situation in Zhdanov's heyday, the Politburo, Secretariat and Orgburo were limited to oversight of the media, science, literature, art, and contacts with foreign Communist parties. Jointly with the State Security Ministry, party offices were to select leading personnel and monitor the fulfillment of top-level decisions.[53] The clout of Agitprop further dropped with its division into four separate offices and the closing of its newspaper, *Kultura i zhizn* (Culture and Life), and journal, *Partiynoye prosveshcheniya* (Party Enlightenment). In June 1951 the doctrinaire Suslov lost the editorship of *Pravda*, whose foreign correspondents were told to avoid crude attacks on host governments and keep from meddling in their domestic affairs.[54]

To keep Malenkov and Beria in check, Stalin recalled Khrushchev from Ukraine to Moscow. Since December 1949 Khrushchev was a CPSU Secretary (for agriculture) and first secretary of the Moscow regional party committee. He explains in memoirs that Stalin wanted him to spy on local officials who, according to an anonymous letter, were involved in a conspiracy. As little as 10 percent of truth in such denunciations was sufficient for Stalin to order investigations and arrests.

Khrushchev was hardly a liberal and arguably a political weathervane for much of his kaleidoscopic career. Ukrainian peasants were neglecting collective work and toiling on private plots to sell food on the free market at high prices.[55] From Kiev, Khrushchev sent a letter to Stalin advising a ban on private farming. This initiative failed, but Khrushchev succeeded in February 1948 with a proposal to exile from Ukraine "harmful village elements," or collective farmers who failed to meet their work quotas. The suggestion was approved and Beria, Khrushchev and Suslov led a commission to work out the details of a new law for the entire USSR. By year's end nearly 2.5 million social undesirables were resettled in remote areas.[56]

A few weeks after Khrushchev returned to the central Secretariat, *Pravda*, (February 1950) criticized Politburo member Andreyev for promoting the small "link" work units on collective farms which tended to encourage independent peasant activity. In 1951 Khrushchev and Mikoyan clashed over a new system that Khrushchev proposed for the collective farms to deliver products to the state. Stalin accepted Khrushchev's ideas "in principle," but the argument resumed and Mikoyan was allowed to rework Khrushchev's draft decision.

Since 1948 Stalin was pouring vast amounts of resources into the modernizing of his war machine and he resented Khrushchev's bid to renovate the country's many backward villages. In *Pravda* March 4, 1951, Khrushchev proposed the building of clubhouses, schools, hospitals, shops, parks, stadiums and bathhouses in collective farm "settlements." Some foreign observers construed the scheme as an effort to discourage peasants from work in their private plots. But Malenkov later criticized it as a consumerist deviation. Only a day later *Pravda* had told readers that Khrushchev's article was run "for purposes of discussion," or was not authoritative.

A party circular in April 1951 called Khrushchev's plan "harebrained scheming," "leftist rushing ahead" and "petty-bourgeois hotheadedness." Stalin privately told both Khrushchev and Beria, who seemed to have made a tactical alliance on this issue, that they were "Bolshevik fellow travelers" and "populists." Khrushchev recanted a few weeks later in a speech at a Moscow party plenum.[57]

Old and infirm, Stalin lacked the vigor or will to address acute domestic problems. The food situation was deplorable in the largest towns, with many waiting in long lines to buy loaves of bread limited to around two pounds each and 40 percent composed of potato and other mixtures. Workers were housed in hated barracks or one-room apartments with shared kitchens. New technologies were seriously lagging and even military output was marked by poor workmanship. Over 2.5 million were in prison camps and those outside the "zone" fearful of police informers.

To defend his legacy, Stalin compiled from old memorandums a pamphlet published in September 1952, *Economic Problems of Socialism in the USSR*. Reformers whom Stalin labeled the "new young forces of the leading cadre" were upbraided for seeking "to abrogate the laws of science and to formulate new laws." The heretics were calumniated as pupils of Bukharin, or wishing either to force development of the consumer industries or to return to the mixed private and state economy of the 1920s. Stalin explicitly rejected the idea of less detailed centralized planning and broader use of the profit motive. He forecast the gradual disappearance of money and introduction of products exchange (*produkto-obmen*) or barter in material goods. Stalin upheld state control of basic farm equipment, and an academic who was critical of that was arrested. Stalin lent respectability to the big gap in supply between overgrown heavy industry and stagnant agriculture, as well as bureaucratic privilege. (The average worker earned less than

1,000 rubles monthly while a state minister got 14,000 rubles in salary and bonuses.) The foreign policy section of Stalin's testament echoed Trotsky's 1918 line of "No War — No Peace."

Malenkov was tapped to keynote the party congress in October 1952. Given Stalin's status of virtual deity it is astonishing that a draft of Malenkov's speech ignored *Economic Problems*, and the Politburo approved the draft. Clearly there were major policy disagreements in the Kremlin. Stalin convened the Politburo and Malenkov distributed a new version of his draft that approved the contents of *Economic Problems*.[58] The congress went smoothly but Stalin raged at some colleagues at a secret meeting of the new Central Committee. He harked back to an incident in June 1946 and rebuked Molotov for bowing to pressure and wrongly making concessions to the western Powers in diplomatic talks. Mikoyan and Molotov were said to have returned from trips to the United States foolishly impressed and intimidated by American economic power. Stalin alleged that behind the back of the Politburo, Mikoyan and Molotov sent a directive to the Soviet ambassador in Washington to yield to the American side in upcoming talks.

At the same conclave Stalin attacked Molotov for urging the Politburo to raise the state prices paid to collective farms for their grain. That reproach harked back to a Molotov demarche in 1946 or 1947 that Stalin had rebuffed. Mikoyan tried to refute the charges against him and denied that substantial concessions were made to the Americans. Beria and Malenkov interrupted Mikoyan in an obvious attempt to curry favor with Stalin. The rift healed in a few weeks' time but Khrushchev told Mikoyan that Stalin was confident that he, Mikoyan, and Molotov were foreign spies.[59]

The scholar Rudolf Balandin has an original view of why Stalin impugned Molotov at the October 1952 Plenum. He affirms that Stalin asked to be relieved of his top party post and was set on downgrading the party as opposed to the state as it had become a magnet for privilege-seekers. Molotov was still a prestigious figure and if he replaced Stalin as the party's foremost Secretary it would be all-powerful. Thus, Stalin is thought to have knocked Molotov to blackball him as party successor. Balandin holds too that the recent decision to rename the party from All-Union Communist Party (Bolsheviks) to Communist Party of the Soviet Union (like a USSR state ministry) reflected Stalin's wish to lower its standing among governing institutions.[60] Neither Balandin nor other close students of Soviet politics echo a remark in the Shepilov memoir that Stalin at a Central Committee Plenum — evidently the October 1952 session — unveiled his charges of sabotage against Kremlin physicians and "someone" (*kto-to*) doubted the evidence.

The future course of events suggests that Stalin's fellow Georgian Beria was under a cloud and rejected the slander of Kremlin doctors. A Politburo decree adopted in November 1951 accused senior officials in Georgia of protecting bribe takers. Those criticized were said to be "Mingrelian nationalists," or members of Beria's regional clan. In June 1952 the state security chief in Georgia was fired. At the close of the party congress Beria's longtime associate V. N. Merkulov, USSR Minister of State Control, was dropped from full to alternate status on the Central Committee.

A new great purge was in the offing with Stalin's arrest of Kremlin physicians and family members on trumped-up charges of treason. That drama started in October 1952 and two months later *Pravda* railed at managers with an attack on "some functionaries" who had "turned their enterprises into their own fiefs, introduce[d] their own order and discipline and thr[e]w party discipline overboard." Malenkov may have bristled with the statement that "people with higher education" who were "practitioners without principles" differed from the "ideologically superior people" who "strictly adhere to party discipline." "Some comrades" were said to "believe wrongly that a person with higher education no longer needs any ideological-political training. They forget that higher professional education does not mean that a person is ideologically enlightened and tempered." This was far more than a war of words between rival clans around Stalin: military tribunals began to sentence economic officials to prison camps for "embezzlement and sabotage."[61]

Disputes over foreign affairs were raising the political temperature. *Pravda* (February 6, 1953) included among "rotten theories" current inside the Soviet Union a belief that capitalist encirclement no longer existed and the capitalist world had ceased trying to subvert the regime. Kremlin policy was declared to be one that "admits of no concessions or little concessions to the imperialist aggressors." Judging from Stalin's censorship of Malenkov in the recent past and upcoming political drama, the Number Two Soviet leader may have been a target of this vitriol.

Running counter to propaganda on behalf of new bloodletting were moves to curb the anti–Semitic propaganda organized around the Doctors' Case. V. Lebedev, head of the newspaper sector in Agitprop, on January 1, 1953, rejected a manuscript sent by V. P. Moskovsky, chief editor of the military daily *Krasnaya zvezda* (Red Star), "Zionism — Spy Agency of American Imperialism." The chief editor of *Literary Gazette*, Konstantin Simonov, on February 16 refused to run an article critical of Israel and a major Jewish relief society as anti–Soviet centers.[62]

Khrushchev's memoirs hold that Marshal Konev was the only prominent military leader who endorsed material that Stalin circulated on the Doctors' Case. Konev sent to Stalin a letter agreeing with the texts and reporting that the Kremlin doctors had done harm to him. Khrushchev thought that this charge strengthened Stalin's belief that the doctors were really a hostile anti–Soviet group.

Someone at top level made an effort to accommodate technocrats concerned about economic prospects. In January 1953 state planners and financiers drafted an analytical memorandum that envisioned less centralized planning with the profit motive playing a limited role. A measure of economic freedom was foreseen for ministries, enterprises and republics.[63] Beria and Malenkov would champion such measures soon after Stalin left the scene.

Stalin had a history of strokes. One occurred in autumn 1945 and recovery took ten weeks. Another was diagnosed in summer 1950 and laid up Stalin for almost five months. The nation was stunned in March 1953 with news bulletins that Stalin had suffered a disabling brain hemorrhage and died. Over a half-century later, the Russian far right was sure that Stalin "was murdered while preparing for inevitable war between the West and Russia, which he had begun to restore to the status of Great Power. He decided to cleanse the country of a real Fifth Column, which is now plundering and ruining it. He readied freight cars [to deport Soviet Jews to Siberia] and was murdered."[64]

Unlike this fantasist, Stalin's principal heirs were realists with the clear-sightedness needed to deal with practicalities. Notwithstanding his borderline madness, Stalin had pushed to the forefront men who had the leadership qualities to keep afloat a leaky ship of state. That after all is the overriding goal of political activity. For all their dreadful moral values, Malenkov and Beria grew knowledgeable about statecraft at Stalin's side during and after World War II. Khrushchev was *de facto* governor of Ukraine for more than a decade and as such responsible for thousands of large factories, mines and grain farms. Now at the levers of power they coped with pressures far better than either Stalin or foreign observers had believed would be the case. First, the incipient terror on the Soviet scene had to be addressed and then the slow drift toward all-out war between the United States and USSR.

CHAPTER 4

Khrushchev: Between Reformers and Diehards

Khrushchev's anti–Stalin campaigns were the cornerstone of Gorbachev's political reforms. Those drives featured glasnost to impugn coercive rule and to argue the urgency of an emergency program to overcome food shortages. As a rule, Khrushchev pursued a course of repairing relations with the United States to slow the costly superpower arms race. But inconsistency and indecisiveness plagued Khrushchev during his Kremlin years. At heart a party supremacist, he remained hostile to civil society, market relations and cultural freedom. As in Stalin's time, mobilization methods were used to tackle social-economic issues. Like Lenin and Stalin, Khrushchev made big gambles such as planting wheat on huge tracts of land in arid eastern regions, erecting the Berlin Wall and emplacing ballistic missiles in Cuba. The influence of conservative associates was one of the reasons for Khrushchev's erratic official behavior. Acrimonious debates raged over institutional and personal authority, resource allocation, nationality rights, diplomatic priorities and how to evaluate Stalin's role in history.[1] The resistant-to-change figures were largely responsible for toppling Khrushchev after he effectively created a second Communist party to enhance the political control of industry.

Stalin was officially reported to have died at 9:50 P.M. on March 5, 1953, and a state coup occurred in his last hours. A meeting of party and state bodies was held and ended at 8:40 P.M. Malenkov was vested with Stalin's titles of premier and party Secretary. Beria was named one of several first deputy premiers and head of the unified security services. (MVD). Beria's strength was underscored by the fact that MVD troops occupied the Interior Ministry at 6 A.M. on March 6, or two hours after Moscow Radio announced that Stalin was dead. They cleared squares and streets, surrounded the Kremlin and isolated the capital from the rest of the country until the

state funeral on March 9. Khrushchev's status as the only top party man without a government post meant that the highest state officials were in charge.

The first of many surprises occurred when Malenkov resigned from the
Secretariat on March 14.[2] The Mikoyan memoirs claim that Malenkov exaggerated the clout of the premiership and voluntarily left the Secretariat in
the hands of Khrushchev. Mikoyan writes that Malenkov and Khrushchev
were on good terms and Malenkov could not have suspected that
Khrushchev would be so disloyal as to plot his downfall. Mikoyan comments that Malenkov should have appreciated that he himself helped Stalin
to make the party bureaucracy all-powerful.

The outer world learned that Malenkov differed from Stalin about the
chances for negotiating an end to the Korean War. That stalemated conflict
had taken the lives of millions of soldiers and civilians over the past three
years. Malenkov paved the way for an armistice in Korea with his statement
to the Soviet parliament on March 15, 1953: "There is not a single controversial or unsettled question which could not be solved by peaceful means
on the basis of the mutual agreement of the interested countries."

Unknown to foreign observers was a skirmish fought over the choice
of continuity or change in Kremlin policy. Malenkov instigated a media
blackout on Stalin that took effect on March 17 and hinted at a desire to
inch away from political rigidity. In contrast, the head of the Komsomol,
Aleksandr Shelepin, age 34, was a devoted Stalinist and urged recommit-
ment to orthodoxy. Despite Malenkov's directive to avoid mention of Stalin
in the media, Shelepin sent a memorandum to the party Presidium (Politburo) on March 26 requesting that the Komsomol be renamed from "Leninist" to "Lenin-Stalin" and its newspaper be called "Stalin's Generation."
Shelepin was rebuffed and Malenkov was ready to go before the Central
Committee and denounce the Stalin cult as a Socialist-Revolutionary vice
of seeing "heroes and crowds" (*eserovshchina*). But a Kremlin majority
opposed castigation of Stalin.[3]

In the hope of reaching out to widen his power base, Beria crafted a
reformist platform. He was keenly aware of the professionals' desire for personal security and had a natural talent for politicking. Nuclear scientist
Vitali Goldansky recounts that as supervisor of the atom bomb project,
"Beria more than other 'top leaders' socialized with the senior technical
intelligentsia. He knew the attitudes of such persons and if these did not
clash with his personal interests he made an effort to win popularity among
them."[4] Beria accordingly sponsored a March 27 ukase that released almost
1.2 of 2.5 million inmates of prison camps.[5]

Historian Gennadi Kostyrchenko examined a Beria memorandum of April 2 reporting to party leaders that security police chief Abakumov and his deputy, Ogoltsov, met with Stalin in December 1947 and Stalin ordered them secretly to murder the world-famous Jewish actor Mikhoels as a renegade. Beria initiated an April 3 decision of the party Presidium that quashed the Kremlin Doctors' Case as a violation of Soviet laws. Thirty-seven physicians and family members were freed and Beria authorized to send an explanatory letter to senior officials. The circular revealed that Stalin had ordered the beating of confessions out of the doctors, one of whom died from the ordeal.[6]

Ironically, Khrushchev, the future arch critic of Stalin crimes, put up roadblocks to Beria's movement toward legality. He allied with Molotov to block a Beria suggestion to amnesty all survivors of Stalin purges. Beria was stopped from reining in the MVD's extra-judicial Special Council, abolished only in September 1953, or after Beria was overthrown.[7]

An undercurrent of the Beria-Khrushchev infighting was renewed disagreement over the relations of state experts and party controllers. Beria told his agents to collect materials proving the incompetence of apparatchiks in handling economic problems. *Pravda* led the charge with a March 27 editorial instructing, "The responsibility of party leaders for the conditions in one sector or another in no way means that they should do the work of others, or assume the functions of administrative and economic personnel. The party firmly cautions its cadres not to stifle the initiative of such personnel and not to exert any petty tutelage over them." Malenkov was on the same wave length and in May lowered the salaries of party officials.[8]

Beria subtly and otherwise flirted with non–Russian elites in the borderlands. He rejected the Russian tradition of personalized leadership and sponsored a May 9 party decree that forbade the display of leaders' portraits in parades and on buildings during state holidays. Chekists were to collect information on the ethnic origins of local chiefs, and Beria aides went to republics to demand that native cadres replace Russian superiors.[9] Special attention was paid to Lithuanian officials who felt themselves victims of discrimination by Russians. The Presidium on May 20 discussed Beria's memorandum on battle with the nationalistic underground in Lithuania and tasked republic party bodies to promote native officials. A halt was called to the practice of appointing ethnic outsiders to the posts of deputy premiers and second secretaries of district and town party committees, as well as deputy soviet chairmen. Lithuanians were to be assigned to the posts of directors of state farms and Machine Tractor Stations. The names of per-

sons lacking knowledge of the Lithuanian language were to be stricken from
the rolls of those eligible to hold public office (*nomenklatura*). All clerical
work in governing bureaus was to be conducted in the Lithuanian language
and Polish used in areas that Poles inhabited. After Beria's arrest this decision was expunged from the master records of the Presidium and decisions
based on it were rescinded as able to "activate bourgeois-nationalist elements."[10]

The power struggle of Beria and Khrushchev got hotter in May–June
1953. Khrushchev client and Russifier Leonid Melnikov was dropped as
party head of Ukraine and Beria named Pavel Meshik republic MVD head.
Beria deputy B. Z. Kobulov told the leaders of Belorussia that Russian first
party secretary Patolichev "should be replaced and Comrade Zamyatin
appointed."[11] A Latvian plenum held June 22–23 ignored an advisory of the
CPSU Secretariat and kept to the Beria line of giving preference to non–Russian candidates for high posts.[12] Another Beria move that angered centralists was to shift from Moscow to local control the rest homes in Georgian
resort areas.[13] The Shepilov memoir reports that around this time Beria sent
a letter to political leaders and intellectuals in the Union and autonomous
republics urging more scope for them to display initiative.

Beria took advantage of new rules that entitled leaders to make proposals in any sector of policy. He trumped Khrushchev's bid to raise the
state prices for potatoes grown on collective farms with a proposal to create special state farms to produce that commodity.[14] With Malenkov Beria
urged a sweeping reappraisal of foreign policy. He aimed at economizing
on both defense and subsidies to orbit states. The Government Presidium
met on May 27 and analyzed reasons for the mass flight of East Germans
westward. An unfavorable political and economic situation was said to exist
in East Germany. For almost a year, leaders there were engaged in the "rapid
building of socialism" and it resulted in a sharp decline of living standards
and increase of arrests. Malenkov and Beria tabled a draft decision for themselves with Molotov and Khrushchev to formulate corrective measures in
three days' time. Molotov disagreed with the directive and Khrushchev's
position is unclear.[15]

Gorbachev's New Thinking about foreign affairs is presaged in the
word of an old Chekist that Beria strove for German unification on Western terms in hope of obtaining from the Allies a $10 billion aid package for
Moscow and the shedding of a $20 billion subsidy that East Germany would
cost the Soviet Union over the next decade.[16] Beria's internal foes doubtless
rejoiced over the plunge of his reputation as spymaster and strategist on the

heels of a worker uprising in East Germany on June 17 that Soviet troops suppressed. The East German leaders accused their Beria-linked secret police of failure to anticipate the insurrection.[17]

Khrushchev's version of Beria's downfall is that he was alarmed over the sudden movement of MVD divisions to the outskirts of Moscow and feared a coup. He recalls having told Malenkov that Beria was menacingly deploying special police units near Moscow.[18] Mikoyan remembers that Khrushchev enlisted his support of Beria's ouster by saying that Beria commanded Malenkov and had turned Kremlin bodyguards into spies. Mikoyan tells that he asked Khrushchev about Beria's fate if demoted and was misled to believe that Beria would be named head of the state oil industry.

On June 26 army troops surrounded MVD forces near Moscow and occupied the Kremlin. At a leadership meeting that Malenkov chaired Khrushchev took the floor and cited a 1938 purge victim to the effect that Beria was a British agent. Before a vote could be taken on the issue of what to do Malenkov signaled armed military officers to enter the room and arrest Beria. Defense Minister Bulganin deployed two armored divisions in central Moscow to prevent Kremlin guards or MVD troops from trying to rescue Beria from his confinement in a military bunker.[19]

Russian archives hold no verbatim record of the meeting at which Beria was arrested. The Presidium unanimously resolved to burn unread the documents in Beria's safe, convinced that compromising material abounded. Malenkov, Beria and Khrushchev had earlier ordered the burning of a large part of Stalin's personal archive, according to historians Roy and Zhores Medvedev. Six months after Beria's arrest a special tribunal presided over by Marshal Konev sentenced the defendant to death.[20]

In 1953 the ousting of Beria and tagging of him as an imperialist agent had to electrify Soviet audiences. Under Stalin the man with the pince-nez and outsized black hat was officially held in exaltation. He was the recipient of five Orders of Lenin, three Red Banner Orders and alone held the title "Honored USSR Citizen." A 1945 song lauded Beria as "true knight," "fearless marshal" and "devoted to dear Stalin." Another in 1946 rhapsodized that "dear comrade Beria protects the gains of 1917, He is sacredly loyal to the Leader's behests and safeguards the Homeland's happiness. A reliable sword is in the hands of a Chekist and soldier." A 1948 work of court painter Nalbandyan showed Stalin briefing the Politburo on his plan for planting shelter belts in steppe regions with Beria seated close to the *vozhd*.

To discredit Beria and his novel ideas an unusual week-long meeting of the Central Committee was held July 2–7, 1953. The charges likely to ring true to the elites were that Beria

- tried to subordinate the CPSU to the MVD (Malenkov and Khrushchev);
- ordered MVD officers to gather embarrassing facts about regional party officials (Kaganovich);
- replaced local MVD chiefs without consulting local party leaders (Z. T. Serdyuk);
- eavesdropped on the conversations of colleagues (Malenkov and Molotov);
- proposed to abandon the building of socialism in East Germany and its merger with West Germany along capitalist lines (Malenkov, Khrushchev and Molotov);
- pressed for the state Council of Ministers rather than party Presidium to be the prime policymaking body in foreign affairs (Molotov); and
- urged the replacement of Russian officials with ethnic nationality personnel in west Ukraine and Lithuania (A. P. Zavenyagin).

Rumors of teenage abduction and rape were to follow the official accusation that Beria cohabited with dozens of women and contracted syphilis.[21]

July 1953 Plenum speeches hinted at new discord among the leaders. Malenkov plugged broader use of material incentives and development of internal trade. He made a rare direct criticism of Stalin for theorizing that money would disappear as the country entered the stage of full communism. But Malenkov chose to keep silent about his advice to Finance Minister Zverev in April to note in his next budget speech to the quasi-parliament that more funds should be earmarked for agriculture and the consumer industries.[22]

Khrushchev at the Plenum took a middle-of-the-road position, shielding Stalin and indirectly knocking Malenkov for assuring the 1952 party congress that the chronic grain shortage was overcome: "What kind of communism is it," Khrushchev asked, "when *there is no bread or butter?*" (italics added). Kaganovich was uneasy about lessening the terror and, embracing continuity, asked that regime doctrine be renamed from Marxism-Leninism to "the teaching of Marx, Engels, Lenin and Stalin."[23]

In Communist parlance the leadership speeches indicated a lineup of Right or reformist (Malenkov), Center or middle-of-the-road (Khrushchev) and Left or conservative (Kaganovich). Khrushchev kept his wartime ties to military leaders and intended to use them to gain the upper hand in ruling circles. He said that Marshal Zhukov and he recently got a plea for justice from a colonel-general who was falsely arrested in 1948 and sentenced to a long term of imprisonment.

The military would have applauded too Khrushchev's rejection of Beria's idea of a German peace settlement: "And what is this treaty worth? We know what treaties are worth. A treaty has force if it is reinforced with cannons. If a treaty is not reinforced by might, then it is worth nothing, they'll be laughing at us, thinking us naïve." Obviously with an eye to his participation in the overthrow of Beria, Marshal Zhukov was promoted to full membership in the Central Committee.[24]

The resolution of the July 1953 Plenum was delivered to regional party offices as a secret letter. Malenkov and Khrushchev stood to benefit from avowal that the new regime aimed at "further improvement of agriculture (livestock, vegetables, etc.)" and "maximal satisfaction of the ever-growing material and cultural demands of the workers." Reactionaries could take heart from the document keeping silent about Malenkov's criticism of Stalin as economic theorist.[25]

In the long run Khrushchev was the main beneficiary of such meetings. During the recesses he drank with barons and told ribald jokes, which made him seem like a trustworthy Goodfella. Agitprop veteran Dmitri Shepilov records in a memoir that his first impression of Khrushchev was that of a simple and good-natured person with a phenomenal memory. Ordinary citizens who saw Khrushchev during his many visits to the provinces admired him as "rough peasant with a head on his shoulders" (*muzhik s golovoy*). One of Khrushchev's brain-trusters recalled him that way: "His broad face with its two warts and his huge bald skull, his large snub nose and his protruding ears could easily have belonged to a peasant from the middle–Russian countryside. The impression of being, so to speak, of the common people was intensified by his thick-set, full figure and his long arms, which [were] almost continually gesticulating."[26] Gorbachev's *Memoirs* offer a darker view of Khrushchev, who in 1958 came to Stavropol in south Russia for an awards ceremony. The young party man was struck by the guest's folksy style, use of expletives and boozing.

Khrushchev was not above the courting of grafting bureaucrats. Malenkov at a rally with managers and apparatchiks in November 1953 criticized bribe-takers. Khrushchev sensed the indignation of auditors and cleared the air by saying, "That's all true, of course, Georgi Maksimilianovich. But the apparatus is our bulwark." The remark drew loud applause, alluding as it did to the necessity of a strong governing caste. The job security of elites would be of less concern to Khrushchev once he felt himself to be in the driver's seat.

Yet at Stalin's funeral Malenkov invoked Lenin's conciliatory slogan of the worker-peasant alliance and seemingly promised the rural class a better deal than was the case since farm collectivization. Malenkov elaborated on the theme of economic well-being with a pro-consumer speech to the parliament in August 1953. He contended that the USSR was "now stronger than ever" thanks to having matched the United States in possession of a thermonuclear bomb. This made possible a double downsizing of the open military budget. Malenkov said that it was unsatisfactory that since 1925 heavy industry grew 55 times and consumer goods only 12 times. He insisted that living standards could be raised in the next two or three years by forcing the development of light industry, using new technologies, streamlining management and closing unprofitable enterprises.

Malenkov announced a new food policy of raising state prices for collective farm products, lowering rural taxation and lifting restrictions on work in the household plots.[27] Visitors to the Soviet Union heard citizens lavish praise on Malenkov for enacting the reforms. An old peasant woman told a journalist that in the countryside things were getting better. She explained that Malenkov had declared he would follow the politics of Lenin and not those of Stalin. The reporter checked and found that nowhere had Malenkov ever said such a thing.[28] But there was a sharp and meaningful difference of emphasis between Stalin's acclaim of heavy industry since 1928 and the pro-consumer speech of Malenkov in August 1953.

In line with Malenkov's thinking, state planner M. Z. Saburov ordered the managers of defense plants to produce watches, refrigerators, vacuum cleaners, motorcycles, bicycles, washing machines, television sets, radios and telephones. Some unprofitable factories of heavy industry were to be closed and costly work was stopped on metro systems that were intended to serve as bomb shelters in the event of war. To increase the purchasing power of consumers, the compulsory state loan to which all workers had to subscribe was halved. Glasnost was used to pressure managers to implement the New Course: statistics were aired detailing the rises in planned output of consumer goods.

As the superpowers were embarking on a military aircraft race that would be very expensive Malenkov insisted on a real chance to avoid nuclear war. The literary journal *Zvezda* (November 1953) ran an article of publicist Gus (pronounced *goos*) suggesting that with the rising power of socialism mankind was able to prevent general war. This was almost certainly a trial balloon to gauge informed public opinion and many found it acceptable.

Malenkov warned in a March 1954 speech that a global conflict would mean little short of the end of world civilization. That seemed to make a case for arms control and other forms of peaceful cooperation. In dispatches U.S. ambassador Charles Bohlen remarked that Malenkov took a calmer view of world affairs than did Khrushchev. American lawyer Marshall Mac-Duffie often spoke to Khrushchev and said he "displayed a shocking rigidity in his thinking about the West — an apparent willingness to swallow the propaganda he himself had helped create."

Khrushchev knew that his luster would dim if the Malenkov reforms picked up steam. He got the leadership to convoke a Central Committee plenum on agriculture in September 1953. There Khrushchev played his glasnost card to reveal that livestock was less than in 1928 and cattle below the number in 1916. His remedy came from the era of collectivization and was to send 30,000 factory workers to serve as collective farm chairmen. Khrushchev, as director of this effort to bring order to the floundering villages, was named CPSU "First" Secretary.

That also symbolized command of the 125,000 apparatchiks who oversaw all forms of social activity throughout the Soviet Union.[29] One of them was Dmitri Shepilov, *Pravda* chief editor, who soon wrote a pamphlet trumpeting Khrushchev's advocacy of restrictions on household plots.[30] A secret government decree adopted in December admitted Khrushchev to the inner state cabinet and named him chairman of a new Bureau for Agriculture and Procurements.[31] Now Khrushchev was the man a regional boss had to see if he wanted more resources to develop his rural infrastructure.

A mistaken illusion of Malenkov was that U.S. President Dwight Eisenhower might offer concessions to the Soviet side in a new round of diplomacy. Unlike the open-minded Churchill, Eisenhower was highly suspicious of Kremlin intentions when the two met at the Bermuda conference in December 1953. Ike had a bad temper and created a stir with a description of Kremlin leaders as the same old streetwalker in a new dress. The Soviet agents in high British quarters are likely to have informed Moscow about the Bermuda discussions and that probably served to strengthen the Khrushchev-led hardliners.

Sustaining the momentum, Khrushchev sent a letter to colleagues in January 1954 reviving an old scheme to plow up and sow to grain nearly 30 million acres of unused and fallow lands in Kazakhstan and Siberia. The so-called Virgin Lands would be three times larger than the area of all land cultivated in the Soviet Union, and equal in size to the farm acreage of Great Britain, France and Spain. A labor force of 250,000 was required, along with 120,000 tractors and 10,000 harvesting machines.

Malenkov and Molotov opposed the plan as too risky in view of the dry climate in the east. They also held that the project underrated the outlook for farms in central Russia. Khrushchev argued that intensive farming there would require greater outlays of resources and knowledge of how to use modern technologies, which peasants lacked. He organized a conference of lower officials and his idea was endorsed. Addressing the Central Committee in February 1954 Khrushchev turned the spotlight of glasnost on rural ills and won a mandate for the New Lands program. The gamble proved to be essentially sound with a few good harvests of fodder grain until soil erosion took a heavy toll.[32]

A negative by-product of the affair was worsening of Slav-Muslim relations in Central Asia. Khrushchev tells us in memoirs that Kazakh party head Zhumabai Shayakhmetov disliked the reclamation program as sure to bring more unwanted Russian and Ukrainian settlers to his homeland. The Slavic apparatchiks P. K. Ponomarenko and Leonid Brezhnev replaced Shayakhmetov. Brezhnev was a subordinate of Khrushchev in postwar Ukraine and on his watch in Kazakhstan a delegate to the republic's party congress who thanked Khrushchev "personally" for "rendering aid to the construction and organization of our state farms." Brezhnev was to remain a flatterer of Khrushchev until even he could no longer tolerate his patron's erratic antics and plotted to oust him.

Khrushchev endeared himself to the party stalwarts and antagonized the reformist intellectuals with a decision to retreat from the post–Stalin curbing of literary censorship. The party Secretariat in obedience to Khrushchev's orders adopted a decree in July 1954 attacking the progressive journal *Novy mir* and removing chief editor Aleksandr Tvardovsky for having read an anti–Stalin poem to friends.[33] Khrushchev's memoirs contend that this action was taken to reassure rattled officials who feared loss of party control of the country.

The pullback from limited cultural freedom was prelude to a cabal to sideline Malenkov, the leader most critical of Stalin and his policies. Khrushchev's set gathered at Black Sea villas during the Crimean vacation season in August and September 1954. Included were civilian Defense Minister Nikolai Bulganin, Moscow mayor during Khrushchev's stint in the capital during the 1930s; deputy premier Mikoyan; regional party heads

Frol Kozlov (Leningrad), Aleksei Kirichenko (Kiev) and Yekaterina Furtseva (Moscow). They agreed to lobby Central Committee members for support of a decision to remove Malenkov from the premiership. In October
Bulganin accompanied Khrushchev on trips to the Soviet Far East, Siberia
and Urals.

A secret decision taken by the CPSU Secretariat in November 1954
marked a breakthrough in the power struggle. A General Affairs Department was created at party headquarters to replace Malenkov's Office of the
Presidium (*Kantselyariya*), which printed and distributed executive documents. Now Khrushchev personally finalized draft resolutions and controlled
the flow of sensitive information.[34]

Khrushchev struck at the heart of Malenkov's policies of consumerism
with detente in his speech to a meeting of youths on January 7, 1955. He
invoked Stalin on need to bolster heavy industry and defenses as the country was surrounded by foreign enemies. A *Pravda* article of January 24 signed
by Shepilov dusted off the Stalinist vocabulary and rued lapse into "justly
condemned ideas of the Right deviation," or Bukharin's pro-peasant platform. Malenkov's views were assailed as "theoretically wrongful and politically harmful." The Central Committee met a week later and adopted the
secret decree "On Comrade G. M. Malenkov." This lacerated the premier
for

- lacking knowledge and experience in economics and local government affairs;
- poorly organizing the work of the government cabinet;
- indecision when facing ripe issues;
- insufficiency of political maturity and firm Bolshevik leadership
  qualities;
- courting cheap popularity by sloganeering for the preferential
  growth of consumer industries;
- harmfully asserting that if the imperialists started World War III it
  would result in the destruction of world civilization;
- close and longtime ties with Beria, and political blindness in following him on many issues;
- moral responsibility for 1949–1950 purges in Leningrad and slandering leaders to Stalin;
- political spinelessness in joining Beria to frame governmental
  changes when Stalin was dying;
- agreeing with Beria to refrain from building socialism in and to

withdraw Soviet troops from East Germany, enabling it to merge
with West Germany as a single, capitalist and neutral state; and
• political responsibility for the backwardness of agriculture, and
blindly trusting fraudsters such as party agrarian A. I. Kozlov.[35]

This largely unconvincing indictment was meant to presage a return to the
clear-cut primacy of heavy industry and supremacy of the party controllers
headed by Khrushchev.

At a meeting of the parliament Malenkov confessed to incompetent
oversight of farm affairs in the postwar period and resigned as premier. He
was given a post in the energy sector but kept his seat on the Presidium.
The listless Bulganin was chosen premier and Marshal Zhukov replaced
him as Defense Minister. Secretly, Khrushchev was named chair of a Defense
Council formed in February 1955 to decide military issues and, as was his
wont, boorishly imposed his personal views on professionals.[36]

Some loose ends were annoying as Khrushchev organized the party
congress due to open in February 1956. He still had to keep abreast of the
opinion of independents along with party sentiment in general. A major
Khrushchev ally was party elder Mikoyan, who was responsible for the huge
task of liberating political prisoners unjustly convicted during the Stalin
era. Historian Roy Medvedev holds that in 1955 there were millions such
inmates in work camps and the normal procedures for release and pardon
took one or two years. The families of many prisoners were pleading for
immediate relief lest the prisoners die (Medvedev and Chiesa 1989).

Khrushchev learned more about Stalin's crimes against the elites when
USSR Interior Minister Kruglov in February 1954 sent to him a memo
reporting the existence of 383 lists with over 43,000 names of officials that
Politburo members had to authorize to be shot or imprisoned in 1936–38.
Stalin, Molotov and Zhdanov most often signed the condemnatory documents while other top men did so infrequently or never (http://Stalin.
memo. ru).

Mikoyan's memoirs tell of contacts with former camp prisoners and
hearing of their torture by NKVD interrogators. Mikoyan states that he
took some freed victims to Khrushchev and told him that if present-day
leaders failed to condemn Stalin's excesses they might someday be blamed
for them. Khrushchev agreed with Mikoyan's proposal to create a commission with access to relevant documents and to assign the panel to draft a
suitable report for the party congress. Unsuccessfully Mikoyan objected to
Khrushchev's choice of party ideologist Pospelov to head the commission

as he was a Stalinist (*prostalinski nastroyennym*). Moreover, anti–Stalinism was bubbling up from the security service. The commandants of prison camps wanted to release many restless inmates to avert more of the strikes and riots that swept the camps in 1954–1955 and could be suppressed only with the help of military units.

The Presidium met on December 31, 1955, to discuss the Stalin issue. A heated dispute arose after premier Buglanin read the letter of an old party member accusing Stalin of the Kirov murder. The ceremonial president and Stalinist Voroshilov shouted "Lies!" Mikoyan spoke and said that Chekists had a hand in the assassination. Khrushchev commented, "It doesn't smell good." A commission chaired by Pospelov was formed to investigate repressions from Kirov's murder to the German invasion (December 1934 to June 1941).[37]

The Stalinist terror was so indiscriminate that Khrushchev's decision to explore it might have raised a threat to social peace. The political control of historical records was a duty of party Secretary for ideology Suslov. His career and speeches make it likely that he would have opposed a reassessment of Stalin's methods. At odds with Khrushchev's second thoughts about Stalin, the Moscow newspaper *Literary Gazette* in January 1956 announced official plans to publish a volume of Stalin speeches inclusive of ones dating to the 1937–1938 purges.

Historical argument resumed in January when the Presidium examined a draft of Khrushchev's keynote to the party congress. Kaganovich objected to "risky propositions" such as one revising Lenin's teaching about the inevitability of war between socialist and capitalist powers. Molotov carped that it was wrong to approve of using parliamentary elections to bring Communists to power without attacking the British Labor party. On the other hand, *Pravda* editor Shepilov certified Khrushchev's text as strictly Marxist-Leninist. The first secretary himself proposed that special party commissions go to more labor camps to free prisoners. Voroshilov was skeptical but Molotov agreed and the motion passed.[38]

Khrushchev made conciliatory gestures toward the Stalinists at the February 1 Presidium. He portrayed Stalin as the mastermind of purges but was forgiving of his retinue. NKVD chief Yezhov was absolved of guilt in the 1938 arrest and execution of Politburo member Robert Eikhe. Khrushchev went so far as to call Yezhov an honest person. Molotov took heart and hailed Stalin as "great." Kaganovich scolded Khrushchev for banning Stalin posters. Mikoyan, however, accused Molotov of complicity in Stalin's crimes. Khrushchev as chair finally tore into Stalin for using barbaric methods that nearly destroyed the party.[39]

An uproar occurred at the February 9 Presidium over the finding of Pospelov's commission that a huge number of Soviet citizens were annihilated in the post–Kirov terror. Molotov stood his ground: "For 30 years the party lived and worked under the leadership of Stalin, industrialized the country, won victory in the war and emerged a Great Power after its conclusion." Kaganovich pleaded extenuating circumstances for his involvement in the mass murders: "We bear responsibility, but the situation was such that we could not object." He stressed that if Stalin was now criticized uncontrollable forces (*stikhiyu*) might be set loose. To avoid that the Lenin Testament had to be kept secret and only top leaders allowed to read it.

Mikoyan urged publishing the Testament and Lenin's criticism of Stalin as a wrong-headed bureaucratic centralist. Voroshilov, who was involved in the decapitation of the Red Army in 1937, said it was best to avoid raking up the past. The technocrat Saburov objected to Stalin's revival of the tsarist aim to control the Turkish Straits and commented, "We lost a great deal because of a stupid [foreign] policy (the Finnish war, Korea and Berlin)." At the end of the day the vote on whether to pillory Stalin at the congress was Noes: Molotov, Kaganovich and Voroshilov; Ayes: Khrushchev, Mikoyan, Pervukhin, Bulganin and Saburov; Abstained: Malenkov.[40]

Khrushchev told the Central Committee on February 13, or eve of the party congress, that the Presidium had decided to add to the agenda a special report on Stalinism. Not until February 18 was work completed on a draft of the report. The next day Khrushchev dictated to a stenographer additions to the draft making Stalin appear to be more primitive than was originally intended. Not until March 1 or after the congress did Khrushchev submit to the Presidium the full text of his speech destroying the Stalin myth.[41] It was read to a late-night session of the party congress that was closed to foreigners. A March 5 decision of the Presidium mandated that almost the entire adult population be briefed on the special report. In the meantime, Khrushchev got the Presidium to order the formation of almost 100 commissions to visit prison camps and free political inmates, over 50,000 of whom were soon released.

The mass readings of Khrushchev's attack on Stalin led to outbursts of indignation. Some workers threw oily rags at portraits of Stalin. A letter to the Presidium from Leningrad commented on reaction at the USSR Academy of Russian Literature:

> The impression which the report created was one of shock and the scene is hard to describe in a few words. The real tragedy lay not in Stalin's personality. The historic reality of one-man rule within the Soviet system must

be viewed as a greater tragedy for the masses, party and people.... We cannot limit ourselves to hearing the report and leaving with our heads bowed. The document was read to us without the right of discussion, merely "for purposes of information." The party must condemn Stalin in a party court.... Allow each party organization to voice its opinion on the Stalin question.... Let each Communist speak up at a party meeting and say if Stalin was a state criminal. Yes, let the party take a vote on this topic. Did he commit crimes against humanity?

A speaker declared at a meeting of scientists who were party members: "The people are powerless. That enabled a small group to establish its dictatorship.... A radical measure to eradicate harmful phenomena in our life is perhaps to arm the people." Another letter-writer saw hypocrisy among the elites: "We talk about the power of the party and authority of the people. There never was any such thing and it does not exist now. With Stalin we could have gone straight to fascism.... Now too we are redoing the personality cult, extolling Khrushchev. His report on the cult was not subjected to intelligent discussion at the congress."

The majority at one party meeting barely voted down a scathing opinion: "Our country is socialist, but not democratic.... We are wrong to compare socialism with capitalism. Why don't we compare it to the slaveholding system? ... In our country, property belongs to the people while power is in the hands of a clique of scoundrels. The state security service is like a child that we've raised and then hits us square in the face." Party booklets were taken from four scientists who shared that view.[42] Historian Geoffrey Hosking reports that a physicist, Yury Orlov, addressed one of the briefings on Khrushchev's report and spoke of "the general lack of honesty and morality" and "need for democratic changes."

An unintended consequence of Khrushchev's secret speech was a fanning up of inter-ethnic rancor. The Caucasus republic of Georgia was rocked by March 4–9 protests against the denunciation of native son Stalin. Unrest occurred in the capital Tbilisi and towns of Kutaisi, Sukhumi, Batumi and Gori, Stalin's birthplace. Crowds estimated at 40,000 persons gathered to pay tribute at the Stalin monument in Tbilisi and demanded that Kremlin leaders be ousted. Around 10,000 tried to storm party and government buildings in the capital. Army troops fired on the crowd and MVD units dispersed 30,000 who besieged police headquarters in search of weapons. Officially, 13 protesters were reported to have been killed and 8 of 63 injured later died. Roy Medvedev disputes these figures, claiming in his Khrushchev biography that 250–300 died and 1,000 were seriously hurt. An authoritative Russian source later put at 381 the number of protesters whom the KGB arrested.

Georgian bosses later reported to Khrushchev that some locals were saying that "the Russians want to destroy the Georgians, and gradually all Georgians will be resettled." Russians were cited to the effect that " Stalin was a traitor; only a small part of the Georgian nation was shot on March 9. More of them should have been wiped out. Half of those Georgians should be deported and new people brought here." Party members who heard Khrushchev's secret speech were divided on the Stalin question. Some shouted at meetings "Untrue!" "Slander of Stalin!" "Stalin's name will not be forgotten!"

Others asked, "Do we need portraits and monuments of a man who so mercilessly destroyed people? By his actions he was an enemy of the people, but one not unmasked until now." One party member foretold a 1961 symbolic gesture and said that the presence of Stalin's remains in the Lenin tomb on Red Square was an insult to the memory of Lenin, and proposed remedial action. Oddly, Mikoyan wrote on a memorandum sent from Tbil-isi, "Purge the Mensheviks in the Central Committee. Menshevik elements have used Stalin's name as a banner."[43]

Drawing on a secret party circular, the April 5 *Pravda* editorial brought the anti–Stalin campaign to a screeching halt. "Under the guise of condemning the personality cult," it stated, "some rotten elements are trying to cast doubt on the correctness of the party's policy.... The party has never tolerated and will not tolerate petty-bourgeois license, much less anti-party statements, in its midst." Events tended to vindicate the cautious Stalinists, and Molotov was chosen to head a commission to evaluate the 1936–1938 Moscow Trials. The panel approved of the melodramatic spectacles with a ruling that defendants "over the course of many years headed anti–Soviet struggle directed against the building of socialism."[44]

Gorbachev 50 years later said that Khrushchev's anti–Stalin speech was a milestone on the road to perestroika and introducing more democratic ways to run the country.[45] Roy Medvedev argues with those who thought that the speech left unscathed the essentials of Communist thought. He felt the demolition of major blocks of the ideology and weakening of regime foundations. True, the situation was largely unchanged, but minds were affected, with joy over learning the truth evoked among some and others deeply troubled and fearful. The future reformer Gorbachev and revolutionary Yeltsin were then 25 years old and probably awakened by the reevaluation of values that swept through Soviet society in 1956.

Khrushchev's foes instigated a damaging whispering campaign. The Yugoslav ambassador learned of talk that Khrushchev was unbalanced, rude and simply unfit to serve as Soviet leader.[46] Off-stage, Khrushchev was defiant. During a Kremlin luncheon of Presidium members and Soviet bloc envoys on May Day he talked about "the contempt Stalin had for people, that a human being meant absolutely nothing to him, that Stalin cared nothing for the opinion of the party, that he relied on whims and his unhealthy instincts, and that by abusing his power he had done much evil in the Soviet Union."[47]

Marshal Zhukov remained contemptuous of the diehards. He sent a letter to Khrushchev on May 19 requesting comment on the draft of a speech meant for delivery to the Central Committee. The draft hit at "some comrades" who felt that criticism of Stalin would "harm the party's cause and that of our Armed Forces, and diminish the prestige of the Soviet people." Stalin was faulted for not putting the Red Army on alert in spring 1941 despite reliable information that Hitler was preparing to attack the Soviet Union. Zhukov urged the exoneration of generals whom Stalin arrested and shot for losing the opening battles of the Nazi-Soviet war. He proposed that civil rights be restored to officers who escaped from German captivity and returned to duty but were later arrested. Khrushchev passed Zhukov's text to Shepilov and Bulganin, who consigned it to the archives.[48]

Zhukov was stubborn and fueled a leadership debate over the continued discrimination against war veterans who had been prisoners of war. As chair of a special commission he submitted a June 4 report blaming Stalin for the injustices. Soviet bureaucrats could be heartless and many of the commission's proposals to aid former POWs were never accepted.[49]

Social discontent was widespread enough for a Kremlin clampdown on liberal intellectuals, national separatists and party democrats. A Presidium commission was formed to compile a circular outlining stricter behavioral guidelines. The orchestrator of this effort was Brezhnev, who recently was promoted to the rank of federal party Secretary. The June 16 draft zeroed in on "demagogic and nationalistic" outbursts at party briefings on Khrushchev's secret speech. Writers and artists were criticized for "statements against party decisions on ideological questions and against the principle of partisanship in literature and art." Enemies were said to have " used inner-party democracy for struggle against the party" and "under the guise of struggle against the personality cult some have gone so far as to deny the role of leaders in general. Their opinion is that collectivity is incompatible with the personal authority of a leader and need to carry out his instructions."[50]

The finalized party decree of June 30 upheld Stalin's draconian policies of the 1930s in terms of the resistance of doomed social classes, the com-
plexity of world politics and factionalism inside the power structure. A few
intellectuals found this apologia for Stalinism unacceptable and began a dissident movement. Over the next generation this school enrolled truth-seek-
ers ranging widely from the reform-Communist Medvedev twins to the
Russian nationalist Solzhenitsyn.

Khrushchev's secret speech threw eastern Europe into confusion. Poland
grew ablaze with strikes for "bread and freedom," release of the Roman
Catholic cardinal from detention and withdrawal of Soviet occupation
troops. Khrushchev flew to Warsaw in October and thanks to saber-rattling
was able to calm party reformers. As liberalization of the regime in Hungary snowballed into armed rebellion a dominoes theory seized the minds
of Soviet leaders. The Presidium met November 1 and Shepilov warned that
if Hungary broke free of Soviet control Czechoslovakia would be the next
satellite to do so.[51] Only Mikoyan disagreed with the consensus to hurl
Soviet tanks and 500,000 troops against the Hungarians. Suslov keynoted
the Moscow rally to celebrate the anniversary of the Bolshevik Revolution
and put one more cross over de–Stalinization: "The services and role of
Stalin in the October Revolution, in building socialism, and in the struggle against the enemies of the people and the enemies of the working class
are well known. " The *Pravda* version of Suslov's speech differed from the
live radio broadcast, omitting the bitter phrase "enemies of the people,"
which Khrushchev's secret speech wrongly condemned as an invention of
Stalin.[52]

A humane alternative to Khrushchev was a utopian desire, and he
assuredly approved the 1958 secret trial and execution of Hungarian reform
leader Imre Nagy in Romania. Yet at the time the Kremlin ordered harsh
repression of protesters inside the USSR. The Presidium met November 4
and discussed "cleansing the higher schools of unhealthy elements." At some
universities there had been rallies to oppose the Soviet invasion of Hungary, and the KGB was told to whip into line the student community. Brezhnev headed a commission that drafted a circular to party organizations on
December 19. The document railed against persons who "under the flag of
struggle 'for democracy' and expansion of the sovereign rights and autonomy of the union republics" were harping on past Kremlin mistakes.

Speeches glorifying freedom and democratic institutions in the West
were made at colleges in Moscow, Sverdlovsk, Kaunas (Lithuania) and
Tallinn (Estonia). Baltic nationalists rhetorically sided with Hungarian insur-

gents, urging liquidation of the Komsomol and its replacement with local-patriotic clubs. The Moscow Writers' Union was scourged for failing to counter the anticensorship speeches of writers Paustovsky and Bergolts. KGB and court officials were instructed to be "merciless" in dealing with "the enemy rabble" and "anti–Soviet elements." Ukrainian party head A. I. Kirichenko demanded that action be taken against former prisoners who had resumed their subversive activities. Kirichenko from Kiev informed the Center that global class struggle was re–energizing nationalistic elements in his domain. Across the country thousands were imprisoned for "slandering the Soviet system" and for "revisionism."[53]

Evidence of the vast scale of intellectual ferment is provided by a November 1956 memorandum that top leaders got from the party Secretariat's Department for Science, Higher Schools and Schools. Broadsides were fired at Dudintsev's *Not By Bread Alone*, Simonov's "Memories of A. A. Fadeyev" and Granin's "Our Own Opinion." The verse of Yevtushenko and a "Literary Bulletin" of students at Moscow University were impugned.[54] Simonov was attacked too in a December 1 memorandum to leaders from the CPSU Culture Department. An October 30 speech he made at a nationwide conference of literature teachers had rejected the 1946 Zhdanov report and subsequent restrictive decrees on literature and film.[55] A blow was struck at westernizers in secret reports that USSR Culture Minister N. A. Mikhailov sent to leaders in December 1956 and January 1957. Celebrities of the Soviet art world were criticized for statements in public and private that

- "collectivization of agriculture in the USSR was the very greatest people's tragedy, accompanied by horrors";
- "for a long time a 'socialist monarchy' existed in the USSR and it narrowed the people's sense of truth and beauty while at the same time the monarchy in Britain existed and exists to cultivate those feelings";
- "extolled the American path of a society's development and said it was superior to the socialist path of the USSR's development"; and
- defied the Party Group of their trade union during the election of delegates to an artists' convention [and the same persons refused to vote for the Group's nominees].

The same documents recognized acute substantive differences between the liberal cultural organs *Novy Mir, Iskusstvo* and *Literaturnaya gazeta*, on the one hand, and the orthodox party outlets *Pravda* and *Kommunist* on the other.[56]

Party conservatives detected or manufactured for ulterior reasons a surge of anti–Communist unrest in Moscow. Historians Aksenov and Zubkova look back:

> At that time international developments strongly influenced our lives. First and foremost the Hungarian events of 1956. Their hasty analysis, without deep probing to the crux of the matter, evoked fear of a repetition of such happenings in our country. Panic overcame some party officials. Rumors flew that people were going around to apartments and compiling secret lists of Communists. It is not too important whether those rumors arose because of "well-intentioned" misconceptions or were whipped up artificially. Something else is important. The Hungarian events, understood mainly as "minuses" for democracy, became a strong card to play in the hands of our conservative forces and fundamentally shook the positions of political leaders. As a result measures of over-insurance were taken and a struggle began with ideological revisionism. The situation grew more acute when it became clear that a crisis of authority was ripening in the country.[57]

A sign of looming political crisis was the exceptional nature of the communiqué of the December 1956 Central Committee Plenum. Khrushchev grew strangely unobtrusive. In contrast to the rising intervention of Khrushchev's party men into the details of management, a State Economic Commission of technicians was authorized to direct industry and planning.

Khrushchev tacked and at a New Year's reception revived the orthodoxy that Soviet Communists were "Stalinists in the consistency with which they fought for communism and Stalinists in their uncompromising fight against the class enemy, as was Stalin, who devoted his whole life to the victory of the working class and socialism."[58] At a Chinese Embassy reception Khrushchev hailed Stalin as "a model Marxist-Leninist and a revolutionary and will always remain so in history."[59]

The same month, however, a state edict restored to their homelands the small nations of the North Caucasus that Stalin had deported eastward in 1944 for alleged collaboration with the Germans. Khrushchev expressed sympathy for them in his secret speech and may have taken this step to help restore his shaken prestige.

A political row flared over Khrushchev's January 1957 policy memorandum to the Presidium urging party-directed streamlining of the command economy. The missive targeted for abolition 50 economic ministries in Moscow and advised that their functions be shifted to 105 regional economic councils. The sectors to remain centralized dealt with armaments, nuclear energy, and technologies.[60] Quite a few observers were skeptical of the proposed change as it failed to provide material incentives for workers and their enterprises.[61] Clearly the political aim was to shatter the technocratic support base of top state leaders in the Kremlin.

Just a day later Molotov and Voroshilov balked at Khrushchev's idea as too risky. Senior economist Pervukhin claimed as advantages of central ministries the large and specialized firms at their disposal, and he cautioned against dividing the management of electric power stations, railroads and military industry The industrialist Saburov also warned against rushing ahead. Brezhnev supported Khrushchev's initiative and the party chief likened it to a blood transfusion and model of real democratic centralism. The Presidium would go no further than to approve Khrushchev's memorandum "in principle" and authorized a commission to study the issue.[62]

The Central Committee endorsed Khrushchev's reform in February and launched a nationwide discussion of "Theses" which provided a wealth of detail. But resistance continued with Malenkov at a March 22 session of the Presidium backing Molotov's proposal for a Supreme Council of National Economy like one that existed during Lenin's tenure. Molotov two days later submitted a memorandum to colleagues flatly rejecting Khrushchev's project as too extreme and restating his demand for a single body to direct industry from Moscow. Upon gaining assurances of support from premier Bulganin and party Secretary Suslov, Khrushchev flung back at Molotov his charge of haste with an accusation that Molotov was hasty during the 1930s destruction of kulaks and military chiefs.[63]

Molotov retaliated with an April 22 *Pravda* article marking Lenin's birthday and whitewashing Stalin's crimes. "We know," Molotov wrote, " that mistakes, sometimes very serious mistakes, are inevitable when such vast and complex historical tasks are being resolved. There are not and cannot be any guarantees given on this score by anyone." Three days later Khrushchev bid for military support by asking the Presidium to issue party booklets posthumously to army leaders shot in 1937. Khrushchev taunted Molotov, Kaganovich and Voroshilov with questions about their roles in such frame-ups. Kaganovich said that as usual a report had been given at a leadership meeting and appropriate decisions were taken. Khrushchev turned on Malenkov for hatching "palace intrigue" that took the lives of many high officials.[64] Nikolai Ignatov, a Stalin agrarian and Khrushchev ally, wondered in *Pravda* (May 6, 1957) if it was worthwhile to keep intact Molotov's State Control Ministry.

The actual overhaul of industrial management was largely boycotted by the USSR Government and almost entirely a work of central and local party machines. This sabotage of a major party venture was bound to culminate in a political explosion. Upon his return from a trip to Finland, Khrushchev was surprised at a June 18 Presidium. Just a few members were present and conservatives had a majority. Bulganin as chair had turned coat and pictured Khrushchev as a man in a hurry who had committed a raft of mistakes:

- failure to clear with the Presidium the text of his secret speech;
- unilateral personnel changes;
- using the KGB to spy on associates;
- rushing the New Lands program;
- hastily merging collective farms;
- restricting work in highly productive garden plots; and
- setting the unrealistic goal of overtaking America in per capita output of meat and dairy products by 1960.

Molotov charged that Khrushchev ignored healthy tradition and gave priority to relations with the United States rather than European states. Others demanded that the post of first party secretary be abolished and chairmanship of the Secretariat rotated. Roy Medvedev's sources told him that Molotov was to replace Khrushchev as party leader and Khrushchev demoted to agriculture minister — if he confessed to errors and resigned; otherwise he would be arrested.

When the entire Presidium met the anti–Khrushchev forces had seven commanding votes: Malenkov, Molotov, Kaganovich, Bulganin, Voroshilov, Pervukhin and Saburov. Khrushchev's bloc was limited to Mikoyan, Suslov and Kirichenko. The Opposition looked so strong that Shepilov joined it. He traced the evolution of first party secretary Khrushchev from humble liberator to conceited know-it-all: "At first, Nikita Sergeyevich, you acted properly. You freed people from imprisonment and restored honor to thousands of completely innocent persons. A new atmosphere was created in the Central Committee and Presidium. Discussion of special questions was conducted in a professional manner, competently, with specialists invited. But now you are an 'expert' on all matters, whether agriculture, science or culture." Shepilov fired a hurtful arrow at Khrushchev: "An illiterate cannot run the state!"

There are several versions of how the Kremlin showdown was settled after four days of argument. One is that Bulganin ordered Interior Minister N. P. Dudorov to send a coded message to regional elites telling them Khrushchev was ousted from the top party post. Dudorov refused to comply and convoked a Central Committee Plenum. Another account is that to rescue Khrushchev party veteran Ignatov created from Central Committee members a Group of Twenty (*dvadtsatka*) that demanded a Plenum to resolve the crisis. Roy Medvedev identifies KGB chairman Serov as leader of the pro–Khrushchev lobbyists. There is general agreement that Bulganin met with the *dvadtsatka* and showered its members with expletives for asking to be admitted to the room where the Presidium deliberated.

Khrushchev learned of the clash and threatened to go alone to a Plenum if delegates of the opposing sides failed to confer. Talks began between the *dvadtsatka* and Voroshilov, Bulganin, Mikoyan and Khrushchev. Medvedev heard that Voroshilov swore at Serov, who grabbed him by the collar and threatened to call the Plenum. Most believe that Serov arranged for military transport planes to fly barons to Moscow for an emergency session of the Central Committee. The importance of Serov is clear from the odd fact that during the June 1957 Plenum the main army newspaper listed his name above those of nine Marshals of the Soviet Union who were guests at Marshal Zhukov's reception for visiting Yugoslav officials.

A backstairs deal rigged the June Plenum. Suslov as chair was far more prosecutor than honest broker. With an eye to the 1954–1955 dispute over investment policy he ridiculed Malenkov's newfangled concern about the priority status of heavy industry. Suslov sparked an outcry of "Anarchy!" by attacking the Opposition's effort to unseat Khrushchev. He denounced the putsch as "entirely unjustified, politically harmful and dangerous, capable of inflicting immense harm to the interests of party and country" and reeking of "monstrous disregard for the fate of our party and country."

Marshal Zhukov was first to be summoned to the podium and warned that the anti–Khrushchev faction wanted to abolish the posts of party first secretaries on the local level. He tore into Molotov, Kaganovich and Malenkov as accomplices of Stalin in organizing mass purges. Zhukov's documents had the signatures of those current-day leaders on lists of thousands condemned to death in 1937–1938. Significantly, the Yugoslav ambassador wrote in his journal: "The fact that Khrushchev had Marshal Zhukov and the leaders of the Soviet armed forces on his side turned out to be of decisive importance."

Although constantly heckled, Oppositionists made a case against Khrushchev for violating cabinet secrecy, among other things. They revealed that in a speech to writers he mentioned disputes with Molotov over such matters as subordinating the KGB to himself. Kaganovich hailed Stalin as stellar Marxist although we have seen that in the 1920s he was widely known in party circles as a vulgar empiricist. Molotov charged that Khrushchev was failing to learn from Lenin and use the conflicts among imperialist states to weaken them.

Khrushchev's partisans acclaimed him for policy initiatives, work style and personal qualities. Special pride was taken in easing the climate of fear and improving the food supply. Khrushchev's trips around the country were praised as efforts to mobilize the masses and keep in touch with their attitudes. The Oppositionists were depicted as "murderers," "sadists," and "wolves." Some attacked them for planning to downgrade Khrushchev to the post of agriculture minister and Suslov to culture minister. Others held that Khrushchev was put in mortal danger when accused of Rightist-Trotskyite deviation.

Isolated, the anti–Khrushchev clique recanted. They admitted it was a political mistake to have sought Khrushchev's ouster, but there were major caveats to their *mea culpas*. Molotov denied a conspiracy and special platform, which was needed to justify invoking the 1921 decree that authorized the dismissal of Central Committee members guilty of factionalism. Khrushchev said he disbelieved the admissions of error but excused titular president Voroshilov on grounds of advanced age and failing mental powers. Suslov later read out statements of the factionalists and was displeased with Molotov for calling Khrushchev's final speech "extremely non-objective."

The victors were not of one mind about what to do with the defeated. Khrushchev and 27 others who spoke or submitted speech texts demanded that Opposition leaders be ousted from the Presidium and Central Committee. Fifteen others wanted to expel one or more culprits from the party. Six of the speeches urged the trial of one or more factionalists. Those urging loss of party membership were not to get their way until 1961–1962; only Molotov and Shepilov got back their party booklets from post–Khrushchev leaders.

Khrushchev prevailed to remove Malenkov, Molotov and Kaganovich from the Presidium and Central Committee, as well as to ditch Shepilov from the Secretariat. He was clearly reluctant to press the issue of bringing foes to trial lest his own involvement in the Stalinist terror be uncovered. Khrushchev's ally Suslov rejected the request of USSR Minister Sheremetev to send a circular to party cells with Zhukov's incriminating documents. The published version of the Plenum decree omitted a passage accusing the losers of personal responsibility for Stalin crimes who tried to conceal their guilt by seizing key positions.

The fear of Kaganovich that he would be shot for plotting a coup was unfounded. He, Molotov and Malenkov were sent to sinecures at remote locations. Co-conspirators like Bulganin and Voroshilov were kept on board temporarily to mask the broad scope of the anti–Khrushchev cabal. Aged 63, Khrushchev seemed to have solidified power with the formation of a new Presidium in which 10 of 15 members were subordinate to him as CPSU Secretaries.[65]

One of the key factors that decided the critical events of June 1957 and the Stalin succession problem was Khrushchev's successful use of scare tactics. Aleksei Kosygin was a top industrialist in 1957 and later told diplomat Oleg Troyanovsky why Khrushchev won his fight against Molotov, Malenkov and Kaganovich. The trio were viewed as outright Stalinists and as such liable again to spill blood if allowed to seize real power. Khrushchev, on the other hand, was seen as forward-looking and unlikely to restore violent methods of government.[66]

If Marshal Zhukov had remained at the top he might have unleashed a campaign of political repentance and sponsored perestroika-like reforms. It is too facile to explain the Khrushchev-Zhukov blowup in terms of personal antagonism between two proud leaders.[67] Khrushchev's version is equally unconvincing:

> when Zhukov joined the Central Committee Presidium, he started accumulating so much power that the leadership of the country began to feel alarmed. Members of the Central Committee Presidium expressed their opinion to me more than once that Zhukov was heading in the direction of a military coup and the seizure of power. We received such reports from a number of military men, who spoke of Zhukov's Bonapartist tendencies. Gradually the facts added up and could no longer be ignored without subjecting our country to a military coup of the kind that happens in Latin America. We were forced to take the step of removing Zhukov from his posts. It was with difficulty that I arrived at this decision, but there was no alternative.[68]

A more acceptable opinion is that Zhukov wanted to bring Stalinist criminals to trial and that raised a threat to Khrushchev, whose hands were unclean. On July 15, 1957 Zhukov made what *Pravda* called a "great speech" in Leningrad and "listed the cases in which ... Malenkov, Kaganovich and Molotov violated the law." This contrasted with the toned-down public version of the June Plenum decree, and Zhukov still intended to make an anti–Stalin speech to the Central Committee.[69]

A policy disagreement between Khrushchev and Zhukov occurred in

August 1957 over the Soviet position to be taken at the United Nations Disarmament Subcommittee. Zhukov agreed with Eisenhower's idea of using aerial photographs to verify the observance of arms control treaties. At a Presidium meeting Voroshilov rejected the notion as apt to give an advantage to the United States. Khrushchev agreed: "The adversary's potential is greater. Whoever can fly higher is more interested in reconnaissance. They don't know everything about us. And what if they accept the offer? It would be a bad thing. What does the adversary lack? Intelligence." Khrushchev wanted the foreign ministry to rework the Soviet proposal.[70]

While Zhukov was visiting Albania in autumn 1957 the USSR president adopted a secret ukaz on Khrushchev's initiative that released Zhukov from the duties of defense minister and appointed in his place the less revered Marshal R. Ya. Malinovsky. Army political chief Zheltov at an October 17 Kremlin meeting criticized Zhukov for bridling him and creating for himself a personality cult. Suslov claimed to have heard from a senior army figure that political officers were babbling for 40 years and like old cats had lost their sense of smell. Mikoyan objected to military rules forbidding servicemen from expressing their own thoughts outside the chain of command. Khrushchev alleged that Zhukov "wants to sit on our necks" and asked that a commission of apparatchiks Suslov, Kirichenko and A. P. Kirilenko explore party-military relations.[71]

The top leaders went to Military Districts on October 22–23 and voiced misgivings about Zhukov. Khrushchev said that Zhukov sought to remove KGB chief Serov and replace him with a military officer. Brezhnev and Marshal Konev drafted a secret circular with such allegations that was sent to party cells and foreign missions. The Presidium met October 26 with Zhukov present and he denied wanting to isolate the armed forces from the party. Zhukov disputed too the claim that he created special forces to seize power, assuring that commando teams existed since 1945 and 17 current ones were in a low state of readiness. Khrushchev said that Zhukov would have ordered the army to subdue the Molotov clique if that was necessary and wished to substitute military officers for party leaders at the Defense Council. A decision was taken to convoke the Central Committee and oust Zhukov from all party offices.[72] Khrushchev forewarned the Yugoslav ambassador and explained that if in June Zhukov threatened to use troops against the Molotov faction he could eventually do the same against someone else.[73]

The Central Committee met October 28–29 and heard a report by Suslov on improving party-political work in the armed forces. Films were shown celebrating Zhukov like one made in July during a parade for the marshal in Leningrad that more than a million had attended. Khrushchev equated Zhukov's ambition and lust for power with that of Beria. Khrushchev enlarged the analogy and charged that Zhukov created on his own a Central Intelligence School: "We don't know why these saboteurs had to be assembled without the knowledge of the Central Committee. Was this a premeditated hostile act? And it was done by a Defense Minister with Zhukov's kind of character. Beria also had a sabotage group and before he was arrested Beria summoned the group of his cutthroats, they were in Moscow, and if he was not unmasked we don't know where heads would have rolled."[74]

It was perhaps at this meeting that a bitter exchange occurred between Zhukov and Marshal Moskalenko. According to Khrushchev's memoirs Moskalenko accused Zhukov of planning to seize power and Zhukov retorted that Moskalenko himself had urged him to seize power. Khrushchev later confided to the Yugoslav ambassador that Zhukov was astonished over his fall and asked in a telephone call why their friendship had ended with such rancor. The disgrace of Zhukov had the effect of lowering Khrushchev's prestige among ordinary citizens.[75]

Like Stalin before him, Khrushchev combined the posts of party and government head. It was Brezhnev who in March 1958 nominated Khrushchev for the premiership and acclaimed his brilliance (*genialnost*). A more rounded picture of Khrushchev emerges from the memoir of diplomat Troyanovsky, who served in Khrushchev's secretariat after he became premier. That inner circle was comprised of Grigori Shuisky (director); Vladimir Lebedev (media and culture); Andrei Shevchenko (agriculture) and Troyanovsky (foreign policy). The industrialist Kosygin as first deputy premier dealt with daily affairs and Khrushchev handled major economic issues, foremost agriculture. Troyanovsky gives Khrushchev high marks for a good memory, powers of observation and accessibility. But he found his boss impulsive, too willing to take risks and painfully lacking a sound knowledge of economics. This source claims that Khrushchev was too sensitive to slights and inclined to threaten the Allied presence in West Berlin so as to catch the attention of Western leaders.

The impulsiveness of Khrushchev was displayed in his reform of the network of machine and tractor stations in rural areas. Initially he said it would take two or three years before the inventories of the state-owned equipment centers might be sold to collective farms. Khrushchev ignored a warning from economists that less than half the farms could afford to buy the machinery. Without trial runs the party regional committees were told to speed the sales and did so in most cases over a span of three months. The sale prices were much higher than expected and a major shift of limited farm resources to the state occurred. Many operators of the machinery left villages for the towns as farms could not afford to pay their wages.

Yet during the MTS overhaul Khrushchev was distressed that some were arguing that state property as a higher form of ownership could not be sold if the letter and spirit of socialist doctrine were to be observed. The chairman bypassed colleagues and issued a statement that regardless of the 1945 Potsdam accords Berlin had to be freed of Allied troops. Khrushchev's hatred of Chinese hardliners was aired at meetings with them after his goodwill tour of America in 1959.

As in Kazakhstan and Georgia, Khrushchev laid up explosive material in Latvia. Stalin annexed the Baltic republic in 1940 and the Red Army took it back from Nazi occupiers in 1944. At the end of the 1950s Latvia had a population of 2,100,000, over three-fifths Latvians and one-quarter Russians. A republic party Plenum in October 1958 regretted that the titular nationality was underrepresented among officials in industrial, construction and police work; only 70 of 314 directors of large state firms were Latvians. That same month deputy premier Eduard Berklavs spoke to leaders in Riga and opposed the policy of expanding local output of railroad diesels and cars for export to other republics. He urged the faster growth of consumer industries to raise local living standards.

Although Khrushchev criticized Berklavs during a visit to Riga the latter refused to truckle. In June 1959 Khrushchev raised the issue at the Presidium and Central Committee. The deputy head of the party in Latvia confessed to the Presidium that forerunners supported Beria in 1953 and discarded Russian-language typewriters and Kremlin leadership portraits. Khrushchev was critical of a more recent Latvian decree barring the issuance of permanent residence permits (*propiski*) to Russians. He told the leaders of Latvia, "Don't force the residents of Russian nationality to learn the Latvian language. They don't want to and won't do it." A team of central officials had investigated and wrote a memorandum about deficiencies in Latvia. The republic's bosses examined the document under the scrutiny of Presidium member and Secretary for nationality affairs Nuritdin Mukhitdinov. In July 1959 Latvian party head Kalnberzins spoke at a Riga Plenum and criticized Berklavs and anti–Russian phenomena in local culture and education.[76]

The Turkic leaders of Azerbaidjan in the Caucasus were admonished at the July 1 Presidium. Khrushchev declaimed against Azeri nationalists as

"Nazis and Hitlerites." One was the writer Mirza Ibrahimov, who had drawn applause from university students by saying that any Azeri intellectual who failed to know or speak his native tongue was a "renegade, scoundrel and traitor." Over 60 percent of the residents of Baku were non–Azeris but few radio programs were in Russian or Armenian. Nationalist demands were heard to replace all non–Azeri personnel in state offices.[77]

Slavic and Muslim youths rioted over harsh conditions at a building site in Temir-Tau, Kazakhstan, in August 1959. Arson and looting accompanied the graffiti proclaiming that "Anarchy is the mother of order." Demands were made for freedom to strike, a six-hour work day and higher wages. Police shot at the rioters and the fire was returned. Army and MVD troops were summoned and that resulted in 11 protesters killed and 52 wounded, five of whom later died. The army and police casualties were reported at 102, 32 by firearms. A central party commission established that 190 arrests were made.[78]

The rumbling in borderlands probably contributed to flux in ruling circles. The Presidium in November 1959 examined a conflict of Khrushchev's Ukrainian protégés Brezhnev and Kirichenko over management of the party Secretariat. Russian conservatives Kozlov and Suslov joined the attacks on Kirichenko as rude and overbearing in making personnel changes. They argued for the observance of collegiality. Khrushchev agreed to the idea of rotating the direction of the Secretariat and this set in motion changes that featured the rise of Kozlov to the rank of deputy party leader.[79] The Presidum resolved in June 1960 that Kozlov chair meetings of the Secretariat and filter materials prior to its meeting.[80]

The Mikoyan memoirs offer a picture of Kozlov that is different from the conventional wisdom of foreigners that he was a devoted Khrushchevite. Mikoyan cites Kozlov as remarking behind Khrushchev's back: "Let him travel around the whole world and we'll be the ones who run things." Kozlov is said to have been a Stalinist who persuaded Khrushchev to freeze an internal document exposing the fraudulent nature of the 1936–1938 Moscow Trials on the ground that a new verdict would embarrass western Communists. Kozlov led a delegation to investigate worker unrest in the south Russian town of Novocherkassk in 1962 and, according to Mikoyan, induced Khrushchev to sanction the use of lethal force against protesters. Mikoyan reports too that in determining terms of foreign trade Kozlov was heedless of the sensitivities of Communist leaders in Poland, Romania and Hungary. A stroke disabled Kozlov in 1963 and this accidental factor may have averted the pursuit of a still harder course of Soviet policy after Khrushchev.

One of the strongholds of conservative opinion was the military high command. In 1956 Admiral N. G. Kuznetsov retired from the naval leadership after Khrushchev overturned a decision for a buildup of surface warships and directed a focus on submarines and nuclear missiles. Khrushchev pushed through in January 1960 a 1.2 million reduction of military manpower, which left 2.4 million in the services. Marshals, generals and admirals wrote a letter to the Central Committee warning that Soviet security could not be guaranteed after such big force cuts. To redress the military imbalance between America and the Soviet Union Khrushchev deployed medium-range nuclear missiles in Cuba in 1962. His backdown in the face of U.S. tactical superiority stirred resentment in the officer corps.

Police resented Khrushchev's decision to abolish the federal Interior Ministry and depend on republic-level ministries. Khrushchev slashed the bonuses and pensions of policemen, then refused to believe that low pay was a disincentive to recruitment. The law-and-order lobby, however, got from Khrushchev the concession of a stricter regime in detention centers. All told, there is something to a generalization about Khrushchev's authority in Gorbachev's memoirs: It is that policy decisions made in the Khrushchev years bore the influence of different political forces and the top man had to maneuver and present measures in a form acceptable to influential groups.

Below the ruling heights there was much grumbling about the quality of life and prevailing social values. As recorded by foreign visitors and residents some complaints during the Khrushchev era were

- *discontent with low living standards*: a Soviet geneticist remarked, "The people are told of these glorious achievements [in the USSR] and then are expected to be content to go home to their six square meters of inadequate, shabby, over-crowded rooms and their poor diet, and their drab, grubby clothes."
- *desire for openness:* during the Cuban missile crisis a Komsomol leader at Moscow University said that all the meetings being held around the USSR to condemn U.S. actions were silly. "How," he asked, "could people vote on condemnatory resolutions when they did not even know what President Kennedy had said?" "The proper way to remedy this defect," he added, " would be to have the full text of the President's speech printed alongside the Soviet government statement and then let the meetings hold their vote."
- *ideological vacuum*: Soviet physicist Igor Tamm was cited to the

effect that "we are no longer dogmatic," elaborating that in the present Soviet state, Marxist values were no longer as true as they had been and that a reconsideration was sometimes necessary; a mid-career official of the Soviet bureaucracy, himself a party member of long standing, said:

> Take the party members. Why do they belong to the party? It is not because they believe in the system or in the ideology of the party. No, not at all. I can state with assurance that 99 per cent of the so-called Communists in the Soviet Union are not Communist at all. They are people who joined the party in order to have a greater opportunity to gain a good position which would be impossible for them to gain without being in the party. That's what it means to be a Communist. Just as previously the party members were truly dedicated to that ideology — fully dedicated — so, now, just the opposite is true.

- *anti–Stalinism*: a 1962 question-and-answer session at Moscow University was the scene of a student asking how Stalin's dictatorship could be considered basically different from Hitler's. The professor who answered the question said that the class structure of the USSR and Nazi Germany made all the difference, but the students appeared to be unconvinced. In 1963 an American visiting the Soviet Union reported that Soviet students had discussed with him the relationship between Stalin and Leningrad boss Kirov. In the students' version, Kirov in 1934 received more votes for the party Secretariat than did Stalin, and Stalin had Kirov eradicated to get rid of a dangerously popular rival.[81]

Khrushchev's fatal misstep was effectively to create two Communist parties to cope with rising shortfalls in production. In September 1962 he spoke to colleagues about his recent memorandum to divide the party into industrial and agricultural branches. The bifurcation was meant to give the economic sectors "equal opportunities for concentrating attention on their development." What Khrushchev meant was that industry was getting too few checkups from party controllers. He knew that traditionalists were eager to stop rocking the boat and in October *Pravda* attacked them with Yevtushenko's poem "Stalin's Heirs."[82]

The experts found fault with Khrushchev's proposal that the USSR State Planning Committee merely "dovetail" the economic plans of the union republics — a departure from the dictation of such plans from Moscow. This scheme was the basis of a decision taken in January 1963. Offsetting that in March was the creation of an All-Union Council of National

Economy to regulate the local economic councils that were Khrushchev's 1957 brainchild. Undaunted, Khrushchev restated his view that party men had to be masters of economic detail. A memorandum he sent to the Presidium in July 1963 contested "the legacy of Stalin, who removed the party and trade unions from participation in drafting plans for capital investment and compiling the national economic plans."[83]

The year 1963 was a time of sharp slowdown in Soviet economy. Return on state investment was at a record low of 15 kopecks for each ruble of input. Harvests were a nightmare because of bad weather, defective cropping patterns and soil erosion in the New Lands, which dictated a reduction in the sown acreage. Statistics were that farm output was down to the 1958 level; cattle herds lower by 1.5 million; and pigs down from 70 to 41 million; hard currency reserves had to be drawn upon to pay for grain imports from the West.

The bad public mood left Khrushchev with a sense of vulnerability. Upon reading a KGB memorandum he ordered that if retired Marshal Zhukov did not stop needling him in memoirs Zhukov would be expelled from the party and arrested.[84] This documented incident lends credence to a Russian journalist's account of an emotional clash between Khrushchev and Ground Forces chief Marshal Konev in the early 1960s: "At a conference Khrushchev angrily shouted at Konev 'Why haven't you signed the document? The [Defense] Minister has signed.' Konev replied 'I will not sign. I have my own opinion.' Their last conversation ended with Khrushchev promising 'I'll make you get down on your knees!'"[85]

In summer 1964 Khrushchev conjured up a whirlwind of changes, He addressed a secret meeting of the Central Committee on July 11 and disclosed an intention to shake up farm management and abolish the Academy of Sciences. Khrushchev sent to Brezhnev, the deputy party leader, a letter advising that nine trusts be created to direct various sectors of agriculture. Brezhnev discarded the letter.[86] Out of character, Khrushchev in a speech to the parliament urged the granting of wide decision-making powers to factory directors. At a session of the government cabinet on July 24 he demanded a rewriting of economic plans to increase the supply of consumer goods.[87]

One of Khrushchev's ideas passed on to Gorbachev was that Soviet armaments should be at a level of "reasonable sufficiency" rather than superiority over the United States. He implied that Soviet military power made it possible to release investment funds from military projects to light industrial development. *Izvestiya* (September 20) assured that the Soviet Union possessed new and formidable weaponry. Shortly thereafter, Khrushchev was reported in *Pravda* (October 2) to have told a joint meeting of the Presidium and Council of Ministers that, in drafting the 1966–1970 economic plan, "it is essential to be guided by the fact that the main task ... is the further improvement of the living standard of the people."

Khrushchev changed his mind about the expediency of personalizing labor organization in the countryside. He told rural officials it was beneficial to assign collective farm land and machinery for long periods of time to small teams or "links" instead of the existing system of managing production through the larger field brigades. The goal was to inspire collective farmers to identify more closely with the land and to develop a greater interest in its productivity, on which their income would be based. The links system was still unpopular among apparatchiks as tending to undermine collective farming and their order-giving rights. Khrushchev also floated a proposal that centralized procurement of certain foodstuffs be reduced in order to permit farms to market part of their crop commercially in the towns.[88]

Gorbachev was to borrow from Khrushchev the idea of constitutional change to establish a Western-style standing parliament and strong presidency. Khrushchev told Mikoyan that the USSR Supreme Soviet should no longer meet twice yearly for a few days to rubber stamp Kremlin decisions. Western politicians, Khrushchev said, tricked ordinary people to believe that parliaments enabled them to influence state policy, and Soviet leaders should borrow that clever tactic. To counter *apparat* resistance to such change a prestigious figure had to be the torch-bearer. Mikoyan thought that he was to be chosen for the mission.

Khrushchev was probably readying new measures to curtail bureaucratic overprivilege. He had abolished special food parcels and cut the lists of persons with the right to use state-owned autos. Just prior to his fall the main party newspaper for economic affairs told factory managers to use company trucks for business trips rather than the autos normally put at their disposal.

The last straw for Khrushchev's colleagues was his intention to renew the leadership. It was known that a Central Committee meeting would be convoked in November to admit to the Presidium theorist L. F. Ilyichov, farm overseer V. I. Polyakov and media strategists P. A. Satyukov, N. A. Kharlamov and Khrushchev son-in-law Aleksei Adzhubei.[89] This had implications for political succession, as Khrushchev in April 1964 had celebrated his seventieth birthday. The most endangered heirs-presumptive were party Secretaries Brezhnev and Podgorny, and former KGB chief Shelepin.

A former Chekist close to retired party official Ignatov told Khrushchev's son, Sergei, that a plot was afoot to depose Khrushchev. While titular president of the Russian Federation Ignatov had traveled around the country and badmouthed Khrushchev, Khrushchev seemed unworried about his son's warning, telling Mikoyan that personal relations among Presidium members were strained — Brezhnev and farm expert Gennadi Vorovov, for example, hated one another. He disbelieved that Shelepin and KGB chief Semichastny were tired of him.

In October Khrushchev and Mikoyan were relaxing at Pitsunda on the Black Sea when Brezhnev telephoned. He told Khrushchev to return to Moscow for a Central Committee Plenum on agriculture. Khrushchev put down the receiver and said to his confidant, "This is not a matter of agriculture. They want to put the question to me. Well, if they're all against me, I won't put up a fight." Khrushchev's doubts were heightened when his plane landed at an airport near Moscow and he saw that only Semichastny was waiting to greet him.

At an October 13 meeting of the Presidium Shelepin arraigned Khrushchev for

- inept food policy (constant reorganizations; depriving peasants of household plots and converting collective into state farms to pressure peasants to do more work);
- division of local party and government offices along urban and rural lines, which led to confusion of who was responsible for what and where;
- unilateral personnel decisions;
- inappropriate award of state decorations to son Sergey and President Nasser of Egypt;
- brinksmanship during the crises over Suez (1956), Berlin (1961) and Cuba (1962);
- instigating collapse of the Paris summit meeting in 1960 by demanding that Eisenhower apologize for an American spy plane flying over the USSR on May Day; and
- government-paid family junkets abroad.[90]

At first Khrushchev was defiant but soon told his aide Troyanovsky that there was no hope that the Central Committee Plenum would come to his rescue as it did in 1957. Khrushchev realized that he had become too brusque with subordinates and mused that he was mistaken to have forgotten the wise advice of onetime mentor Kaganovich to meet weekly with two or three local party secretaries.

The next day Khrushchev humbly confessed to mistakes at a Presidium meeting. Brezhnev and Suslov denied his request to address the Central Committee. Brezhnev opened the Plenum on October 14; Mikoyan was the chair and Suslov delivered the report "On the abnormal situation in the Central Committee Presidium in connection with the wrongful actions of Khrushchev." The Chairman was accused of promoting a cult of his own personality. Suslov claimed that in 1963 the central press ran Khrushchev's portrait 120 times and in nine months of 1964 that occurred 140 times. Stalin's visage was said to have appeared in Moscow newspapers only 10 to 15 times yearly. Suslov alleged that Khrushchev used divide-and-rule tactics: "Khrushchev systematically engaged in intrigues, trying by all means to set the Presidium members against one another. But one cannot for long spin intrigues and go unpunished. And at last everyone was convinced that comrade Khrushchev was playing an unworthy game."[91] Suslov charged that Khrushchev's son-in-law Adzhubei harmfully meddled in foreign policy during a recent trip to West Germany. (Rumor said that Adzhubei told officials in Bonn that Khrushchev might tear down the Berlin Wall.) Stalin's criticism of Khrushchev for "harebrained scheming" was revived and the Plenum heard the text of a letter of resignation that the Presidium had written for him.[92]

Some in the audience interrupted Suslov with shouts of "Expel him from the party! Put him on trial!" Mikoyan proposed that Khrushchev be kept aboard as premier for at least one year. He felt that Khrushchev had gained political capital abroad and was dedicated to the pursuit of de–Stalinization. As premier, Mikoyan reasoned, Khrushchev's impulse to make frequent personnel changes would be checked. But others feared his decisiveness and the only acceptable solution for them was to keep Khrushchev at home and under KGB surveillance. The first sign of the existence of a really hardline group in the leadership was noticeable to insiders from the deletion of a clause in the Plenum's secret decree, "On Comrade N.S. Khrushchev," praising Khrushchev for the uncrowning of Stalin.[93]

In December Mikoyan, at a local party meeting, harped on Khrushchev's restlessness. Age and sclerosis made Khrushchev leave his office after three hours and go on inspection tours. He constantly improvised and took decisions on the fly. An organizational itch caused Khrushchev often to revise standard operating procedures.[94]

Brezhnev gave an inkling of the tighter secrecy that would be observed under his stewardship. In a brief address to the October 1964 Plenum he asked that party meetings avoid detailed discussion of Khrushchev's ouster and tell non–Communists only what the press would report. Brezhnev promised deliberation in policymaking and to reverse the division of party and state bodies along urban and rural lines. The reckless planting of certain crops would be terminated — an allusion to Khrushchev's corn-as-silage panacea.

The communiqué of the October 1964 Plenum attributed the unprecedented impeachment to " advanced age and health reasons." Adzhubei lost his seat on the Central Committee for "errors in work" and was banished from the practice of journalism. Brezhnev was elected party first secretary and Kosygin would assume the premiership. Brezhnev later summoned Khrushchev and told him to expect a pension, housing, Kremlin medical treatment, special food ration and car. KGB surveillance was to be enforced around the clock.

The falling of the curtain on Khrushchev's ballyhooed "Great Decade" pleased high and low alike. Bread shortages, higher prices, wage freezes, strikes, administrative chaos and foreign crises had exasperated many. Biographer Roy Medvedev got numerous letters from Khrushchev-haters who were Stalinists, peasants and intellectuals who preferred gradualism to risky leaps. It is surprising that in less than a quarter century Khrushchev would be officially honored as fighting progressive. That happened because of the morass of bureaucratic corruption and economic inefficiency into which the USSR sank under its next personalized leader.

CHAPTER 5

Brezhnev:
Restoring Stability

The 1977 USSR Constitution paid lip service to modernity and pledged more transparency in governance. In reality a golden age of bureaucracy began with Khrushchev's fall and cynicism grew rampant. The local bosses amassed hefty sums of graft in exchange for support of party chief Brezhnev. The arrests of dissidents and greater outlays for armaments assured too for Brezhnev the support of the KGB and military brass. It is indeed wrong to talk of the eighteen-year Brezhnev era as a time without struggle for power in the Kremlin. The elite conflicts raged for more than five years after Khrushchev's demise, or until the military threw its weight behind Brezhnev.

Collectivity resurfaced only after Brezhnev grew increasingly infirm in the mid–1970s and power-sharing returned under the auspices of a small group of caretakers. The major policy issues were resource allocation, economic management, center-periphery relations and foreign affairs. The investment decisions reached after Kremlin wrangling were usually of a pragmatic conservative nature and hyperregulation further ensured that the economy would stumble as was earlier the case. Gorbachev vaulted to power thanks to unanticipated contingencies. These included a slew of top-tier deaths among elderly leaders and Gorbachev's skillful wearing of a mask of middle-of-the-roader that concealed the innermost thoughts of a radical reformer.

Khrushchev's plan to emphasize butter rather than guns was unacceptable to the new collective leadership. Brezhnev quickly signaled that defense industries would not lose resources in a crash program to benefit the consumer. Speaking in Red Square he redefined Khrushchev's "main task" of "the further improvement of the living standard of the people," asserting, "The party considers that its main task in internal policy is *the development of the productive forces* of our society and unswerving improvement *on this basis* of the prosperity of the Soviet people" (italics added).[1] The USSR's stockpile of intercontinental missiles jumped from around 224 in 1965 to over 1,000 by 1969.[2]

Now any thought of transforming the party into a technically functional institution was viewed as its "depoliticization, " or neglect of its usual duty of mass indoctrination.[3] The Stalinist idioms "commercialism" and "pure empiricism" were used to reject Khrushchev's bid for party staffers to delve into economic planning and management.[4] CPSU Secretary Podgorny keynoted a Central Committee Plenum in November 1964 that reunited separate branches of party and government. The division was said to have caused "confusion of the functions, rights and duties of party, soviet and managerial bodies" and "pushed party committees into substituting for managerial bodies."[5]

Brezhnev launched a tougher national-security policy with his November 6, 1964, speech for the anniversary of the Bolshevik Revolution. "In implementing the policy of peaceful coexistence," he said, "we base ourselves on the might of the countries of the socialist camp and we shall maintain our defense potential on the highest possible level." That same month the Kremlin reversed its withholding of large-scale Soviet military support to North Vietnam. Brezhnev downplayed the value of nuclear deterrence and allowed for conventional war between the superpowers. Taking a swipe at Khrushchev he agreed with military professionals that "we consider it premature to 'bury' the infantry, as some people do."

Diplomat Troyanovsky is certain that the break with China played a role in Khrushchev's fall. Some elites believed that Khrushchev went too far in his anti–Stalinism and relations with the United States should have been sacrificed for the sake of restoring friendship with the Chinese hawks. Troyanovsky writes in his memoir that Soviet leaders were euphoric to hear that Chinese premier Chou En-lai would visit Moscow for celebration of the Bolshevik Revolution anniversary in November 1964. Chou, however, was stubborn in his talks and Marshal Malinovsky angered him at a Kremlin reception when the Soviet defense minister told him "we've gotten rid of Khrushchev and now it's your turn to get rid of Mao."

Soon a major disagreement broke out in the Kremlin over whether to go the extra mile to mend fences with the Chinese. In January 1965 the Presidium reviewed instructions for a Soviet delegation that was to attend a meeting of the Warsaw Pact's Political Consultative Committee. The text had been drafted by Foreign Minister Gromyko and Yuri Andropov, who was in charge of relations with ruling foreign parties. Premier Kosygin and party Secretary Shelepin objected to the wording as too conciliatory toward the West and neglecting a chance to make up with China.

Kosygin was unable to persuade Brezhnev to head a peace mission to China and himself undertook the task.[6] Mao Zedong remained combative and spurned the olive branch that Kosygin extended to him. The Russian's suspicion of America probably rose when he visited Hanoi and American warplanes bombed the North Vietnamese capital at that very moment. Returning to Peking from Hanoi, Kosygin met with Mao, who was sarcastic to the verge of insulting his Soviet visitor.[7]

Either Kosygin or Shelepin, and maybe both, sometime in 1965 urged the Presidium to offer China a friendship and cooperation treaty. The accord was to promise that any attack on China would be regarded as an attack on the Soviet Union. Opponents argued that the Maoists could use such a treaty to drag the USSR into war with the United States. They held too that China would see the move as indicative of Soviet weakness, or Moscow's inability to get along without it. A majority of leaders found the proposal unacceptable, according to Mikoyan's memoir.

The posture of Defense Minister Marshal Malinovsky that May was decidedly bellicose. At the Presidium he assessed the U.S. bombing of North Vietnam and armed intervention in the Dominican Republic as prelude to an American probe of Soviet weak spots. Malinovsky warned of aggressive U.S. plans against Cuba and outlined Soviet countermeasures. These would include shows of force in Berlin and on the border with West Germany. Soviet airborne troops would have to be sent from home bases to Germany and Hungary. Malinovsky advised that a strike against West Berlin had to be contemplated and said that "we should not fear to take the risk of war."

The critics of this scenario included Kosygin, Podgorny, Suslov and Mikoyan. The premier reminded that Stalin blockaded West Berlin in 1948, had to retreat and the result was a decline of Soviet prestige. Khrushchev was criticized for having acted rashly about Berlin in 1958 and 1961; after a speech by President Kennedy the number of Allied troops in the city increased and Soviet prestige again fell. While Mikoyan's account is silent about Brezhnev's role it does record that Foreign Minister Gromyko asserted that the international situation was like that before World War II, or perilously volatile.

Westernizing intellectuals took advantage of the interregnum to circulate their viewpoint. A bridge to the Gorbachev era was the plugging of multicandidate soviet elections in the journal *Soviet State and Law* (No. 2, 1965). Chief editor A. Lepeshkin argued,

> Soviet election law does not limit the number of candidates proposed as soviet deputies. The practice of elections for the soviets of all levels has been formed in such a way that only one candidate, for or against whom the voters of a given electoral district vote, is on the voting list for deputies. Numerous articles and suggestions of our readers raise the question of the advisability of leaving on the ballot paper not one, but several candidates proposed by the voters for election to one vacant seat of a Soviet deputy for a given electoral district. Of course, the democratism of any electoral system is not measured only by the number of candidates put on the voting list, that is one or two. Nevertheless, this is not a problem of minor importance and its correct solution under our conditions is of great importance for the development of the democratic principles of the Soviet electoral system.

Party monitors grew suspicious of Lepeshkin and around June 1965 he lost his editorial post.

On questions of economic planning Kosygin was aligned with the central establishment. He remarked in a March 1965 speech that republic-level planning under Khrushchev "was not always in harmony with general state interests, especially when localist tendencies were strongly manifested in the plans." This deficiency was blamed on Khrushchev's idea of "dovetailing" the republic plans in Moscow.[8] This kind of admonition earned for Kosygin the repute of independent professional wedded to the time-honored power vertical (*vlastnaya vertikal*).

Russian centralists humiliated Ukrainian federalists at the Presidium in August 1965. Kiev party head Petro Shelest had sent a letter to the Kremlin stating that many countries that avoided commerce with the Soviet Union asked Ukrainian officials to sign trade accords with them. The letter noted that Ukraine was a prestigious founding member of the United Nations and entitled to freedom of action in the field of foreign trade. Kosygin-type figures, however, defended the centralized trade monopoly. Now Shelest was in Moscow and, bowing to party discipline, recognized his letter as wrongful.

Russian officials hammered the Ukrainians and party leaders such as Brezhnev, who had long worked in Ukraine. P. N. Demichev, party secretary for culture, charged that nationalism was rampant in Ukraine, where almost no Russians were in the leadership. Demichev further accused the Shelest group of sponsoring a letter of Ukrainian intellectuals demanding that nationality languages be taught in all schools and universities of constituent republics. Streets in Kiev once named "Moscow" and "Soviet" were said to have been mistakenly renamed to honor Ukrainian writers. Demichev criticized Ukrainian Chief of Party Propaganda Skaba for a speech he made six months earlier to a central party conference. He objected too that Podgorny recently proposed that the USSR minister of cinematography go to Kiev and discuss ideological questions of film-making.

Shelepin criticized Podgorny for approving the Shelest letter on behalf of world trading rights. Shelepin said that Ukraine officials violated plans for the delivery of goods to other republics while overfulfilling their own targets. He alleged that all speeches were in Ukrainian at a meeting in Sevastopol awarding a decoration to the Black Sea Fleet, which he called the "fleet of Russian glory." Shelepin complained too that while most residents of Crimea were Russians radio and television programs were in Ukrainian. One or two Presidium members, he concluded, should go to Ukraine, convene a Plenum and gather material for a Kremlin evaluation of the mistakes of Shelest and Podgorny.

Kosygin and Brezhnev calmed the waters. The first secretary dismissed the suggestion to convoke a special Plenum in Kiev and rejected Shelest's bid for independent trading rights (Mikoyan, 1999). In 1990 the premier of the Russian Federation would demand for his republic the right to trade freely on the world scene and Russian president Yeltsin pushed for a republic-level foreign trade agency.

The half-reform of economic management that Kosygin announced in September 1965 was based on opinions of academic economists whose controversial press articles were filtered by staff aides.[9] The Troyanovsky memoir suggests that a Presidium commission drafted the reform plan and included party Secretary Kirilenko, a longtime associate of Brezhnev who apparently was told to slow the reform process. The changes promised enterprise managers fewer planning orders from Moscow and the opportunity to dispose of increased sums of working capital. Plan fulfillment would be based on sales and profits rather than on physical volume of output. But the ability of enterprises to make effective use of these new rights was hindered by the center's retention of control over investment and price policy, as well as over the physical distribution of many categories of producer goods. Kosygin rejected a proposal that firms be permitted to fix their own wage funds; this would impair the state's authority to regulate purchasing power and the output of consumer goods.[10]

The 1967 reform of wholesale prices gave little incentive to increase quality or improve production technology, still leaving managers without a reliable guide for production and investment decisions. Moreover, a Kosygn-led streamlining abolished republic-level councils and Moscow state committees standing above regional economic councils. The Stalin-era ministerial system was restored and by 1967 there were 25 all-Union and 27 union-republic ministries in Moscow, with only eight republic ministries in the Russian Republic which answered to no central body. (At the moment of Stalin's death there had been 30 all-union and 22 union-republic ministries.)[11]

Gorbachev's memoirs inform that Brezhnev and Kosygin disagreed over economic issues. Kosygin wanted CPSU Central Committee departments for supervision of varied branches of the economy to be transferred to his government. Brezhnev saw this as an effort to take the levers of management away from the party leadership and leave it with propaganda alone. Anatoli Lukyanov was a legal adviser at the time and learned that Suslov, Podgorny and Kirilenko often clashed with Kosygin at Politburo meetings and nullified his economic corrections. The ideologue Suslov was concerned about a major doctrinal anomaly that *Pravda* featured in September 1965. Aleksei Rumyantsev, chief editor of the party daily, wrote two articles on the intelligentsia that assigned to it the central role in societal progress. This meant rejection of the Marxist-Leninist dogma of the party's leading role as vanguard of the people. The articles were pegged to Kosygin's reform and implied that the brains of economic planners and factory managers — "technical intelligentsia" — were superior to those of party officials. Proofs of the articles were sent to top leaders for their comments and one of Brezhnev's aides told the author that publication was undesirable. Rumyantsev felt protected and ran the pieces, but was later reassigned from *Pravda* to the Academy of Sciences.[12]

Like Khrushchev before him, Brezhnev took charge of agriculture, but ignored his old patron's advice for reorganizing farm labor and lending flexibility to product marketing. Instead a course was set toward pragmatic conservatism. A series of stop-gap measures were taken to halt deterioration of the national diet. These included the easing of restrictions on private plots, abolition of taxes on privately owned livestock, release of reserve fodder to feed livestock, and increased purchase prices for milk.[13] (In 1965 about two-thirds of the potatoes and eggs, and about 40 percent of meat, milk and vegetables came from the private plots, which constituted 1–2 percent of cultivated land.) At the March 1965 Plenum Brezhnev announced a doubling of state investments in agriculture during 1966–1970 as compared with the total for the preceding five years, increases in crop delivery prices, and stable delivery quotas for several years.[14] (The investment program ran into serious difficulties with at least $8 billion earmarked for farming in 1966–1970 redirected into defense-related projects). Collective farmers were offered a guaranteed monthly wage to replace the old system of deferring payment until crop deliveries were made to the state.[15]

To the dismay of liberals, Brezhnev named his longtime aide S. P. Trapeznikov to head the CPSU Science Department. Trapeznikov proposed discarding the term "personality cult" or suspending criticism of Stalin and his policies. A tightening of censorship coincided with an unsigned *Pravda* article of April 29, 1965, that condemned "onesidedness" in the treatment of historical events and personalities. Suslov reportedly convinced Brezhnev that writers Daniyel and Sinyavsky had to be brought to trial for having published their anti–Soviet works abroad under pseudonyms. Suslov opposed an initiative to honor a victim of postwar purges, party Secretary Aleksei Kuznetsov, on occasion of his 60th birthday. Historian Pikhoya knew what Moscow theater figures thought of Suslov and his companions: "these people were justified in viewing the party ideologues as their enemies.... Under the influence of Suslov the bureaucrats from the Central Committee and Moscow [party] Committee were just brutal police chiefs."

A step to reconnect with the past was a *Pravda* editorial of January 30, 1966, which, like Trapeznikov, rejected the anti–Stalin epithet "period of the personality cult." The term was said to have demeaned "the heroic efforts of party and people in the struggle for socialism." Striking a pose of cool common sense, Brezhnev avoided making any pronouncement on the Stalin issue at the party congress that opened in March, and left it to other speakers to praise the late dictator. The congress underlined continuity with the Stalin period by decreeing that the Presidium should again be named the Politburo and that the title of party general secretary, which Stalin held, should be resurrected.[16] Former party adviser Shakhnazarov says in memoirs that he lost hope of political reform when Stalin's post of general secretary was restored and the ban on apparatchiks holding key posts for more than two consecutive terms was dropped from party Rules.

The regime showed itself to be intent upon a limited rehabilitation of Stalin while retaining for itself a monopoly of the right to criticize various aspects of Stalinism. Thus, the Theses for the 50th anniversary of the Bolshevik Revolution repudiated Stalin's subjugation of the Politburo and the blood purges;[17] yet, Professor Aleksandr Nekrich was expelled from the CPSU for assailing Stalin's conduct of diplomatic and military affairs during the Second World War.[18] Again, a *Pravda* article on the occasion of

Stalin's 90th birth anniversary in December 1969 called the former leader a "great theoretician" — the highest tribute a Communist could receive — but also noted "theoretical and political errors that became serious in nature during the latter period of his life."[19]

Agitprop leaders knew that a nation's historical memory thrives on positive images, so film epics such as *Liberation* depicted Stalin pacing his wartime office in deep thought, and helped to create the popular illusion of him as an architect of victory in 1945. Khrushchev watched from afar and bitterly commented that people with a slave mentality still admired Stalin as an iron-fisted ruler whose viciousness was pardonable.[20]

Brezhnev's rivals objected to his prima donna instinct with an unusual article of party consultant F. Petrenko. He stressed the importance of observing equality of status in the relations between the members of a party body: "The secretary of a party committee is not a commander and he is not endowed with the right to command. He is only the senior person in the organ of collective leadership elected by the Communists. He has greater responsibility, but in solving problems he has only as many rights as other members of the committee."[21]

Taking advantage of the diffusion of power, Dmitri Polyansky, the Politburo's farm overseer, expressed his disagreement with a policy decision that went against the countryside. He challenged in *Pravda* (March 3, 1967) "some people" who were "beginning to argue that collective and state farms can now develop even with less material aid." Nevertheless, the leadership decided to cut back the outlays on agriculture by 13 percent below the level targeted in the directives for the 1966–1970 Five-Year Plan. Polyansky voiced his disapproval in an extraordinary article in the journal *Kommunist* campaigning for an "uninterrupted increase" of investments in agriculture.[22]

Brezhnev heeded the advice of Suslov to use the defection of Stalin's daughter Svetlana to the United States as a pretext to sack KGB chief Semichastny, a former collaborator of Shelepin. In May 1967 the KGB was put under Andropov, who had worked closely with Suslov in the central party office for dealings with foreign Communists.[23] Like Brezhnev and Suslov, Andropov hated the dissident intellectuals, some of whom were confined in psychiatric hospitals and abused with the use of narcotics. The KGB shakeup benefitted Gorbachev, who as party head of Stavropol region in the North Caucasus ingratiated himself with Andropov during the latter's holidays in the area.

In June 1967 Shelepin counted on striking a blow at Brezhnev just after the defeat of the Kremlin's Arab clients in a six-day war with Israel. Mos-

cow party leader Nikolai Yegorychev made the running for Shelepin during a plenary session of the CPSU Central Committee. He insinuated that
Brezhnev was abetting a reckless Egyptian leader:

> I would like to express the desire that in our relations with the United Arab
> Republic and with President Nasser personally we should show a little more
> exactingness in providing aid for that country. Some of our friends are often
> very careless and irresponsible. What is the value, for example, of President
> Nasser's irresponsible statements that the Arabs will never agree to coexist
> with Israel, and about total war by the Arabs against that country, of the
> statement made on Cairo Radio on the first day of the war to the effect that
> at last the Egyptian people were giving Israel a lesson in death. This kind
> of irresponsibility combined with lack of concern can lead the world to
> even more serious consequences.[24]

Yegorychev implied that Brezhnev as chairman of the Defense Council had grown arbitrary and complacent: "Perhaps I am overemphasizing the
issue and that I am incorrect in some things because of my lack of information. But I do believe that the country's defense is too important a matter, and therefore if we here in the Central Committee were to overemphasize
an issue it would be only for the good of things.... I am worried, for example, about the status of the capital's air defenses. The present system is
becoming increasingly obsolete. Modernization will not produce the effect
required. The development of a new air defense system for the capital is too
slow.... Perhaps it is time as we continue the line of the Central Committee's October 1964 Plenum [to observe collective leadership and] to hear a
report at one of the upcoming plenums, in closed session, about the status
of the country's defense and the tasks for party organizations, civilian and
military."[25]

Yegorychev tacitly rebuked Brezhnev for indifference to interethnic
tensions. Ukraine was still a tinder box of anti–Russian sentiment and in
July 1965 40 Ukrainian intellectuals were arrested for advocating local independence. Open trials for some were held in January and February 1966,
but protest demonstrations stopped those trials. Now Soviet Muslims were
angry over the latest defeat of Arab armies at the hands of Israel. "Events
in the Near East," Yegorychev said,

> have evoked certain unhealthy attitudes among the most backward part of
> our population. I am talking primarily about the disgusting phenomena of
> Zionism and anti–Semitism. In order to prevent them from developing fur-
> ther we should not pass over them today as if we do not notice them. For
> unhealthy manifestations of nationalism and chauvinism in whatever form
> are very dangerous. Vladimir Ilyich Lenin always paid great attention to the

nationalities question. Now, with the development of our socialist, multi-national state relations between the nations are becoming richer and more diverse. Sometimes some complex phenomena emerge in these relations, particularly under conditions of the intensified ideological struggle between the two world systems. Thus, nationalities issues are a living process in social development. And it can hardly be right that for some decades no work has been done on them, in all their diversity. Most often the matter is limited to the theme of friendship between the peoples of our country. Yes, the friendship of the peoples is a very great achievement of the party's Leninist nationalities policy. At the same time, in-depth theoretical research on the nationalities question in general can be very useful, particularly for us, the party practical workers.[26]

It is noteworthy that Yegorychev in spotlighting official neglect of ethnic problems ignored Stalin's responsibility in the closing of the USSR Nationalities Affairs Commissariat and special offices in the central party apparatus.

Bad feelings between Muslims and Jews in Uzbekistan were rising and tens of thousands of Bokhara Jews later emigrated to Israel. The KGB saw as ethnic hotspots the Baltics and western Ukraine, areas most penetrated by hostile foreign radios. The Chekists mistakenly thought that nationalists from one of those regions set off an explosion in the Moscow metro in January 1977 and was the work of Armenian extremists. Nearly everywhere in the Caucasus national Communists, dissident intellectuals and underground businessmen were becoming assertive. Mountain tribesmen in the region were feuding and that prompted a 1973 CPSU decree "On anti-social nationalistic manifestations in Grozny city" of the Chechen-Ingush republic. A follow-up edict in 1982 noted that mass demonstrations had occurred in North Ossetia over the resettling there of Ingushi. A two-day riot in the town of Ordzhonikidze was marked by attacks on state buildings and urban transport. The USSR MVD chief ordered confiscation of firearms and daggers in North Ossetia and the Chechen-Ingush area.[27] Jacob Beam, U.S. Chief of Mission in Moscow at the time, was keenly aware of the significance of such phenomena. National discord, he rightly prophesied, would create major problems for the Kremlin and nationality problems would be among the strains accompanying forthcoming change.[28]

The Shelepin faction miscalculated that Yegorychev would set off a political firestorm. CIA's version of a secret Soviet report was that Brezhnev at the June 1967 Plenum defended the regime's diplomatic effort to settle the Arab-Israeli crisis by peaceful means and eschewed the violent methods that Shelepin favored. Brezhnev was quoted as saying that the regime avoided loud threats and saber-rattling because "the aggressors and their allies well understand that the Soviet Union consistently comes out for a stable peace in the Near East and ... if necessary will resolutely come to the defense of the victims of aggression." CIA reported a Moscow rumor that Yegorychev read statistics to the Plenum to prove that Moscow was inadequately defended against a missile attack. Brezhnev interrupted Yegorychev to ask when he had last attended a session of the Military Council of the Moscow Military District, to which Yegorychev replied "never." Brezhnev then requested an intermission and assembled the Politburo. Returning to the Plenum, Brezhnev accused Yegorychev of carelessly revealing state secrets. The critic was swiftly demoted and exiled to the post of ambassador to Denmark.[29]

Victor Grishin, new party leader in Moscow, was reputedly mired in corruption and thereby at the mercy of Brezhnev as topmost KGB overseer. In July Shelepin was named head of the powerless Trade Union Council, and foreign diplomats in Moscow inferred that this was Brezhnev's retaliation for Shelepin having opposed his policy in the Middle East.[30] That September Shelepin was dropped from the CPSU Secretariat but kept his seat at the Politburo until expelled in April 1975 for rumoring about Brezhnev's poor health and urging his replacement.[31]

Still unclear was a dispute over censorship in the same time frame. Solzhenitsyn circulated a letter to delegates at the Writers Congress in May 1967 decrying the censorship as illegal. The poet Andrei Voznesensky read a work attacking censorship at the Taganka Theater. Unexpectedly, the Komsomol daily on June 30 ran an article by Khrushchev advisor Burlatsky and a former Komsomol secretary rejecting theater censorship. The Komsomol leadership later (July 8) published an editorial in the same paper ruling that the anticensorship article was "a crude ideological mistake" on the part of the editorial board. Evidently a liberal party faction tried to capitalize on Politburo infighting and was mauled.

The regime strongly reacted to ascendance of reform Communists in the neighboring satellite of Czechoslovakia. In January 1968 Alexander Dubcek became party leader in Prague. His scrapping of censorship and introduction of parliamentary government frightened Soviet bureaucrats, who feared a spill-over effect. General Staff officers in Moscow worried that a gap might open on their strategic flank with NATO. A former insider relates that Brezhnev and Kosygin were unsure about how to deal with the situation. He identifies as Politburo hawks urging military intervention to stifle the Prague reformers Suslov, Grishin, Shelest and titular president Podgorny.[32] A source with access to Kosygin and Gromyko has identified the Kremlin hardliners as Shelest, Arvid Pelshe (old Latvian Communist), Polyansky, deputy premier Kirill Mazurov and CPSU Secretaries Dmitri Ustinov (defense industries), Konstantin Katushev (relations with ruling foreign parties) and Demichev (culture). Almost all of the army marshals who were Central Committee members are said to have requested military action.[33] On August 20 Soviet troops occupied Prague and major Czech towns. The Prague Spring was frozen over and more Soviet intellectuals estranged from their masters.

A few months later Brezhnev sought to terminate whatever freedom of action Kosygin still enjoyed. The general secretary sternly criticized the Government's direction of the economy at the December 1969 Plenum and effectively demanded that party men take the reins of management. This offensive accounts for an ideological change in the Theses for the Lenin birth centenary, published on December 23, 1969. The Theses stated that the party "accomplishes its tasks *both directly and* through the soviets, state bodies and public organizations" (italics added). This nullified the balanced formula of the 1967 Theses for the 50th anniversary of the Bolshevik Revolution, which had stipulated that the party fulfilled its leading role in society "through the system of state and public organizations."

A *Pravda* (February 13, 1970) editorial warned that criticism of economic deficiencies ought not to take the form of "demagogic fault-finding, squabbling, and squaring of private accounts." Rumor had it that Suslov and Shelepin disagreed with Brezhnev's speech at the December 1969 Plenum. They wrote a letter to the Politburo accusing Brezhnev of "politically harmful" meddling into matters that were beyond the range of his competence. A proposal was made for discussion of the issue at a Central Committee Plenum in March.[34] Brezhnev was on good terms with Defense Minister Marshal Andrei Grechko, who in March led army maneuvers near Minsk. Ignoring the rest of the Politburo, Brezhnev attended a critique and parade following the maneuvers. The Oppositionists surmised that Brezhnev and Grechko had struck a deal and withdrew their letter to the Politburo.[35]

Anatoli Lukyanov informs that Brezhnev avoided the nursing of a grudge against Suslov and often telephoned him about the 1977 draft Constitution, asking if the liberals (*liberaly*) had gone too far in new formulations of political doctrine. In any event, a new Leader was recognized in April 1970. A cult of Brezhnev's personality got off the ground and his speeches for the Lenin birth centennial overshadowed those of other leaders. A two-volume edition of Brezhnev speeches and articles covering the 1964–1970 period was released on May Day, conferring upon the party chief a distinction enjoyed by no Soviet leader since Khrushchev.[36] There was also an effort to diminish the prestige of Kosygin. A report in *Pravda* (April 30) on the nomination of candidates for parliamentary elections relegated Kosygin to the role of a mere "organizer," while rating Brezhnev's personal contribution to Soviet achievements on a par with that of the Politburo as a whole. Kosygin was further slighted by receiving fewer nominations to the parliament than Podgorny, whom he had surpassed in this regard in 1966.

Gennadi Voronov as premier of the Russian Republic demanded a say in senior bureaucratic appointments. At a Politburo meeting in June 1971 Voronov asked that his office be consulted prior to the naming of regional leaders. Party Secretary Kirilenko responded that CPSU headquarters decided personnel questions and there was no reason to rearrange things.[37]

Voronov resurfaced the decentralizing idea of using small work teams on collective farms. He claimed that as few as a dozen team members were able to cultivate 5,000 acres on their own and ensure the observance of crop rotation. Brezhnev supported the apparatchiks who feared the teams as "rebirth of the kulaks," whom Stalin had liquidated. He ordered the withdrawal from circulation of a manual about the teams that Voronov wrote and wished to distribute at a nationwide conference of farm workers.[38]

Brezhnev and Voronov disagreed no less over the management of natural resources. A project dear to Brezhnev was to build a dam and power station at Chebokssary on the Volga that required the flooding of vast tracts of farmland. A Politburo commission was formed under Kirilenko, who met with members on an individual basis and alleged that defense interests required their approval. Voronov recalls that after Kirilenko had won a majority to his side, he left a session at which he, Voronov, was to speak. Brezhnev used a similar method to push through decisions to abandon thousands of small villages as futureless and to divert the flow of northern and Siberian rivers to Central Asia — a costly venture that Gorbachev later scrapped.[39]

Voronov's last assignment was to head the USSR People's Control Committee, which investigated reports of bureaucratic malfeasance. He was informed that Brezhnev loyalists who were first secretaries of republic-level party organizations — Geidar Aliyev (Azerbaijan) and Saraf Rashidov (Uzbekistan) — were involved in large-scale racketeering. When Voronov was told from above to ignore the allegations he resigned from the Control

Committee. He later heard that Brezhnev exulted "Voronov's gone. Now we have unanimity!"[40]

Brezhnev's racist fear of Chinese expansionists nudged him to adopt a conciliatory stance in dealings with the west Europeans. He accepted U.S. President Nixon's hand of friendship that was given in the hope that Moscow would help settle the Vietnam conflict. As if to guarantee that detente would be controlled, Brezhnev convoked the Central Committee in April 1973 on the eve of his visit to the United States and raised to full Politburo membership Defense Minister Grechko, KGB chief Andropov and Foreign Minister Gromyko. Ambassador Dobrynin was Brezhnev's interpreter in America and to his discomfort Brezhnev in a drunken state told Nixon that it was hard to be general secretary as Kosygin and Podgorny were trying to undermine his position.[41]

A Podgorny-Grechko alliance was indeed struck in the midst of a foreign policy crisis. War broke out between Egypt and Syria, on one side, and Israel, on the other, in October 1973. The Politburo met on an emergency basis when the Israelis disregarded a U.N. Security Council resolution for combatants to return to cease-fire positions and attacked the Egyptian Third Army Corps. This threatened collapse of President Sadat's rule in Cairo, and Grechko with Podgorny urged a "demonstration of our military presence in Egypt and Syria," which meant the deployment of airborne troops from the Soviet Union. Brezhnev, Kosygin and Gromyko were afraid of a collision with the United States and successfully opposed this proposal.[42]

Nevertheless, Brezhnev was quick to show that detente was strictly limited to nonideological matters. He addressed the Politburo in January 1974 and attacked the dissident intellectuals. Brezhnev said of Solzhenitsyn's *Gulag Archepelago*,

> This is a crude anti–Soviet lampoon. We must consult about this, what we should do now. Under our laws we have full grounds for putting Solzhenitsyn in prison, inasmuch as he has cast aspersions on what is most sacred — on Lenin, on our Soviet system, on Soviet power, on everything that is precious to us. In the past we imprisoned Yakir, Litvinov and others, sentenced them, and that put an end to it. Kuznetsov, Alliluyeva, and others went abroad. There was some noise at first, and then everything was forgotten. But this hooligan element, Solzhenitsyn, has let himself go. Lashes out at everything, doesn't stop at anything. What shall we do with him?

Andropov claimed that the existence of tens of thousands of hostile elements in the USSR made Solzhenitsyn's work dangerous and he advised the writer's expulsion from the country, which soon occurred.[43]

Brezhnev's commitment to the defense sector led him to reject Kosygin's bid to offer more consumer goods during the 1975–1980 planning period in order to raise worker productivity. The result was that in 1980 the share of consumer goods in the total volume of industrial production stood at only 26 percent, or less than was the case in the Khrushchev years. Kosygin's son-in-law remarks that the premier "was outraged by the magnitude of expenditures for the Armed Forces, he said that the arms race would end in our complete ruin."[44] In the meantime, an unofficial supply network for household items, which were produced in illicit workshops or stolen from state firms, eased the hardships of ordinary citizens. The "proletarian life style" of many also served to offset the chronic shortages of basic commodities.

A drinker and smoker, Brezhnev suffered from circulatory disease. He was stricken while seeing off U.S. President Ford near Vladivostok in December 1974. Brezhnev later had memory and speech lapses that were enfeebling. Health Minister Chazov tells of his report on Brezhnev's diminished capacity to the KGB chief and senior party secretary: "I informed both Andropov and Suslov — who ran for cover — about Brezhnev's grave condition. Everyone knew what was happening. But the 'stability' united everyone. All of them said: 'If we remove him now, a power struggle will begin, everything is now calm and peaceful in the country, whereas there would be a commotion then. For the sake of stability, we need to keep Brezhnev.'"[45] Gromyko and Brezhnev aide Konstantin Chernenko agreed and helped to prop up Brezhnev.[46]

In 1977 a new Constitution was adopted and Article 6 went beyond the party-supremacist clause of the 1936 edition, proclaiming that the CPSU was a "leading and directive force of Soviet society, core of its political system, state and public organizations.... [It] determines the course of society's development, the line of USSR domestic and foreign policy, guides the lofty creative activity of the Soviet people, gives a planned and scientifically based character to its struggle for the victory of communism." But political volatility recurred as Brezhnev's health worsened. Gorbachev's memoirs inform that upon coming to work in Moscow in 1978 he was told that Brezhnev was looking for support in rival factions fighting for power. On Brezhnev's side were Defense Minister Grechko and party Secretary Kirilenko. A later contingent of Brezhnev loyalists included party Secretary Ustinov, KGB chief Andropov and republic party heads Shcherbitsky (Ukraine), Kunayev (Kazakhstan), Rashidov (Uzbekistan) and Aliyev (Azerbaijan). Though not a struggle between reformers and conservatives, Gorbachev points out, standing up for Brezhnev tended to strengthen conservative trends. Yeltsin's memoirs are more lurid, claiming that Brezhnev in his last years was mindless and easy prey for highly placed grafters.[47]

The galloping corruption in high places became common knowledge and evoked an idealized view of the past. Eminent analyst of Soviet affairs Wolfgang Leonhard reflected on Russian public opinion:

> There has been such a disintegration of the official ideology that it is not too much to speak of a spiritual psychological vacuum. Western scholars have searched far and wide and found "not a single Marxist in the land." No one believes anything any more. Signs of the "vacuum" can be found in the phenomena of civic resignation, rising alcoholism, and signs here and there of a search for "alternatives" (essentially in nationalist or conservative traditions). I have seen letters which record how people, old and young, are on the move, traveling hundreds of kilometers to visit some old fortress or ancient church. Some of this has to do with a new religiosity, and I do not mean the piety of the aged grandmother from Zagorsk [a medieval town near Moscow] but rather the theological bent of the educated young and indeed the offspring of party functionaries.[48]

Russian nationalism had subversive counterparts in the borderlands. One motive behind the Kremlin's 1979 invasion of Afghanistan was a desire to prevent Islamic fundamentalism from infecting Muslims in the Soviet Union's Central Asian republics. Georgians staged mass demonstrations against Moscow's wish to drop a constitutional proviso that Georgian was the republic's state language, and the Center retreated.

The death of Kosygin in December 1980 should have opened a door for younger political leaders. New premier Nikolai Tikhonov, however, was 78, and his appointment in line with a leadership consensus to stick with gerontocracy: 12 of 14 Politburo members were over 70. One of the two upstarts was Gorbachev, who in 1978 had succeeded Fyodr Kulakov, party secretary for agriculture upon Kulakov's sudden death. Gorbachev was born in March 1931 into a peasant family in south Russia. His father was a farm mechanic and grandfather a collective farm chairman; both were party members. Gorbachev's grandfather was arrested when he, Mikhail, was 9 and held for 14 months, during which time he was tortured and beaten. A grandmother told him that collectivization led to hatred inside families with brother against brother and son against father.

Mikhail did hard physical labor on a collective farm from the age of 13. In 1950 he finished school and entered the law department at Moscow State University (MGU). He was a member of the Komsomol committee at the law department and joined the party in 1952. Soon Gorbachev became secretary of his Komsomol unit and member of the MGU party committee. In 1955–1956 he was deputy chief of Agitprop in the Komsomol leadership in the Stavropol area. Gorbachev was regional Komsomol head in 1960 and two years later a secretary of the Stavropol territorial party committee. Five years later he completed a correspondence course from an institute and qualified as farm economist (Gromyko's educational background).

The party job enabled Gorbachev to meet high party officials like Andropov who visited the North Caucasus spas for the health benefits of their mineral waters. In 1971 Gorbachev was picked for the CPSU Central Committee and in 1980 for voting Politburo member. An aide later remarked that Gorbachev for years had little respect for stale party dogmas: "Long before his Moscow appointment Gorbachev had been inwardly prepared for the crumbling of Marxist-Leninist orthodoxy."[49]

Travel, reading and conversation were sources of Gorbachev's wide-ranging knowledge of foreign and domestic politics. During the 1970s he made trips to Italy, France, Belgium and West Germany. Gorbachev read translations of the works of socialist and Eurocommunist scholars. The books included Aragon's *Parallel History of the USSR*, Garaudy's *French Model of Socialism*, and Boffa's *History of the Soviet Union*, and the *History of Marxism*, as well as volumes about Italian leftists Togliatti and Gramsci. This broadened Gorbachev's horizons, as did his readings of Karl Marx on worker alienation and the minutes of Lenin-era party congresses. Talks with old-time party officials such as Leon Onikov helped Gorbachev to satisfy his curiosity about Stalinist politics. Gorbachev at age 25, of course, was familiarized with Khrushchev's anti–Stalin speech at the 1956 party congress and he was a delegate to the 1961 congress at which Khrushchev reopened the discussion of Stalin crimes. In addition, American travelers to the Soviet Union reported that Gorbachev was familiar with the writings of American liberal scholars who saw a prosperous future for the USSR if the Kremlin revived Lenin's New Economic Policy of 1921–1929. The travelers heard this from employees of the Institute of World Economics and International Relations in Moscow, which sent to Gorbachev the American liberals' works.

Gorbachev in power would be a fierce critic of Stalin. He avoided use of the term *stalinizm*, which implied an ideological current within the framework of Marxism, and bristled at *stalinshchina*, a term connoting the dark times of the historical personality in question. The original closeness of Gorbachev to the land makes it possible that he was influenced by the literary movement that interpreted Stalinism as a violent reaction of urban Russia against the peasantry. The writers of this school saw Russian Marxism as so hostile to village ways that it sought the "depeasantification" (*raskrestyanivaniye*) of their country.

What Gorbachev learned from secret reports in Moscow convinced him of the failure of threats and pressure as management tools. A basic indicator of efficiency was the return on the state's capital investment, and from 1970 it was in a downward spiral of 3 percent annually. Output on farms was plunging and the same was true of productivity at nearly half of all industrial firms. Academician Aganbegyan describes the general economic situation in the late 1970s and early 1980s as catastrophic and the slackness of workers terrifying.[50] It will be seen that he would become a vocal champion of perestroika.

The Brezhnev circle was unyielding in defense of routine. During preparations for the 1981 party congress Siberian factory director Tengiz Avaliani wrote a letter to Brezhnev asking him to step down and allow sober review of failed policies. Avaliani warned against making the congress one more "great and boastful theatrical spectacle." The letter was passed along to Chernenko who ordered local party officials to investigate. Avaliani was ousted and his worst fears about the party congress realized.[51]

Gorbachev is likely to have been among those in Moscow alarmed over new instability in the outer empire. The review of a Moscow stage play that centered on Lenin was featured in *Pravda* January 12, 1982. The Workers' Opposition of 1921–1922 reappeared, wrongly urging the independence of Soviet trade unions from the state. Reference was made to "belching of the 'Workers' Opposition' concept" in connection with "current-day Polish events" or rise of the Solidarity free-trade union.

A debate in the Soviet academic journal *Voprosy Filosofii* (Problems of Philosophy) pitted reformers against conservatives. One side argued that internal strains under socialism might become antagonistic and provoke revolution. Others held that only in capitalist states might the tensions escalate to the point of explosion. Gorbachev's later observation that the USSR was in a "pre-crisis" mode under Brezhnev suggests that he too may have feared the advent of a homegrown version of the Polish unrest.

The death of Suslov in January 1982 intensified presuccession maneuvering. Andropov with the information resources of the KGB in hand began to match wits with the Brezhnevists. In late February an investigation was made into charges of bribery on the part of the USSR's top circus administrator, Anatoli Kolevatov, who was a friend of Brezhnev's daughter, Galina

Churbanova. She was married to Colonel-General Yu. M. Churbanov, first deputy interior minister, who would later be arrested for embezzlement and ties to the criminal underworld. According to the stories in circulation, Kolevatov allowed performers to make trips abroad on the condition that they bring back for him high-value items that fetched extraordinary black market prices in Moscow.[52] This was only the tip of an iceberg of crime involving senior officials who had become racketeers and foreign currency speculators (*valyutchiki*).

Chernenko seemed best positioned to replace Brezhnev. Aged 70 and a federal party Secretary, he was officially shown to be involved in the oversight of military, police, agricultural, trade union and foreign affairs.[53] This circumstance must have alarmed serious officials as Chernenko was little more than a faithful clerk. He was born in September 1911 of Siberian peasant stock. In the 1930s he served as a border guard on the Chinese frontier and upon discharge embarked on a party career in Agitprop. Chernenko met Brezhnev in 1948 while both were in Moldavia, a Rumanian corner of the USSR. Brezhnev took him to Moscow in 1956 and he became editor of the low-grade magazine *Agitator*.

The colorless Chernenko served as Brezhnev's chief of staff for a decade and landed in the General Department for documentation work after Brezhnev replaced Khrushchev. By 1978 he was a Politburo full member. Now seemingly poised to lead the party, Chernenko made a number of public statements that indicated resolve to forestall the dissidents' vision of the convergence of Soviet and Western systems. Like a stolid conservative he disparaged "pragmatism" and "excessive trust in material stimuli alone."[54] Chernenko harped on the danger of the party's transformation from integrating force of society into a loose coalition of interest groups.[55]

Although largely self-taught, KGB chief Andropov was a polished rival of Brezhnevists Chernenko and Kirilenko. He was born in 1914 in south Russia, the son of a railway official. Educated at the Rybinsk Water Transport Technical College, Andropov initially worked as a Volga sailor. He joined the Komsomol in 1930 and the party in 1939. Andropov was Komsomol leader in the Soviet Karelo-Finnish Republic from 1940 to 1944. During World War II he took part in guerrilla activities. He was promoted to work in Moscow in 1951 and served as Soviet ambassador to Hungary during the 1956 revolution, a traumatic experience that is reported to have left him with serious reservations about hastily undertaking reforms. Andropov entered the orbit of Suslov as head of the CPSU office for contacts with ruling foreign parties and apparently became head of the security service with Suslov's backing.

In May 1982 Andropov replaced the deceased Suslov and took control of censorship guidelines, party bureaus for propaganda and foreign affairs, and policy research institutes. To build a power base he exploited the discontent of younger party men with the Brezhnevists' protection of grafters. Sergei Medunov, profiteering boss of Krasnodar region in south Russia, was arrested a short time after Andropov joined the party Secretariat.[56] Just as suddenly Kirilenko lost his high party posts for "reasons of health and in connection with a personal request."[57] Earlier rumor was spread that he protected a corrupt ex-magnate in Baku, who paid under the table with luxury goods and special vacation trips. The ritualistic sacking of a top figure at a Central Committee Plenum was ignored, perhaps to avert a backlash from corrupt barons.

As old guarders sang thanks to Andropov, Young Turks rose. Gorbachev was tapped to give a major report on farming to the Central Committee Plenum in June 1982. Scholars at the Institute of the Economies of the World Socialist System suggested that he include in his speech support for the family contracts that were popular in China. Gorbachev cautioned against rushing ahead and promised that in the future he would raise more important issues (Ellman and Kontorovich, 1998). He might have had in mind a rebirth of the leasing of land as during the NEP era, a measure he was to champion during perestroika.

Brezhnev died on November 10, 1982, and the Politburo supported the view of Defense Minister Ustinov and Gromyko that Andropov be elected to the post of general secretary.[58] Chernenko accepted his setback with a bad grace, and at the Central Committee Plenum on November 12 nominated Andropov to lead the party as embodiment of "the Brezhnev style," "the Brezhnev concern about the people's interests" and "the Brezhnev attitude towards cadres."[59] The audience, however, gave Andropov an ovation out of respect for his superior intelligence and extensive knowledge.[60]

In his inaugural Andropov promised to win the war in Afghanistan and deal firmly with the Reagan administration. Like Khrushchev and Brezhnev who once courted military favor, Andropov said, "We know very well that peace cannot be obtained from the imperialists by begging for it. It can be upheld only by relying on the invincible might of the Soviet armed forces."[61] The new leader kept his word and deployed SS-20 intermediate-range nuclear missiles in response to Reagan's stationing of similar weapons in western Europe. The accelerating arms race was driving down the growth rate of popular living standards.

Nevertheless, Andropov stuck to an anti–Western position. The party intellectual Shakhnazarov in his memoir recalls trying to persuade Andropov that in view of the extreme poverty of many in the USSR its leaders should economize on defense and rely on minimal nuclear deterrence. Andropov upheld the building of an ocean-going navy with bases in Vietnam, Angola and Yemen. He viewed the third world as the main theater of the Cold War and saw future need to land Soviet ground forces on distant shores. Andropov dismissed as "pacifists" the foreign policy consultants like Shakhnazarov. In other words, Andropov was like some Western anti–Communists of his era, wrongly believing that the superpowers would decide the future of the world in Asia and Africa.

Andropov had an incurable kidney disease and his tenure lasted only 15 months. He devoted most of his limited energy to the enforcement of lax social discipline. Brezhnev's son-in-law in the police hierarchy was arrested for corruption, as was his superior, Interior Minister N. A. Shchelokov, accused of protecting Rashidov, grafting potentate of Uzbekistan, who committed suicide.[62] Andropov won popularity by ordering police roundups of Moscow officials who spent working hours at cinemas or saunas.

He set a tone of policy gradualism in a theoretical article sent in draft form to colleagues. Upon receiving "The Teaching of Karl Marx and Some Questions of Building Socialism in the USSR," half the Politburo members struck from their copies the word "socialism" and substituted for it the word "communism."[63] Andropov insisted on keeping the original text and prevailed. Evidently, the disagreement was over the time needed to reach general prosperity and minimize official coercion. Andropov's insistence that socialism was still a work in progress contrasted sharply with the Khrushchev-Brezhnev smug view of material progress and denoted belief in the need for strong state bodies.

Andropov may have envisioned some kind of reforms once he consolidated power. He sponsored a party resolution adopted in August 1983 that anticipated Gorbachev's campaign for inner-party democracy. "The party's electoral assemblies," according to this document, "are conducted in accordance with a pre-existing script, without serious and frank debate. Candidates' declarations have been edited beforehand; any initiative or criticism is suppressed. From now on, none of this will be tolerated."[64]

In her study of the KGB, Russian journalist Yevgenia Albats notes that under Andropov a group of economists was attached to the government's Interagency Council to Study the Experience of Socialist Countries and analyzed economic reforms in China, Yugoslavia and Hungary. It advised revamping the Soviet economy and was disbanded when Andropov died.

Russian analyst Yevgeni Vertlib also holds that Andropov intended to introduce a variety of market socialism, in particular the Chinese experiment with "free economic zones."

Kremlin insider Vadim Medvedev reports that Andropov recognized his poor knowledge of economics and entrusted to Gorbachev an analysis of the economic situation (Ellman and Kontorovich, 1998). Gorbachev, however, maintains in *Memoirs* that Andropov was unlikely to have set his sights on radical reforms. He is portrayed as a man of his time and unable to break through the barrier of old ideas and values. Gorbachev adds that to the discredit of Andropov he ignored Stalin's crimes and failed to challenge Brezhnev's efforts to revive Stalin's image and model of organizing society. A similar view of Andropov as cautious apparatchik stands out in the memoir of diplomat Troyanovsky. He recalls hearing Andropov shudder about his experience as ambassador to Hungary in 1956 and watching mobs ready to devastate everything in sight.

During the last months of Andropov, Gorbachev played a double game of covert malcontent and party loyalist. He visited Canada in 1983 and met Soviet ambassador Aleksandr Yakovlev, the Agitprop official who a decade earlier was sent into diplomatic exile for criticism of Russian ultranationalists. In a 1995 interview with foreign journalists Yakovlev recalled one of his private talks with Gorbachev at the time: "We were in an open field waiting for the arrival of an official. We discussed everything, we interrupted each other and said, 'That thing must be changed and that one's intolerable.... Everything's intolerable.'"

Back in Moscow Gorbachev could be difficult with colleagues on questions relevant to his portfolio of agriculture. He differed with Politburo members who wanted to drop from the draft of a Brezhnev speech a reference to the idea of giving some independence to collective farms: "If they don't accept it, people will solve the problem themselves." That was a paraphrase of Tsar Alexander II's rebuke of those opposed to liberating the Russian serfs.

But Gorbachev was careful to avoid offending heavyweights on the most sensitive issues. At a meeting of the party Secretariat in April 1983 he agreed with the KGB that a stage play had harmful ideological content and its production showed "lack of control and an absence of political alertness."[65] The Politburo met in September to discuss the Soviet downing of a South Korean airliner in which 269 persons died. Soviet media had justified the action and only Gromyko and party Control Committee chairman Mikhail Solomentsev suggested a statement of sympathy with the families of the victims. Gorbachev sided with the chauvinist majority and urged a tough stance.[66]

A conflict of temperaments between Marshal Ustinov and Gorbachev prevented Andropov from designating Gorbachev his political heir. When the Politburo met after Andropov's death on February 9, 1984, Ustinov laid a hand on the shoulder of premier Tikhonov and said "Kostya [Chernenko] will be easier to get along with than the other one [Gorbachev]."[67] An eyewitness describes the atmosphere at the February 13 Plenum held in the Kremlin's Sverdlovsk Hall to elect a new general secretary. The barons were hardly a clutch of walking *Pravdas*. They shouted greetings, loudly kissed one another and chatted about the weather and outlook for the next harvest. Tikhonov spoke on behalf of the Politburo and announced the selection of Chernenko to replace Andropov. The audience responded with "a weak, formal, very brief round of applause" that contrasted with the ovation that Andropov got on the last such occasion.[68]

Brezhnevism was on its last legs but still a force to be reckoned with. In April 1984 Chernenko called a secret meeting to talk about the drafting of a new Program to be adopted at a party congress.[69] He vilified "renewers" and "improvers" of socialism, and professed faith in the "great creative forces which are to be found in the consciousness and ideological convictions of the masses." Chernenko insisted that he would prevent the CPSU from deteriorating into an amalgam of pressure groups.[70] A British scholar later presented a lineup of existing Soviet lobbies in the approximate order of their importance:

- nuclear scientists, managers of nuclear plants, heads of the military nuclear services and those in charge of outer space experiments;
- the chief planners and managers of heavy industry and of engineering;
- the trade union lobby, organized in the All-Union Council of the Trade Unions;
- the lobby of municipalities to press the demand for living accommodations;
- directors of the state-owned farms and weaker spokesmen of the collective farms;
- the officers' corps of the conventional military forces;
- the leaders of academic institutes; and
- journalists and literary figures.[71]

In support of Deutscher's reporting, former Soviet insiders routinely told scholars Ellman and Kontorovich about the military industrial complex lobbying the Olympus. This reality of informal bureaucratic pluralism runs counter to Professor T. H. Rigby's "mono-organizational" model of Soviet society in which top party officials regimented all institutions. In any event, one of Chernenko's last official acts was to restore party membership to old Stalinist Molotov.[72] Declining health forced Chernenko to miss Politburo meetings with increased frequency, and Gorbachev every week waited for a phone call from him in expectation of having to stand in for the general secretary.

Gorbachev had a hand in the Politburo adopting in April 1984 a concept of economic management that included ending the state monopoly of foreign trade and legalizing cooperatives and private services within the framework of central planning (Ellman and Kontorovich, 1998). But it was the death of Defense Minister Ustinov in December 1984 that strengthened Gorbachev's power position.[73] As the new chief ideologist, Gorbachev made a liberalizing speech at a leadership conference held around the time of Ustinov's death. He criticized dogmatic notions of economic management, and supported fresh initiatives, openness and socialist democracy. This extraordinary departure from orthodoxy was kept out of *Pravda* and published only a half year later, after Gorbachev had risen to the highest post.

In March 1985 Chernenko succumbed to lung disease, the third general secretary to expire in less than three years' time. Historian Pikhoya learned that Gorbachev struck a deal with old guarder Gromyko to succeed Chernenko. Gorbachev's intermediaries in winning over Gromyko were the institute directors Yakovlev (World Economics and International Relations), Anatoli Gromyko (Africa) and Yevgeni Primakov (Eastern Studies). KGB deputy chairman Vladimir Kryuchkov later joined the talks, which centered on the idea that once Gromyko nominated Gorbachev for the top party job he, Gromyko, would be named ceremonial president.

When the Politburo formally met to choose a successor to Chernenko the Moscow party head Grishin nominated Gorbachev to be chairman of the Brezhnev funeral commission, which signified imminent election of Gorbachev to the general secretaryship. At the ensuing Central Committee meeting Gromyko spoke and endorsed Gorbachev as a stellar nominee. The audience was relieved that a mediocrity like Grishin was passed over and broke into an ovation even louder than the one at Andropov's election. Speeches of endorsement followed from Grishin, party Secretary for heavy industry Romanov, Russian Republic premier Vorotnikov, party Secretary for world affairs Ponomarev, KGB chairman Chebrikov, Georgian party head Shevardnadze, Culture Minister Demichev, party Secretary for personnel Ligachev, and USSR premier Ryzhkov. Gorbachev had the last word and deceptively promised to maintain continuity of policy.[74] Eventually Gorbachev was often blamed for the meltdown of the Soviet Union as he dismantled the control mechanisms that held together the Kremlin's inner empire. But whether the political inheritance of Gorbachev was sustainable will be endlessly debated.

CHAPTER 6

Gorbachev: Turning Point

Only a political philosopher would think that Gorbachev's greatest historical achievement was to renounce the Marxist belief that class struggle holds primacy in the conduct of international relations. Gorbachev's all-important feat was to dismantle the Soviet party-state. He did so by undermining the institutions that were essential foundations of autocracy: Communist party, KGB, censorship, economic planning and ministerial bureaucracy. Gorbachev stripped the ruling party of its operational direction of the command economy and relinquished its monopoly of political power. The party had to compete with others in genuine elections that decided who was to legislate in a standing parliament. The KGB was no longer empowered to arrest those suspected of sedition and fabricate cases against them. Censorship was rolled back to the meager status it held in the last years of tsardom. The planners and ministers lost control of firms as greed and boldness seized managers whose harnesses Gorbachev had loosened.

All this amounted to the culmination of nearly a century of struggle for freedom inside Russia on the part of martyred or exiled liberals, Social-Democrats, borderland nationalists and reform Communists. Stalin was their arch persecutor and Gorbachev spent much effort knocking the old dictator off the pedestal that admirers kept erecting for him. Yet, Gorbachev's reforms would have gone for naught had Boris Yeltsin as president of the Russian Federation not thwarted the 1991 coup attempt of Communist elites. Yeltsin's populism, anti–Communism and Russian nationalism proved to be far more appealing to broad circles of Russian society than either Gorbachev's neo–Menshevism or the coup plotters' neo–Bolshevism.

When the man from Stavropol came to power he puzzled many Western and Soviet observers. A British scholar was sure that he was an outright conservative.[1] America's ambassador to the Soviet Union inferred from Gorbachev's low-keyed debut that he was an ideologue.[2] Even after he promoted great reforms a former adviser was uncertain about whether power politics or idealism motivated him.[3] But a onetime dean of the diplomatic corps in Moscow shrewdly drew a distinction between previous rulers of the USSR and Gorbachev. Robert A. D. Ford sized up the new general secretary as representative of a new generation of urbane officials eager to grapple with neglected domestic problems.[4]

The cited recollections of Yakovlev and Chernyayev attest that Gorbachev for some time was skeptical of party cant. Upon gaining a working majority at the Politburo, he destroyed basic pillars of the regime — censorship, centralized planning and the party's monopoly of power. As a result, the economy flew apart and the populace grew demoralized, Gorbachev's major concessions to the republics in drafting a new Union treaty incited hardliners to attempt a coup that Russian president Yeltsin thwarted and used as a springboard for the overthrow of Communist rule.

At the moment of Gorbachev's accession, around 10,000 persons occupied strategic positions and many held old-fashioned ideas about politics. The highest policy makers were the 30 or so members of the CPSU Politburo and Secretariat, 15 to 20 of whom were from the essentially conservative party machine. Leon Onikov was a longtime apparatchik and remarked that most were afflicted with "ideological blindness" and under "hypnotic power of the Stalinist idea of need for the party control of literature and art." Gorbachev, like other post–Stalin leaders, would find it necessary to shape opinion among the following in order to enact new measures that stood a chance of being successful:

- 800 leaders of the central party apparatus, USSR Government, largest ministries (Defense, MVD and Foreign Affairs);
- 1,000 state ministers and deputies, members of ministerial boards and USSR agencies, higher representatives of the USSR Government: army, KGB, justice, industrial ministries; science; and central party departments for propaganda and culture;
- 2,113 chiefs of party departments in union republics and regional committees; and
- 4,000 Moscow and local industrial firm directors, commanders of Military Districts and large military units, KGB administration chiefs.[5]

Like Gorbachev, the majority of power elites were born in the 1930s. As many as 40 percent were of bureaucratic antecedents, and this figure rose to 70 percent among those born in the 1940s. Only 4 percent had worker or collective farm backgrounds and most vulnerable to idealistic party slogans. Slavs accounted for 70 percent of the senior bureaucrats, Muslims 15 percent, Armenians and Georgians 4–5 percent, and Balts 3–5 percent. The vast majority had graduated regional polytechnics, agricultural institutes or the Higher Party School rather than quality universities. The main criterion for their promotion was public relations skills rather than professional know-how. The talent scouts from party offices who selected them were looking for persons with few independent thoughts and unquestioned loyalty to party superiors. Careers often began at soviet-party work and novices sent to study courses which they usually failed to complete. By the heyday of Gorbachev it was usual to pass over for key jobs the offspring of high-level bosses, who were better informed than average citizens and sometimes became dissenters. These distrusted scions of the upper crust sometimes went from universities to privileged jobs at institutions such as the Foreign Affairs Ministry.[6]

Gorbachev had a formidable brains trust. Unlike Brezhnev, whose aides and speechwriters were mostly journalists, Gorbachev favored specialists with advanced degrees. An idealist in the kitchen cabinet was historian Yakovlev, who was named Agitprop chief in July 1985 and sent to Gorbachev a revolutionary memorandum proposing the creation of a two-party political system and powerful presidency. Other key advisors were V. I. Boldin (private secretary and journalist); M. B. Bikkenin (philosopher and journalist); V. A. Medvedev (party theorist and economist); I. T. Frolov (philosopher and journalist); G. K. Shakhnazarov (lawyer and political analyst); A. S. Chernyayev (world affairs specialist); A. I. Lukyanov (lawyer); and economists L. I. Abalkin, S. S. Shatalin and N. Ya. Petryakov, as well as Aganbegyan.[7]

Departing from Brezhnevism, Gorbachev urged more rights for the directors of enterprises. He did so at the April 1985 Central Committee Plenum and a June 1985 conference on problems of science and technology. The Plenum registered Gorbachev's headway in building an alliance with independents to isolate conservatives entrenched in the government cabinet (Tikhonov), foreign ministry (Gromyko), and party organizations in Moscow (Grishin), Ukraine (Shcherbitsky) and Kazakhstan (Kunayev), as well as Romanov, CPSU secretary for heavy industry. Now Politburo membership was granted to Andropov clients like CPSU Secretary Ligachev, KGB chief Chebrikov and industrialist Nikolai Ryzhkov. After the Plenum one of Gorbachev's aides overreacted in his journal: "In this Politburo he

[Gorbachev] has a strong majority of eight faithful friends."[8] In fact, Ligachev, Chebrikov and Ryzhkov were cautious personalities.

Under Brezhnev it was usual to conduct campaigns against alcoholism and put limits on the sales of spirits. Andropov decreed penalties for drinking on the job although his regime introduced a new cheap vodka that was known as "Andropovka" and cropped up in workers' tool boxes. Ligachev as party boss of Tomsk region in Siberia proclaimed his area a "zone of sobriety" and convinced Gorbachev to insist a fight had to be waged against drunkenness. The social, biological and genetic evils of alcoholism were pointed up at the April Plenum. A state planner, however, warned that if a dry law was passed 5 billion rubles in state revenues could be lost. That led Gorbachev to fire back "You want to go to communism [universal prosperity] with the use of vodka!"

Gorbachev won this round and a party-state edict adopted in May closed many wine shops, beer taverns, bottling plants and vineyards. The tipplers resisted and a boom in homebrewing caused shortages of sugar, and thousands of poisonings. In the wake of huge speculation on the black market Gorbachev in 1988 halted the push for sobriety. The loss of state revenue is put at around 100 billion rubles.[9]

Gorbachev raised eyebrows in May with a walkabout in Leningrad. This too was a break with the style of Brezhnev, who communed only with war veterans at scripted reunions. The new party chief won popularity too for criticism of "theoreticians" who rejected as a survival of capitalism the desire of ordinary people to run their own small businesses. He spoke to Leningrad party staffers and told them to undergo psychological perestroika. That advice was televised but kept out of the local press, which used the word perestroika only in connection with need to produce more consumer goods.

The visit to Leningrad was the first of many tours of the heartland. Towns and areas inspected included Samara, Tolyatti, Kuybyshev. Vladivostok, Komsomolsk-on-Amur, Khabarovsk, Murmansk, Krasnoyarsk, Ukraine, Irkutsk and Kirgiziya. Usually Gorbachev reported back to the Politburo on local woes such as food rationing, housing shortages and obsolete machinery. On the eve of such journeys Gorbachev tasked his aides to write talking points, and once told them to remind him to relate how Stalin twisted Lenin's sound idea of building cooperatives in the countryside. Occasionally Gorbachev reported to the Politburo his discovery of social tension in the regions, which raised the specter of labor unrest if food and other supplies were not delivered. It was a well-kept secret that since the death of Stalin there were dozens of instances when the police or army violently suppressed public protests.[10]

In May 1986, too, Gorbachev made a stinging attack on the Soviet diplomatic corps. He spoke at the Ministry of Foreign Affairs and found fault with the diplomats' abilities to negotiate, reach compromises and appreciate the interests of interlocutors. The traditional Russian vices of corruption and abuse of power were said to be rife at the MFA and foreign trade agency, which soon lost its first deputy head, Yuri Brezhnev, the late general secretary's son.[11]

Gromyko personified the old hard-nosed style of Soviet diplomacy and in July 1985 left the MFA to take up the titular presidency. His replacement was Shevardnadze, party leader of Georgia and a friend of Gorbachev. Shevardnazde later told journalist Paul Quinn-Judge that when Gorbachev tapped him to be foreign minister, "I was mind-blown. I had been abroad three times in my life: Portugal, India, and somewhere else. I told them, 'I don't even know where the ministry is.'" Shevardnadze was trustworthy enough for Gorbachev to secure him full Politburo membership while that status was denied to Defense Minister Marshal Sergei Sokolov. In any event, Gorbachev became dominant in the formation of Soviet diplomacy, and in August 1985 the Kremlin declared a unilateral moratorium on nuclear testing.

Incriminating evidence of wrongdoing was used to dismantle roadblocks to change. Romanov was ousted from the Politburo and rumored to have borrowed Imperial dinnerware from a state museum for use at a family wedding. Grishin reputedly protected Nikolai Tregubov, head of the Moscow Trade Council, whom federal investigators accused of severe crimes and was eventually sentenced to a 15-year prison term.[12] Grishin lost his Moscow top party job in December 1985 and a few months later was dropped from the Politburo. Perhaps unrelated to illegal actions was the resignation of elderly premier Tikhonov. Out of public view, Gorbachev sanctioned the arrest of Brezhnev's private secretary, G. D. Brovin, who was seized at party headquarters and sent to a KGB prison, where officers told him to confess to corrupt practices or face summary execution. Gorbachev foes were hardly napping: an unauthorized search for compromising material (*kompromat*) on Gorbachev in his home region of Stavropol led him to sack Interior Minister Fedorchuk at a January 1986 meeting of the Politburo.[13]

A fateful personnel change was the promotion of Urals party leader Yeltsin to the post of CPSU secretary for the construction industry. He was a man of less cultural depth than Gorbachev, a fighter by nature and capable of mobilizing resentments of the lowly against elites. Yeltsin like Gorbachev was born in 1931, into a family in the village of Butko in Sverdlovsk province. He spent his childhood on a collective farm at a time of crop failures and hunger. Boris's father was arrested in 1934 and sentenced to three years in a prison camp for anti–Soviet agitation. The community was home to outlaw gangs and often a scene of violent crimes The Yeltsins moved to a crowded communal hut at a building site, where the father had found work after release from camp.

Rough and quick-tempered like his father, Boris too worked as a construction laborer. After vagabond rail trips around the country he spent five years in the department of civil engineering at Urals Polytechnic Institute. There he played for and organized men's and women's volleyball teams. In 1955 Yeltsin graduated from UPI and ran a large industrial complex. He was recruited to head the department for construction of the Sverdlovsk regional party committee and in 1976 advanced to the post of regional party first secretary. The industrial area under Yeltsin's command embraced a population of 5 million and was the third largest province of its kind in the country. The leadership style of Yeltsin in Sverdlovsk was harsh. He severely penalized laggards and conducted many bureaucratic meetings, worker rallies and inspections of recreational facilities. Although Yeltsin organized subsidiary farms at enterprises, food shortages in his area were chronic and only two pounds of meat was available for ordinary citizens perhaps three times a year, on national holidays.

The former Soviet journalist Vladimir Ardayev reports that Yeltsin urged his superiors in Moscow to grant some economic freedom to Sverdlovsk but was scolded for trying to restore Khrushchev's regional economic councils. Yeltsin first met Gorbachev while both were *de facto* governors and exchanged metal and timber from the Urals for food products from Stavropol.[14] Gorbachev nominated Yeltsin to the post of central party secretary for construction at a Politburo meeting in June 1985.

Over the next few months Gorbachev made some headway toward renewing the power mechanism. Yeltsin replaced Grishin as party leader of Moscow and entered the Politburo as candidate member. Ryzhkov exited the Secretariat and succeeded Tikhonov as premier. A nondescript technocrat, Lev Zaykov, was named party overlord of defense industry. Others in the Secretariat running the country on a day-to-day basis were Georgi Razumovsky (party organizer), Medvedev (Agitprop deputy chief) and Lukyanov (controller of documents).[15] Onikov tells that Razumovsky in autumn 1985 sent to regions a detailed order for criticism of party leaders. Medvedev rejected the isolationist custom of "indiscriminately brushing aside the experience accumulated by capitalism," and encouraged "a serious reassessment of the practice of present-day Social-Democracy in defending the social and democratic attainments of working people."[16]

Gorbachev's slogan of "acceleration" was old wine in new bottles. Emphasis was still given to the long-favored machine building industry. Drawing on the example of the military-industrial complex, several ministries and agencies were unified and the Government newly disposed of bureaus for machine building, fuel and energy, chemicals, social development and agro-industrial affairs. Patterned on military industry was a new form of quality control designed to cut the output of defective goods (*brak*). This tended to lower wages and provoked worker strikes. Unpopular too was the curbing of "unearned income," or private commerce, such as renting rooms in seaside cottages.

Behind the scenes, Gorbachev was raising controversial issues. In April 1985 he asked the Politburo for more spending to satisfy consumer needs and update infrastructure. Gorbachev cited statistics on the underdeveloped condition of the food industry, housing and municipal facilities.[17] All these sectors lagged as a result of overspending on defense, and Gorbachev's memoirs put military outlays at 40 percent of the real state budget and 20 percent of the national income. Of 25 billion rubles in total expenditure on science, 20 billion went to the military for research and development. These figures are similar to those in the memoir of Shakhnazarov, who reckons defense outlays at 16 percent of national income and 4 percent allocated to the KGB and Interior Ministry.

With an eye to cutting defense outlays, Gorbachev publicly challenged the military over threat perception. Chief of the General Staff Marshal Nikolai Ogarkov had drawn Andropov's wrath as "little Napoleon" and was ousted in September 1984. Seven months later he sent a grim message in the pamphlet *History Teaches Vigilance*. It implied a high level of war danger and need for acute military readiness. Ogarkov said that the current international situation "*to a certain degree* reminds one of the years which preceded the Second World War" (italics added). In contrast, Gorbachev told the 40th VE Day rally in Moscow on May 8, 1985, that despite certain dangers, "the present world is *absolutely unlike* that of the nineteen thirties" (italics added).

Gorbachev effectively supported defense cutbacks in his keynote to the party congress in February 1986. Almost repeating verbatim the controversial words of Malenkov, he said, "It is impossible to win the arms race and nuclear war itself." The world appeared very different to Defense Minister Marshal Sokolov and he endorsed less than unconditionally Gorbachev's plan to meet with President Reagan to normalize Soviet-American relations. At the Politburo in April Sokolov approved of a summit but voiced reservations. "The Americans are acting in an insolent way," he warned, "proposing that we reduce our personnel at the United Nations and encroaching on our territorial waters in the Black Sea. We need to act so that they feel that they are dealing with the Soviet Union. We must not be silent." Sokolov had submitted a memorandum requesting "shows of force to simulate an attack on U.S. vessels by missile-armed long-range aircraft of the USSR Navy."

Gorbachev rejected the proposal and a little more than a year later replaced Sokolov after a young West German piloted his small plane through Soviet air defenses and landed it in Red Square. The Soviet military brass viewed the ousters of Sokolov and Air Defense chief General Koldunov as retaliation for their having taken a hard line on talks with the United States by opposing the closing of a radar station under construction at Krasnoyarsk in Siberia.[18]

Under the direction of Yakovlev the press broadened its coverage of liberal policy views. A well-connected scholar who grew more vocal was Erik Pletnev. He was director of the political economy department of the All-Union Academy for Foreign Trade. In the 1970s Pletnev had argued for expanding commerce with the West, which he saw as a way of bolstering world peace. Pletnev disagreed with old-school colleagues who accented East-West divisions and refused to recognize the existence of a single world economy. He argued that economic contacts between the Soviet and Western systems proved the existence of a universal economy in a real sense. The practical significance of this theory debate was a rift over the policy question of whether the USSR should intensify trade deals with the West or step up the pace of economic integration among Communist countries. Pletnev was making a case for enlarging Soviet economic ties with the Atlantic community. In *Pravda*, March 29, 1985, he advised against a narrowly sectorial approach to managing the Soviet economy. That meant disapproval of the Stalin-Brezhnev practice of maintaining dozens of central ministries and state committees to carry out the running of industry and agriculture from Moscow. Pletnev urged increased contact between firms and sectors outside of the centralized structures. This was in the spirit of Kosygin's 1965 half-reform, which had attempted to bestow more rights on local managers but was nullified owing to the resistance of Brezhnev and his entourage.

Pletnev spoke out again during the public discussion of the draft CPSU Program in November. He complained that it had failed to mention the word "world" or "universal" economy and should be duly amended. This idea, Pletnev said, was supportive of international detente insofar as it laid an economic foundation for that kind of foreign policy. Pletnev thought that arms control, too, was more likely to make headway if the Great Powers were economically interdependent. While Pletnev's opinion on the single world economy was not included in the finalized Program, he would have welcomed the adoption in January 1987 of procedures allowing joint enterprises with Western countries. An idea initially championed by Pletnev, the meshing of the Soviet Union into a global economy was to become one of Gorbachev's major policy thrusts.

Politburo candidates had different ideas about the tone to be set in the new party Program. Boris Ponomarev, party Secretary for foreign policy, addressed the Politburo in June 1985 and stressed the twin foreign dangers of imperialism and militarism. Gorbachev hit back at Ponomarev during a Politburo session, insisting on immediate replacement of the vapid textbook on party history that Ponomarev edited. Ponomarev himself would lose his post as party overseer of foreign affairs to Anatoli Dobrynin, Soviet ambassador to the United States for almost 25 years and less suspicious of the outer world.[19]

Academician Aganbegyan was the only economist selected to address a Gorbachev-led conference on science and technology. Over the past 30 years he had identified the basic causes of Soviet economic woes as overspending on defense and excessive reliance on command methods of management. He had advocated the use of small-scale, family-based private enterprise operating under state control and a consequent de-emphasis on larger economic units that utilized hired labor. Aganbegyan also stood for an upgrading of cash incentives in the economy's socialized sector.

Tatyana Zaslavskaya also came to the fore thanks to Gorbachev's rise. She had earlier pushed for a policy of agrarian individualism, urging that collective farms be divided into a number of small units, each worked by families whose incomes would be determined by their output. Zaslavskaya defended the economic effectiveness of "links" in the state newspaper, *Izvestiya* (June 1, 1985). Gorbachev himself at a Politburo meeting in March 1986 would plug for tolerance of both private farming and individualized labor. Two years later Zaslavskaya was named director of a new public-opinion institute. The appointment of pro–NEP writer Sergei Zalygin as editor-in-chief of the main literary journal in 1986 further hinted that Gorbachev aimed at revitalizing the collective farm system.

Pravda backed *tovarniki* like those of the early 1930s who respected the profit motive and autonomy of firms within the context of central planning. On August 23, 1985, it warmly reviewed a book of selected works by economics professor Aleksandr Voznesensky spanning the years 1921 to 1941. The review stressed that Voznesensky's approval of cash economy was "worthy of special attention."

The new Draft CPSU Program would no longer feature the doctrinaire formula that commodity-money relations would become outdated and wither away, as did the 1961 basic document. Gorbachev in his speech to the Central Committee in January 1987 was to take issue with Stalinist "prejudices against the role of the relationship of goods to money and against the law of value [profit motive], which is often presented as contrary and extraneous to socialism."

Despite Gorbachev's westward-looking posture, KGB chief Chebrikov vigorously complained against foreign influences at a January 1986 meeting of the Politburo. The session was to review a draft of Gorbachev's political report to the imminent party congress. Chebrikov wanted stronger comment on the struggle with outside ideas and the urgency of conducting atheistic propaganda. Islam and Catholicism were said to have become more aggressive foes of Soviet control ideology.[20]

Gorbachev rebuked the critics of glasnost in his keynote to the congress in February 1986. Gorbachev's note takers record that three months earlier he had told a party headquarters conference that information from ministries and local bodies exaggerated and distorted the facts. "Ambassadors tell lies," he snapped. Moreover, the varnishing of realities was to stop at party election meetings and Central Committee plenums. Now at the congress Gorbachev replied to critics of his demand for sincerity: "Sometimes when the topic of glasnost comes up one hears calls for more cautious talk about our shortcomings and omissions, about the difficulties inevitable in any important work. There can be only one, Leninist, reply to this — Communists always and in everything need the truth."[21]

A fresh and realistic approach to arms control was a demand that Gorbachev made in March 1986 during a talk with aides. He said, "We really want to achieve detente and disarmament. A dishonest game is now impossible. No one can any longer fool the other side. In reply to our proposal about nuclear disarmament the other side brings up the issue of conventional armaments. We are ready to solve that question too. We are for a balance of armaments, including conventional ones, and we are for control but control over disarmament, not over the perfection of armaments. We are against turning negotiations and disputes into endless discussions."

Gorbachev was trying to rectify the Kremlin blunder of deploying intermediate-range ballistic missiles. That step led to the United States installing quick and devastating "Pershing" missiles in western Europe that raised fears among Soviet strategists. Dobrynin, former ambassador to Washington and new CPSU secretary for international relations, in October implied in a speech to the Politburo that Soviet diplomats had wrongly engaged in bluffing and demagogy in the conduct of foreign relations.[22]

Openness bloomed thanks to a chance occurrence. In April 1986 an explosion resulted from a test at the nuclear power plant near Chernobyl in Ukraine. During one week millions were exposed to radiation, around 4,000 died and Pripyat, a Soviet town of 50,000, was evacuated. Two opinions about the disaster grappled at the Politburo. Some were for giving out information gradually to avoid panic. Gorbachev was sensitive to concerned foreign governments and wanted the release of reliable information as it arrived. Gromyko and Chebrikov, however, remained wedded to the old fiction of an accident-free USSR.

Gorbachev came to grips with Chernobyl in a public speech on May 15, and secretly at the Politburo on May 29: "We shall face everything. We must crack down severely on arrogant boasting. We shall openly tell the whole world what happened."[23] Yakovlev joined the fray in June and said at a party headquarters meeting that local officials did not want to keep citizens informed as they embraced secrecy as an instrument of social control.[24]

Gorbachev resumed the drive for glasnost at a Politburo meeting on July 3 attended by scientists and nuclear experts: "The [Soviet] system was plagued by servility, boot-licking, collective [rather than personal] responsibility, persecution of critics, boasting, favoritism, and clannish management. We're now putting an end to all this.... Under no circumstances will we try to conceal the truth, whether in solving practical problems or in answering the people.... There should be complete information about the disaster."[25] Returning from a trip to the Far East in August, Gorbachev told his colleagues, "We shouldn't be afraid of our own people. Let's give a free hand to the local press. Glasnost is true socialism."[26] In memoirs Gorbachev looks back at Chernobyl as one more convincing argument in favor of radical reforms as it showed the harmfulness of concealing accidents, irresponsibility, carelessness, slipshod work and wholesale drunkenness.

Gorbachev made scathing remarks about the political class in a speech to writers in June 1986. He sounded like Trotsky fighting with Stalin: "A ruling stratum lies between the leadership of the country and the people, who wish for change, who dream of change — the apparatus of the ministers, the apparatus of the party, which does not want transformations, which does not intend to lose certain rights tied to privileges."[27]

This attack on smug bureaucrats was barred from Soviet media and only leaked out to foreign communist newsmen. Insiders, however, knew that at a meeting with senior party officials Gorbachev was annoyed that too many were preoccupied with jobs, cottages, cars, special phones and other perks that were valued more than the country.[28] A whiff of hypocrisy can be discerned from the fact that Gorbachev and his fashion-minded wife liked to vacation at a mansion that was built for them at Foros near the Black Sea.

Gorbachev and Chebrikov remained on different wavelengths. The KGB chief spoke at a secret meeting of top leaders in September 1986 and attacked a story of writer Bykov for casting doubt on the wisdom of farm collectivization. By way of contrast, Gorbachev praised the work as "a sign of springtime and renewal." The disagreements over glasnost, democracy legality and pruning the swollen bureaucracy were acute enough for Gorbachev to tell the Politburo, "A real battle is going on. Both at the center and locally, people are slowing down perestroika."[29]

The idea of democratizing Soviet society was floated in a nationally televised speech that Gorbachev made while visiting the south Russian town of Krasnodar in September 1986. An elaboration in *Pravda* (October 31, 1986) objected to the formal nature of Soviet elections and seemed to hark back to a need for a multicandidate electoral system. But several years would have to pass before that radical-reformist practice was introduced.

A tense session of the Politburo in October 1986 dealt with bitter letters from the public. The food shortages were objects of many complaints. There was indignation over private shops that sold state goods at higher prices. The latest price increases for alcoholic drinks and meat products were other irritants. Gorbachev was offended that people were accusing him of creating a new personality cult. What drew special notice was an anonymous letter from Moscow comparing the Soviet Union to ancient Rus devastated by the Mongols. Obviously from a Communist purist, this document attacked Gorbachev for utopian projects that led to a total disruption of party policy. The writer further damned corruption and speculation, viewed the acceleration slogan as senseless, and was alarmed at a capitalist lifestyle taking root.

The Stalin question was hotly debated at this meeting. Ligachev stormed at the unpublished novel *Children of the Arbat* by Jewish writer Anatoli Rybakov. He thought it too negative about Stalin and his policies during the 1930s. Ligachev objected to the version of the Kirov murder that pointed blame at the Leader. Chebrikov was angry that persons he labeled mentally disturbed were spreading anti–Soviet leaflets. In particular he charged that someone wanted to publish banned works that were supportive of the kulaks. Gromyko counseled, "We cannot be do-gooders (*dobrenkimi*)!" He opposed praising writers who suffered in Stalinist times and chided party Secretary for agriculture Nikonov for asking the Politburo to rehabilitate Old Russia economists such as A. V. Chayanov, theorist of the rural cooperative movement, whom Stalin liquidated. Gromyko denounced the Chayanovs as friends of kulaks and recalled that as a teacher of political economy he personally unmasked intellectuals who defended private farming. Gromyko also denied need for a new Politburo commission to exonerate Stalin purge victims. Gorbachev implied that Gromyko was one of those he pitied as "woebegone theorists of Marxism."[30]

Reagan lent small encouragement to the reformers in Moscow. After a disappointing session with the American leader at Geneva in November 1985 Gorbachev told a secret conference of party officials that defense industries remained the "holy of holies" and the military officer corps deserved better housing.[31] In September 1986 a new Reagan-Gorbachev meeting was looming and Yakovlev told Gorbachev that British writer Graham Greene believed that Reagan was a "clown." Gorbachev commented, "And that is dangerous."[32] Reagan's Strategic Defense Initiative (SDI) or Star Wars aimed at the building of an antimissile system in outer space and so challenged the fixed idea of missile parity in the superpower arms race. Gorbachev tried to block SDI and reach an agreement for a 50 percent reduction of strategic missiles at the U.S.–USSR summit held in Iceland that October. He failed on both accounts and responded with a resumption of nuclear tests after a moratorium of nearly 18 months.[33]

Andrei Sakharov, nuclear scientist and human rights activist, was a world-famous critic of SDI whom Brezhnev had exiled to the provinces for protesting the Soviet invasion of Afghanistan. After a Politburo decision, Gorbachev telephoned Sakharov in December 1986 and told him that he was free to return to Moscow. This action harmonized with Gorbachev's intention to release from captivity all political prisoners, and soon 140 were freed. A tormentor of dissident intellectuals, Brezhnev was negatively portrayed in an article that *Pravda* ran for his 80th birth anniversary.

No less than its predecessors, the Gorbachev leadership during 1986 was out-of-touch with the situation in ethnic republics. The CPSU Secretariat in May discussed the situation in the diamond-rich Siberian province of Yakutia. A three-day riot in Yakutsk pitted Russian teenagers against Yakut college students. Hundreds of natives demonstrated at the regional party building with chants of "Yakutia for Yakuts!" and "Down with the Russians." A Russian policeman was beaten and the local MVD headquarters put under siege before order was restored.[34]

A Politburo decision was taken in December to substitute a Russian for the corrupt native leader in Kazakhstan. That sparked rioting in the capital of Kazakhstan and posters were seen declaring, "Enough dictation!" "For each people — its own leader!" "Kazakhs too have smart people!" and "Remember perestroika!" A Central Committee decree blamed "Kazakh nationalism" for the riots and that verdict was kept on the books until revoked in May 1990.[35]

Obtuseness likewise marked Kremlin policy in the neighboring republic of Uzbekistan. Under perestroika nearly 70 party officials were sent there to leading work and all were Slavic. Only one had experience in a nationality area and that was true of 15 of 19 named to government posts. Onikov expands that "the crude and tactless struggle with Islam intensified the anti–Russian attitudes ... [and] led to a sharp activization of Islamic fundamentalism, extremism and aggressiveness, and engendered an underground Muslim clergy."

At the same time, economic policy was fluid. The Politburo was deadlocked over whether to raise retail prices. Gorbachev favored the move and carried five others with him. Deputy party leader Ligachev mustered a group opposed to a price increase on grounds that 25 million citizens lived on a monthly income below 50 rubles and 50 million had earnings below 80 rubles. Gorbachev recognized that the disagreement threatened a split and shelved the issue.[36] But a draft law approved of the election of factory managers and worker councils like those in Yugoslavia that Soviet ideologues had categorized as anarcho-syndicalism. Premier Ryzhkov said that preparers of the legislation heard objections from state ministries and trade unions. A provision enjoining firms to work on a profit and loss basis was questioned because industries handling raw materials invariably operated on state subsidies. When the law took effect management and worker councils often failed to reach agreement on hours and wages.[37]

At Gorbachev's instigation the Politburo in 1987 took a resolute stand for legality. KGB head Chebrikov offered a snapshot of his agents' misdeeds

in the January 8 *Pravda*. A senior officer in Ukraine was dismissed for help-
ing to frame a journalist probing local corruption. Where official lawlessness could lead was suggested in a party edict of September 28 that forged
a Politburo commission to reopen files on arrests that the security services
made from the 1930s through early 1950s.

Gorbachev's aides were undecided over how far to push for democratizing the party. Private Secretary Boldin and party Secretaries Yakovlev and
Medvedev were told to write a speech for Gorbachev to deliver on the subject at a Central Committee meeting. After Gorbachev rejected several drafts
the speechwriters agreed with him that multicandidate elections should be
held at all levels. A dispute over the finalized text broke out at the Politburo in January 1987. The text targeted Brezhnev for impeding domestic
progress: "The CPSU Central Committee, the country's leadership, primarily for *subjective reasons* could not in a timely manner and fully understand
the need for changes and the danger of the growth of crisis phenomena in
society" (italics added).

Yeltsin protested that this formula too narrowly affixed blame and
absolved of mistakes all Politburo members of the Brezhnev era, whose personal performance should be evaluated. Yeltsin criticized the work style of
party headquarters under Ligachev as accustomed to exerting pressure on
lower bodies. Distancing himself from Gorbachev, Yeltsin traced to chronic
deviators Bukharin and Trotsky the phrase in Gorbachev's draft saluting
"production democracy." Yeltsin carried less political weight than Ligachev
and Gorbachev countered that Yeltsin was an emotional person and too
fond of leftist phraseology.[38]

In the run-up to the January 1987 Plenum Gorbachev used his residual authority to broaden the scope of civil liberties and rally around himself millions of persons outside the conservative establishment. The media
let it be known that

- after a senior KGB officer in Ukraine was sacked for fabricating
  a case against a local journalist the regional party head was
  retired;
- film censorship was lifted and this presaged the virtual end of
  taboos designed to prevent the rise of public awareness of social
  ills;
- Russian-language BBC broadcasts would no longer be jammed;
- foreign travel restrictions were to be eased, and new rulings followed; and

- local party officials were censured for preventing religious citizens from building a church.

Gorbachev opted for radical perestroika in his speech to the January 1987 Plenum. It espoused the idea of mass involvement in the running of public affairs and strict observance of the rule of law That meant that officials were no longer to be untouchables when it came to enforcing laws and party secretaries were forbidden to tell prosecutors whom to indict. Gorbachev rejected the practice of party hierarchy and urged multicandidate elections to party and soviet bodies. The party elections were to feature the secret ballot and open nominations, as was the case during the early 1920s.

Gorbachev criticized social scientists — historians, philosophers and economists — for marking time over the last half century. Like Malenkov and Kosygin before him, he attacked Stalinist refusal to allow cash transactions and the profit motive to count for much in running the planned economy. A quarrel arose over the limits of free expression. Gromyko cautioned against writers depressing their readers with negative images. He was seconded by Ivan Polozkov, party boss of Krasnodar region, and future head of the Russian Communist Party. On the other hand, U.S. expert Arbatov spoke for more glasnost. Boldin later viewed the January 1987 Plenum as the start of a party struggle that eventually reached critical dimensions.[39]

One episode of that struggle were the speeches of Ligachev and Cherbrikov at the Politburo in March 1987. They demanded a return to central party control of scientific discussions and the writing of textbooks and scholarly works. Party Control Committee chairman Solomentsev joined them with a Politburo speech in May critical of Academician Samsonov for finding fault with the high command's direction of the critical battles for Moscow and Stalingrad during World War II.[40] But a stream of newly released films and books was devoted to infamies of Stalinism. Gorbachev urged the Politburo to rename places honoring Brezhnev, and the Brezhnev district in Moscow got back its old name, Cheremushkinsky.[41]

No less adamantly, Gorbachev regretted to the Politburo high spending on defense. He said over the last 15 years it had driven Soviet living standards to below the levels of Bulgaria and Romania. Gorbachev criticized Soviet marshals like Grechko for making bellicose statements that unnerved Western statesmen and sowed distrust of the USSR. He set the goal of military sufficiency rather than superiority, and assured that no country would attack the country since an unacceptable retaliatory strike would follow.[42]

Ligachev was distressed by the rewriting of history and at the Politburo a week later redefined perestroika as the strengthening of socialism.
He wanted critical evaluation of the past to be toned down and soon objected
to the very word "reform," preferring "basic perestroika." But Gorbachev
spurred on the political archeology. He was convinced that Kosygin's
revamping of industrial management in 1965 failed because leaders failed
to heed the advice of tsarist finance minister Witte to launch changes both
deeply and swiftly.[43]

Radical reformers got support from Razumovsky, chief of the central
party office for organizational-party work. In June he sent to the Politburo
a memorandum on local elections that reproduced voters' comments on
their ballots. Muscovites told the authorities to "appoint non-party people
to leadership posts as the Communists have proven themselves to be
scoundrels in things small and big"; "as long as there is one party nothing
good can be expected"; and "Authority must reside in the soviets and not
in the party." Ukraine voters wrote: "We have a one-party system and need
a multi-party one so that one party cannot pressure the soviets of people's
deputies"; "Elections are strictly a formality, our deputies in the soviets are
invisible. Actually all power is in the party bodies and [soviet] executive
committees, which decide everything and for everybody." The electorate in
Estonia complained: "Get Soviet forces out of Afghanistan. End Russian
neo-colonialism of the union republics"; "Russians go home!"; and "I don't
believe in Soviet justice." The Politburo discussed local election results and
members were upset over absenteeism and the failure of district party secretaries to be elected to soviets.[44]

Ligachev hoped to clear himself of the reproach that his truculence was
leading to a party rift. He sought a middle road acceptable to Right and
Left. On the one hand he told Moscow-based editors that "The Soviet people will never forgive or justify the repressions of the late 1930s."[45] On the
other hand to provincials he censured "some in the USSR" who "try to discredit the entire history of the building of socialism in the Soviet Union,
through their talk of unjustified repressions." His gut antireformism was
wrathful of "class enemies" who wished to see the Soviet Union "move
toward market economy, pluralism, and Western-type democracy."[46]

Like Ligachev, Chebrikov in public accentuated the positive. He
scolded those who were " raising problems of collectivization and dekulak-
ization," complaining, "All this is viewed negatively, as crime against the
nation. Even victory in the war is subjected to distortion. It is god-build-
ing [a new kind of religion]. We need a dependable analysis of historical

facts made by the competent organs."[47] The battle lines were forming between those who saw Stalin as Joseph the Cruel and others convinced that he was Joseph the Wise.

The pretense of leadership unity was shed in a private journal entry of Gorbachev aide Chernyaev. He recorded that Yakovlev was incensed over a leaflet of the fascist Pamyat Society that had criticized him: "All that scum has the direct support of Ligachev and [Russian Republic premier] Vorotnikov. And I'm sure that this leaflet came out with [KGB chief] Chebrikov's help."[48] Gromyko privately demanded reprimand of a television program in which Khrushchev adviser Burlatsky had appeared.[49]

Gorbachev submitted to the June 1987 Plenum proposals for economic change that won approval. A draft Law on State Enterprises would loosen Moscow's grip on profits and prices. The state firms were to be granted rights to supply private small businesses operating as cooperatives. Taking a leaf from Malenkov's book, Gorbachev told the managers of defense plants to convert to the output of goods for the consumer and food industries. In a year's time the largest enterprises for the first time could freely engage in joint ventures with foreign works. All this brought Soviet economic activities a few steps closer to the revival of Lenin's New Economic Policy.

Aware of bureaucratic discontent, Gorbachev attacked "voices" that said, "Not everything is going badly, that maybe there's no reason to dramatize." A conservative who spoke at the meeting was Yu. F. Sokolov, party leader of Leningrad, who wanted to rein in local informal associations that started out as protectors of historical sites and got involved in government affairs. The informals soon numbered in the thousands and allied with reform Communists, grew into the Popular Fronts that became energizers of change in the Baltics and Caucasus.

One informal still active is Memorial, which sponsors the study of Stalin-era dark pages and honors the victims. By the end of 2008 it had posted on the Internet the names of 2,700,000 who perished in the Stalinist terror. Yet under perestroika many unauthorized publications on a wealth of topics were issued in hundreds of copies.

To the left of Gorbachev and Sokolov, Yeltsin faulted Ligachev's management of the party Secretariat for red tape and bullying. Gorbachev tightened his grip on power with the elevation of party Secretaries Yakovlev, Nikonov and Nikolai Slyunkov (economics) to voting status in the Politburo.[50]

The secrecy rules were loosened in July 1987 when a party and government decree on statistics declassified much economic data unrelated to military production. But Gorbachev sensed that he was engaged in political trench warfare and could only inch his way forward. He met with Central Committee secretaries and department heads, and told them it might take 10 to 15 years to accomplish perestroika. The bureaucrats, who numbered about 18 million, were represented as fearful of losing privileges if democratization went forward. Stung by the charge of letting glasnost undermine faith in the party's benevolence, Gorbachev defended Lenin as friend of peasants because he supported the agrarian program of the Socialist-Revolutionaries. Gorbachev, however, was unforgiving of the crimes of Stalin, whom he called the Grand Inquisitor. He criticized Brezhnev, Andropov and Chernenko for obstructing reviews of the 1936–1938 Moscow trials, and assured that a new effort would be made to rectify those injustices.[51]

Ligachev was just as adamant in his defense of unbridled party power. He inspected the newspaper *Sovetskaya kultura* for two days in July and demanded that writers adhere to traditional guidelines for the arts. Gorbachev struck back at a meeting with media leaders and ruled out forgiveness of Stalin crimes. In August the Ligachev view was aired in a one-page article of *Pravda* staffer Vera Tkachenko, who scorned the new fascination with old purges and sniped at Jews desiring to emigrate to Israel: "There is only one fatherland; to say that the land of your ancestors is somewhere else and to want to go there is nothing more than a cover for treason." Ligachev himself met with intellectuals in September and criticized disrespect toward the heroic builders of socialism and liberal editors who failed to give equal print space to conservatives.[52]

The new-age phenomenon of freedom of assembly was a mixed blessing for reformers, broadening their support base, but raising a threat to ethnic peace. Hundreds of informal associations and perestroika clubs sprang up. None of the public protests staged earlier in Moscow by small minorities such as Baptists or Estonians were as powerful as the 1987 affairs. Taking to the streets of the capital were Jews wanting to leave for Israel (February); Pamyat bigots (May); Crimean Tatars asking for restoration of their homeland that Stalin dissolved (July); and Balts vilifying the Hitler-Stalin pact that led to the loss of their countries' sovereignty (August). A leadership delegation met with the Crimean Tatars and promised to make amends. But Gorbachev told the Politburo in July 1987 that rebirth of the prewar Crimean Autonomous Republic was unacceptable because of Tatars' wartime collaboration with the Germans. When the Tatars in August renewed their protests in Moscow Gorbachev firmly directed the closing of key areas to them and further justified his view on the issue with a reminder that Slavs then comprised almost 85 percent of the Crimean population.[53]

The guardians of order remained on edge. Chebrikov spoke to KGB officers in September 1987 and threw suspicion on intellectuals' blackening of Soviet history. He alerted the Politburo that among the 32,000 unofficial groups behind perestroika there was one with 600 members who took orders from abroad and printed hostile leaflets.[54] Ligachev complained to media leaders about negative views of the past and named editors who published the calumnies of foreign ill-wishers. Gorbachev held his ground and at the Politburo went back to the 1920s in his recitation of unacceptable "bloody deeds" of the system.[55]

Aloof from Gorbachev and Ligachev, Yeltsin built a third force of populism in Moscow. He closed special dining rooms and consumer goods outlets for officials. Hundreds of trade managers were arrested for diverting food products from state stores to costlier farm markets. Twenty-three of 33 secretaries of district party committees were sacked for negligence and corruption. The Moscow KGB and police chiefs were replaced as were their deputies.

Yeltsin campaigned to remove the party from economic management. At the party congress in February 1986 he demanded retooling the switchboard of power over two years before Gorbachev did so: "Party bodies have 'crept into' economic affairs so deeply that at times they lose their positions as political leadership bodies.... The structure of Central Committee [Secretariat] departments has become a virtual copy of the ministries.... There is a wholesale duplication of the State Planning Committee and the Council of Ministers.... A need has ripened to change the structure of the party Central Committee [Secretariat] as a whole."[56]

The first crisis of perestroika was a tussle of Yeltsin and Ligachev, who clashed when Gorbachev was on leave and Ligachev chaired the Politburo. Their differences ranged from Ligachev's demand that a Moscow brewery be closed and a cutback of sales of wine and beer in the capital to Yeltsin ignoring the Politburo when making the rules for holding public rallies and demanding an end to elite privileges. In a letter he sent to Gorbachev on September 12, 1987, Yeltsin attacked Ligachev's work style as "unsystematic and crude." He blamed Ligachev for a lack of comradely atmosphere in relations between the CPSU Secretariat and local party committees. In an unprecedented move of voluntary retirement, Yeltsin requested that he be released from the duties of Moscow party head and Politburo candidate member.[57]

Gorbachev was set to present a more or less realistic account of Soviet history in a speech marking the 70th anniversary of the Bolshevik Revolution. The Politburo discussed a draft on October 15 and a heated debate arose. Premier Ryzhkov harked back to the messages scrawled on ballot papers of recent elections to local soviets. He disagreed with "a certain group of people who are trying to exploit democracy.... [They say] Let's have a second party, a third party."

Ligachev feared a revival of the old Oppositionists that fought for freedom within Bolshevism: "I would like once more to stress that it is very important that precisely now a correct, principled Marxist-Leninist evaluation be given to the party's ideological struggle with Trotskyism." Ligachev attacked Bukharin for proposing in 1928–1929 a slower rate of industrialization, which supposedly could have hindered progress toward socialism.

Gromyko forgot about the hungry years of World War II and afterward: "There can be no argument about how things would have been if we hadn't had collective, socialist agriculture. How would the country have looked during the war and what state would it have been in at the end of it?"

Chebrikov was intolerant of agitation for institutional reform that Gorbachev later championed: "A group has emerged, they don't reflect the mood of the people, of course, but they're distributing leaflets about the need for a new constitution. Here's one of them. It says our Constitution doesn't correspond to perestroika, that it's the constitution of a totalitarian regime, more like army regulations, and that the country is like a barracks. They also attack Article Six, on the leading role of the party."

Yeltsin extolled Bukharin for providing the theory to combat Trotsky's anti–NEP sentiment and honored the Bukharin-led faction that in 1928–1929 opposed Stalin's antipeasant rage.

Gorbachev was angry that Yeltsin had as many as 20 reservations about his draft speech.[58]

When the Politburo reconvened to examine Gorbachev's report on Soviet history, Ligachev took issue with Yeltsin for his praise of Bukharin. The gruff Siberian charged that Bukharin gravely erred by resisting farm socialization. Ligachev argued that liquidation of the kulaks as a class was strictly in accord with the teachings of Lenin. If the Bukharin faction had won, Ligachev said, industrialization would have faltered, and Bukharin never fully recanted his errors.

Gorbachev rose to the defense of Bukharin and condemned Stalin for unleashing the 1937–1938 purge to win an internal power struggle. The mood at the 1934 party congress, Gorbachev said, alarmed Stalin and he used criminal methods to keep power. Gorbachev thought that Stalin was also protecting his authority when he destroyed Leningrad officials in the late 1940s.

Party elder Gromyko had the last word about Stalin. He was mildly critical of his benefactor for telling Roosevelt and Churchill at the 1945 Yalta Conference that Beria was the Soviet version of Nazi police chief Himmler. Then Gromyko praised Stalin for his loyalty to socialism and having fought for Soviet interests.[59]

A festive air was expected at a Central Committee Plenum to hear Gorbachev outline his upcoming anniversary speech. Yeltsin spoiled the mood with a speech accusing Ligachev of sabotaging his work and criticizing Politburo members who flattered the general secretary. Yeltsin announced he was quitting high party posts and drew a spate of epithets. Ligachev called Yeltsin a liar and accused him of falsely alleging that Soviet people were losing confidence in perestroika. A regional leader took pride in having begun his career under Stalin and called Yeltsin a deserter. Another rebuked Yeltsin for meeting with foreign journalists and diplomats. Ryzhkov attacked Yeltsin for dividing the Politburo and courting the West. Chebrikov saw Yeltsin as egotistical and providing grist for the mills of western analysts. The radical reformer Yakovlev played moderate, falling on Yeltsin for "Left revisionist" phrases and personal ambition. Another Gorbachev man, Shevardnadze, objected to Yeltsin using "conservatism" as a bogey in defense of his extremism. Summing up, Gorbachev hit at Yeltsin for planning a grassroots challenge to the leadership. The Plenum's resolution declared Yeltsin's speech "politically erroneous" and instructed the Politburo and Moscow party committee to examine his request for resignation. Both ruling bodies toppled Yeltsin.[60]

The awakening public no longer indifferently reacted to senior personnel changes. A demonstration in Yeltsin's old base of Sverdlovsk protested his demotion. Leaflets were distributed around the city in his defense. Gorbachev addressed the Politburo and diagnosed Yeltsin as suffering from an "infantile disorder" of ambition and euphoria over positive changes.[61] But a petition was circulated at Moscow University demanding Yeltsin's return and the publication of his speech at the October Plenum. Urals factories were rocked by rallies and strikes in support of Yeltsin. Gorbachev retreated and named Yeltsin a deputy chairman of the State Committee for Construction Affairs, with ministerial rank. The independent Zaykov was chosen to lead the party in Moscow and admitted to the Politburo.[62]

Gorbachev damned Stalin's terror in his November 1987 survey of Soviet history. Using archival sources, he painted in strong hues the violent methods Stalin used to collectivize farming. He questioned the validity of the Stalinist theory of intensifying class struggle inside the Soviet Union which served to justify the terror. Stalin's crimes were again declared unforgivable and it was announced that a commission was formed to examine them more deeply. Gorbachev raised Khrushchev from political purgatory for having dethroned Stalin and faulted him only for hesitating to stick to democratization. Rumors were spreading that Old Bolsheviks Bukharin, Zinoviev and Kamenev would be cleared of the verdicts of treason brought against them at the Moscow Trials.[63]

The attack on Stalin's farm policy is relatable to worsening of the food situation. None of the 60 decrees on agriculture taken under perestroika were fulfilled and long lines were usual in front of urban stores selling bread and milk. The available sausages were disdained as of such poor quality as to make them unfit for the consumption of household pets. As early as 1985 an independent Movement for Socialist Renewal had urged the leasing of farmland with repayment to the state of a part of the crops. Now Gorbachev and Ryzhkov approved of leasing land to peasants for 50 years, but farm chairmen and specialists (*ortodoksy*) were usually against doing so.

The conservatives were pushing back on the history issue. Directors of the State Publishing House for Political Literature reprinted without change a work that praised some rabid Stalinists. A seventh edition of Aleksei Abramov's book *At the Kremlin Wall* was sent to press December 3, 1987, with a print run of 200,000 copies. As in the 1974 edition the author said of Stalin's cultural whip, Zhdanov: "Under his leadership Leningrad successfully struggled for premature fulfillment of the plans of the second and third five-year plans.... In 1948 the city of Mariupol [Zhdanov's birthplace] was renamed in honor of Zhdanov, outstanding figure of the Communist party. In Moscow, Zhdanov's name is borne by a street, metro station and the 'First Model Printing Plant.' The same is true of streets and factories in many other of the country's towns and settlements." Kudos were bestowed too on Andrei Vyshinsky, prosecutor in the Moscow Trials, and Lev Mekhlis, Stalin's Minister for State Control.[64]

Kremlin disputes over economics heated up. Premier Ryzhkov and Ligachev got into a wrangle and Gorbachev aide Chernyaev in November 1987 wrote a letter to the general secretary critical of his deputy: "Yegor Kuzmich [Ligachev] personalizes the gross output [central planning order], slave-driving, shock work approach.... Ligachev epitomizes the old approach. Thus his panic, thus his dire warnings of failure and the collapse of the five-year plan. He is a slave to the old ways, the old methods of evaluation, the old style of doing business. It's been obvious for some time now that he elicits a deep and barely contained personal hostility, and not only from Ryzhkov. And this is something dangerous among the leadership, because it's nearly always irreversible."[65]

Gorbachev and Ligachev grew increasingly apart over the rights of factory managers to increase their profits. Ligachev's memoir argues that especially harmful was the shift to free prices without creating a tax system or market infrastructure to cushion the leap. "Collective greed," Ligachev wrote, "burst into full bloom, cooperative ties started to break and supply became unbalanced."[66] This suggested that Gorbachev had put the country between the two stools of centralized planning and free market system.

U.S. Secretary of State George Shultz visited Moscow in April 1987 and got from Gorbachev a major concession in talks on intermediate-range nuclear missiles. Shultz convinced President Reagan that profitable deals could be struck with Gorbachev. The American and Soviet leaders met in Washington in December and signed an Intermediate Range Nuclear Forces treaty. It allowed on-site inspection to monitor the reduction of nuclear arms rather than just putting a ceiling on them.

Speaking about his U.S. trip at the Politburo Gorbachev rejected the old Soviet notion of Western statesmen as little more than puppets of vested commercial interests. That stereotype harmonized with Old Russia's attachment to the Roman maxim of wisdom to prepare for war in order to keep the peace. Under the mantra of New Thinking, Gorbachev preached the decisive importance of "universal human values" in the shaping of world politics. This meant that if a Western leader assured that he hated war, he or she was probably sincere and could be expected to act responsibly. Gorbachev's philosophizing is explicable in terms of need to underpin intellectually any major break with standard Kremlin theology.[67]

In 1987 the Center received many reports of ethnic strains in the Chechen-Ingush and North Ossetia republics of the Russian Federation.[68] One of the telegrams was especially lurid. Over 100 nationalistic incidents were registered since 1984. The murder of Russians and vandalizing of their cemeteries were commonplace. Tribesmen in remote villages were thought to be holding Russians as slaves, and many Slavs were leaving the area. The local police tolerated a high level of drug sales and use. Muslim rituals were noticeable even among party members. Authorities felt compelled to enlist

Muslim clergy to resolve family disputes and recruit manpower for construction projects.[69]

The most serious flash point was the Nagorny Karabakh region of Azerbaijan in the Caucasus. It was an enclave of majority Armenian-Christians inside Turkic-Azerbaijan that resulted from Turkish diplomacy in the 1920s. In 1987 Armenian residents demonstrated for unification with Armenia. Violence flared in February 1988 and many Azeris fled the area. The Politburo discussed the situation and found that Armenian and Azeri party leaders were siding with their ethnic counterparts. After a decision to keep the status quo, Azeris rampaged through the Armenian quarter in the Baku suburb of Sumgait, killing 32 and injuring over 100. Arson, looting and rapes were commonplace. The local police sided with rioters and 16 of 20 detainees were released from custody. To restore order military cadets were summoned and some fainted upon viewing mutilated corpses. In March the Politburo accepted a proposal of Ligachev to replace the party heads of both Armenia and Azerbaijan for their nationalistic attitudes. The party officials in both republics began to join separatist movements that were emerging as dual power centers.[70]

The fluid political situation across the country was to be addressed at a Central Committee meeting due in February 1988. On the eve of the Plenum blows were struck from the reformist and conservative sides of the house. On Gorbachev's initiative a history-making decision taken on January 1, 1988, weakened the party Secretariat, whose meetings were chaired by Ligachev. The usually powerful body was forbidden to discuss policy issues that the Politburo would later approve.

Reactionary party historians in turn defended Stalinism in the newspaper *Sovetskaya Rossiya* (January 28, 1988). Their review of a Moscow stage play rejected the opinion that Stalin wrongly strayed from Lenin's sound course of mixed state and private economy: "The party had no alternative than to leap over the distance between backwardness, on one side, and developed industry and cooperative agriculture, on the other, in the shortest possible time."

At the February 1988 Plenum Gorbachev insisted that the party had to use only democratic methods in solving problems and a free contest of opinions was essential. He regretted that the most important values taught to Communists had been the determining role of the party, state property, and central planning with an eye to tons of steel and wheat, kilometers of railroad and meters of cloth. Many barons were distressed to hear from Gorbachev that party supremacy was not given for all time. Gorbachev's *Mem-*

oirs disclose skepticism about party officials' real commitment to Marxian theory. He thought that arguments of party ideologists about the reality of socialism in the USSR masked a concern for privilege and were no longer persuasive.

Gorbachev assembled his aides on March 1, 1988, and shared his thoughts about the upcoming party conference. His revolutionary message was that the mission of the party had to change and its officials no longer dictate to executive, legislative and judicial bodies. The people were to rise up from their lowly status of "cogs" (*vintiki*), a word that Stalin used to describe his lowly subjects. Under Gorbachev's new order the soviets as popularly elected councils were to take charge of governance. The party first secretaries would have to pass the test of balloting to hold the posts of soviet chairmen if they wished to stay in the saddle. Gorbachev later explained that if a party first secretary failed to be elected to a soviet chairmanship he would have to leave his party post.[71] Graybeards predicted that such changes would dissolve the vanguard party of disciplined and proactive elites into a society teeming with inert rabble.

A political bombshell had burst with the February announcement that the USSR Supreme Court invalidated the conviction of Bukharin and nine others executed for treason in 1938. Now the liberalizing teachings of Bukharin against bureaucratism and state feudalism were made respectable for party members. This kind of revisionism deeply offended Leningrad chemistry teacher Nina Andreyeva.[72] She sent a letter to party headquarters brimming with Stalinist simplicities, and the text went to Ligachev, who was delighted. The experienced journalist V. Denisov was sent to Leningrad to enlarge the letter into an article that *Sovetskaya Rossiya* published on March 13, 1988. The title was wry as it came from a phrase in one of Gorbachev's speeches: "I Cannot Forsake My Principles." The New Thinking about foreign affairs was ignored and peaceful coexistence narrowly interpreted as "no more than a class struggle in the international arena." The Central Committee decree of June 1956 that Brezhnev drafted and that justified Stalinist misrule was held up as a beacon for Soviet scholars and propagandists. Jews were pilloried with a reference to Karl Marx: "On the basis of a class approach he was not ashamed to make damning judgments about a number of nationalities, including the one he himself belonged to." A Russian Jewish playwright and writer were condemned for pointing to Stalin as responsible for the murders of Kirov and Trotsky.

Moscow was alive with rumors that Ligachev got a reworked version of Andreyeva's original text and directed the chief editor of *Izvestiya* to publish it. He refused unless the order was put in writing. Ligachev wanted to protect himself and redirected the article to *Sovetskaya Rossiya*. Insiders elaborate that on March 18 Ligachev met with newspaper editors and told them that Andreyeva's letter was the new party line. Ligachev notified censors to bar the publication of dissent, and Agitprop workers were told that the article was authoritative. Many lower party officials sent messages to Ligachev thanking him for rebuffing the slanderers. Some regional dailies reprinted the article and conferences at Moscow University supported Andreyeva, who was preaching to the converted at the KGB school in Leningrad.

Upon his return to Moscow Gorbachev realized that perestroika was at a crossroads and convened the Politburo to strengthen his authority. Gorbachev asserted that the Andreyeva article was a destructive, anti-perestroika platform. Ligachev admitted that he liked the Andreyeva letter but denied a hand in promoting it. Russia premier Vorotnikov stood with Ligachev and upheld airing the letter in terms of the new freedom of choice in editorial decision making. Yakovlev agreed with Gorbachev that Andreyeva's screed was "an anti-perestroika manifesto."

At a second Politburo meeting the next day Ryzhkov attacked the article and suggested that Ligachev lose his share of the ideology portfolio. Ligachev won support from Solomentsev, Nikonov and Lukyanov, Gorbachev's college classmate, whose actions Gorbachev later said grieved him. At day's end a majority stood with Gorbachev, and Yakovlev was asked to write a rebuttal to *Sovetskaya Rossiya*.

After a three-week silence *Pravda* on April 5 entered the fray and ran Yakovlev's rejoinder to the hardliners. The Opposition was said to be allergic to rule of law: "By defending Stalin they fight to maintain in our life the practices and the methods he created for a 'solution' to problems.... Above all they defend the right to use power arbitrarily." Repudiated again was the canard that Stalin was unaware of orders for mass liquidations — a Soviet counterpart of the myth that Hitler did not instigate the Holocaust: "Not only did he know about [the illegal acts] but he orchestrated them. This is an established fact. The responsibility of Stalin and his entourage for the repression of the masses and for the violations committed cannot be forgiven by the party and by the people."

Ligachev refused to capitulate. He asked the Politburo for a Central Committee Plenum to clear the air. Gorbachev was wary of a stampede and met separately with groups of Central Committee members from April 11 to 18. He was uncompromising about the great terror of the 1930s: Stalin was a criminal who ordered the shooting of one million party activists and sent three million others to work camps; the push for farming collectives destroyed millions more; Stalin-type socialism was unacceptable. Estonian party head Vaino took his cue from Gorbachev and remarked that in 1949 farm collectivization was needlessly performed in his republic and 80,000 families, or perhaps one-quarter million persons, deported to Siberia.

Chebrikov was undaunted and made a speech to backwoodsmen attacking glasnost and democratization. He attributed fighting between Armenians and Azeris to the subversive work of Western intelligence services. A few days later (April 15 and 16) Gorbachev met with the Politburo and, to forestall a party split, the reformers and conservatives papered over their differences. Ligachev had to share with others the right to chair weekly meetings of the Secretariat and was deprived of a voice in media oversight. But he kept the status of Politburo chairman in Gorbachev's absence and the chief editor of the reactionary party daily *Sovetskaya Rossiya* went unpunished.

CHAPTER 7

Gorbachev:
Demolishing the Pillars

The Soviet liberals dismissed as fleeting the latest Kremlin truce and expected a reactionary putsch. One of the first signs of a Khrushchev syndrome and proof of the supreme importance of historical memory was an article in the reformist weekly *Moscow News* (No. 18, 1988), "1953–1964: Why Reform Didn't Work Then." A plea was made for institutional safeguards against the contingency of old guarders seizing power: "The fate of the country and people is in jeopardy if it depends to such a great extent on the alignment of forces in the upper echelons. This alignment will be precarious and variable until the democratic mechanisms of legality, elections, openness and responsibility are put in play." Khrushchev's son, Sergei, discussed hidden aspects of the conspiracy that toppled his father.[1] Suslov, instigator of Khrushchev's removal, was linked to Stalin, termed "ideologist of stagnation" and ridicule heaped on a cultish museum in his home village.[2] One of Khrushchev's advisers dealt with the backstairs politicking that worked for Brezhnev: "It is time to put an end to a system in which people assume the leadership of the country not by a normal democratic procedure, and public activity in the party and state, but by way of covert maneuvering and in particular by way of conspiracies and bloody purges. Experience has shown that in such a situation it is not the most capable leaders who come to power, but rather the most cunning Odysseuses [a willful and arrogant figure in Homer's *Iliad*], masters of group struggle, intrigue, and even outright corruption."[3]

Behind the scenes the conservatives were making their case for moderation. The Politburo in May 1988 discussed Gorbachev's draft Theses for the imminent party conference. The memoirs of Shakhnazarov inform that Ligachev took a confrontational stance against the West, urging that class interests get top billing along with universal human values as foreign policy determinants. Leningrad party boss Soloviev wanted an expression of faith in the indestructibility of the one-party system. And Ukraine party head Shcherbitsky inquired how the party would retain power during the campaign for democratization.

On the surface antimarketeers in the government cabinet obstructed rebirth of the cooperative movement. In May 1988 the parliament passed a law that legalized 10,000 cooperatives set up on the basis of an emergency decree; Finance Minister Boris Gostyev sponsored a bill that raised to 90 percent the tax on the income of a successful cooperative worker. When enacted as law this act forced the closing of many cooperatives and legislators finally annulled it.[4]

That same month Gorbachev indicted Stalin at a meeting with editors, writers and cultural figures. Referring to recent praise of Stalin as military strategist, he observed that with a different Leader the Soviet Union could have defeated Germany faster and with fewer casualties. Evidently with Gorbachev's backing the Politburo feted the anti–Stalinist Marshal Zhukov by ordering that a statue of him be built in Moscow.[5]

When Reagan visited Moscow in June 1988 Gorbachev's words to the Politburo were measured. The American president was said to have become a realist who had overcome preconceptions about the USSR and rectified odious assessments. Gorbachev and others clearly had not forgotten that Reagan the anti–Communist fire-eater once looked forward to the USSR winding up in the trash heap of history.[6]

Gorbachev used the June 1988 party conference to demand the building of a strong state legislature and presidency. He proposed to the tension-filled meeting that a USSR Congress of People's Deputies (CPD) be the highest organ of representative power and formed partly through multicandidate elections. To prevent the CPD from becoming an unruly national assembly, 750 of its 2,250 members would be appointed by the CPSU, Komsomol and trade unions. The CPD was to meet several times annually and elect a Supreme Soviet of 542 deputies that was to be a permanently sitting legislature.

Gorbachev was to replace Gromyko as chairman of the Supreme Soviet Presidium and his tenure limited to two consecutive terms. To neutralize angry party bosses, Gorbachev proposed to combine the offices of the first secretaries of local party committees and chairmanships of corresponding soviets. This was supposed to convert the CPSU into a party obtaining at local elections a public mandate for its control of operational power bodies. Thus, Gorbachev sought to inaugurate a version of the guided democracy familiar in third-world countries and he avoided the introduction of full-fledged political pluralism.

Ligachev and Yeltsin crossed swords in speeches to the party conference. Ligachev drew on a conservative writer's metaphor about perestroika as "a plane that was given instructions to take off but none on where to land."[7] Yeltsin elbowed his way in as delegate from a northern region and made revolutionary appeals for

- a national referendum on Gorbachev's proposal to combine the functions of party and soviet leaders;
- direct and secret elections of all party and state leaders from top to bottom;
- limiting the tenure of elective office to two terms, without exception;
- setting an upper age limit of 65 for the membership of all ruling bodies, including the Politburo (Ligachev was born in 1920 and would have to retire);
- published accounts of the transactions of Politburo and Secretariat, with the exception of topics involving state secrets; how leaders spent their salaries; and the results achieved by each leader for the sector for which he was responsible;
- regular appearances of leaders on television;
- published summaries of workers' letters to party headquarters;
- Central Committee Plenums to discuss expenditures of party funds (hundreds of millions of rubles) and a ban on party spending for the building of luxurious houses, villas and sanatoriums on a large scale;
- material shortages to be felt in equal degree by everyone and no special food packages given to party officials; and
- reduction of the regional party apparatus by two or three times and of the CPSU Secretariat by six to ten times, including the abolition of departments that dealt with various branches of the economy; and hand over to young people whole areas of leadership.

Yeltsin effectively called for repeal of Lenin's 1921 ban on factionalism, asserting that "The existence of a distinct minority opinion will not destroy but only strengthen the unity of the party."[8] This put Gorbachev in the shade, who secretly told journalists in 1986 that factions could become a kind of political opposition to offer second opinions and policy options.[9]

With masks off the ruling party was breaking up along ethnic lines.

In the Baltics demands were made for publication of secret protocols of the 1939 Hitler-Stalin nonaggression pact. The protocols assigned Estonia, Latvia and Lithuania to the Soviet sphere of influence. Details of how those countries were forcibly brought into the USSR in 1940 was an issue on which pressure was being exerted. Separatist-minded People's Fronts arose and legislatures proclaimed the national languages as state languages in place of Russian. Belorussia experienced a nationalist rebirth and demands were made to resurrect from the 1920s the local cultural heritage.

A speech that Shevardnadze made at the Foreign Affairs Ministry in July 1988 angered hardliners. He avowed that "the philosophy of peaceful coexistence as a universal principle in international relations has a different content. The New Thinking places it in the context of the realities of the nuclear age. We are right to refuse to see in it some specific form of the class struggle." Ligachev retorted in August speeches at Gorky and Tula, centers of armaments output. He restated orthodoxies that blocked adoption of Western approaches to property ownership and foreign affairs. Ligachev insisted, "We must assume the class character of international relations. A different statement of the issue only brings confusion into the minds of Soviet people and our friends abroad." Yakovlev spoke in Riga and his ideas differed with Ligachev's about markets.[10]

Gorbachev pushed through a massive reduction of central party officials. He told the Politburo in September 1988 that half or more of 3,000 such bureaucrats who commanded 700,000 to 800,000 local equivalents should be dismissed. All central party departments for controlling government operations would be closed. Apparatchiks left at party headquarters were to serve as advisers to policy-making commissions of Central Committee members. One of the few remaining departments of the Secretariat was for the direction of agriculture. Gorbachev proposed that Ligachev take charge of farming, ostensibly because "This is something that he knows well." Ligachev surly predicted that Gorbachev's party reform would lead to uncertainty, decline of discipline and localism. But he observed tradition and got back into ranks.

Chebrikov was to leave the KGB and become federal party secretary for legal reform. Yeltsin claims that Chebrikov kept an eye on the KGB and "still had the psychology of the KGB man; he saw Western subversion and spies everywhere, didn't want to let anyone go abroad, and treated everyone as a potential defector."[11] The new KGB chief was Vladimir Kryuchkov, an elderly specialist in foreign intelligence work, indicating a lesser role for the security services inside the country.

Gorbachev asked for the resignations of conservative Politburo members Gromyko and Solomentsev. The shakeup was approved at a Central Committee Plenum, and the Supreme Soviet elected Gorbachev chairman of its Presidium.[12] Some foreign observers were misled into thinking that Gorbachev had consolidated his power and become unchallenged head of the country.

Destabilizing consequences of Gorbachev's overhaul of the party machinery exceeded even the grim forecast of Ligachev. Trotsky's 1936 vision of a bureaucratic counterrevolution inside the USSR became reality. Many of the sacked officials looted state property and opened their own business concerns and commercial banks. The number of banks in the USSR indeed rose from six, each state-owned, in 1985 to over 1,400, almost all private, in 1991. Russian Republic Minister of Metallurgy Kolpakov was rapidly compared to the German magnate Krupp for having created 10 to 15 large private firms from pilfered state assets. The absence of relentless party pressure on remaining state enterprises caused shortages of essential goods to increase and the public cursed Gorbachev along with officials thought to be sabotaging perestroika.

Gorbachev found the criticisms hurtful and grew still more responsive to consumer complaints. He read to the Politburo a letter from a village soviet deputy who was indignant at bureaucrats who ignored citizens' demand for a natural gas facility.[13] He pressed harder for shifting resources from the defense to consumer branches. By 1987 the share of consumer goods in the total volume of industrial production stood at 24.9 percent, or below the level in Brezhnev's time.[14]

Gorbachev rhetorically asked the Politburo in November 1988 why the Soviet Union needed such a big army in spite of a leadership decision to withdraw troops from Afghanistan. "Our military expenses," Gorbachev said,

> are two and one-half times larger than those of the United States. No country in the world — except the "underdeveloped" ones, whom we flood with arms without ever being paid back — spends more per capita on the military sector.... We won't solve the problems of perestroika if we leave the army as it is. As before, it still gets the best scientists and technical talent, the best financial support, always provided without question.... Without reductions in the army and the military-industrial complex we won't be able to deal with the task of perestroika.... There is no question about it, we can't afford not to be militarily strong. But for purposes of security, not intimidation.[15]

These remarks were kept secret and military outlays cut back to one-quarter of the national budget. Gorbachev was more successful in rebuffing the appeal of the Estonian parliament for state sovereignty and erasing the names of Brezhnev and Chernenko from Soviet towns and institutions.

The stock of perestroika had so declined that in January 1989 the Central Committee heard Gorbachev wonder if Politburo members might be blackballed in a genuine election of the 100 Communists due to be seated at the Congress of People's Deputies. Party Secretary Razumovsky drew up a list of the "Red-hundred" and it was distributed to barons for their approval. Now many former party officials were joining the departments and secretariats of the CPD, forming a secret power center in the country.[16]

Yeltsin emerged as a strong political force in the run-up to the March election of CPD deputies. Demonstrations of up to 12,000 people in Moscow chanted his name and shouted "Down with Ligachev!" Yeltsin on the stump was uncompromising in his fight with authorities: "The democratization of the Communist party is way behind that of Soviet society. The party has become completely isolated from the people.... Various privileges enjoyed by senior officials are at the expense of the usurpation of the people's property.... Marxism and Leninism are thoughts of the past. They should not be taken doctrinally.... Politburo member Ligachev is a cancer on perestroika.... If elected, I will form a faction in collaboration with colleagues." One of the planks in Yeltsin's platform was the creation of a multiparty system in the country.[17]

The central *apparat* struck back with talking points to activists on how to discredit Yeltsin. District party secretaries read to staffers a pamphlet accusing Yeltsin of "favoring the most authoritarian methods in his handling of personnel matters" and associating with Pamyat Society fascists. Yeltsin was damned for "total lack of principle" and said to be motivated by "injured pride, ambition (which he has so far been unable to satisfy) and a lust for power." A worker-aristocrat rebuked Yeltsin at a Central Committee Plenum for slandering the party and criticizing the Politburo. Gorbachev proposed setting up a commission to investigate Yeltsin's statements at meetings with voters.[18]

The old-style blackening of Yeltsin helped him to win a landslide victory with almost six million, or 90 percent, of all the votes in Moscow cast for him. He realized that many voters were grudging in their support. Yeltsin observed that all Soviet people knew that a career party man had to avoid independence and behave in line with orders from on high. A Communist official, Yeltsin regretted, had to learn to say one thing while thinking something else.[19]

At Politburo meetings held to discuss the CPD election there were recriminations over the defeats of apparatchiks. Thirty secretaries of party regional and town committees lost their races; antiparty majorities were recorded in Moscow, Leningrad and Sverdlovsk. In military districts 14 commanders failed to win election to soviet posts. Leningrad secretary Soloviev and Ligachev argued that the Kremlin might have saved party men from humiliating losses. Ligachev blamed the media for electoral setbacks, called the situation very dangerous, and compared it to Hungary in 1956 and Czechoslovakia in 1968 or when journalists supposedly triggered anti–Communist revolts.

Gorbachev reasoned that Communist candidates were rejected because voters were disillusioned with perestroika. He criticized the humbled big shots for treating ordinary citizens like cattle. Gorbachev said he knew that from letters sent to him by petitioners who spent years in official waiting rooms. The top leadership, Gorbachev added, would not protect such malefactors.[20]

Gorbachev took seriously the rumors of hardliner plotting and at the April 1989 Plenum removed 110 elderly members from the Central Committee. He failed to obtain the right to promote from candidate membership around 25 new members since that was a prerogative of the party congress that met every four years. Ligachev blocked Gorbachev on this issue and barons aired grievances over what they understood to be the party turning into a discussion club, economic chaos, media license, army dissolution and bitter anti–Russian feeling in the Baltics. To counter the protests Gorbachev was allowed to publish minutes of the Plenum and this tactic gained for him some sympathy with the party rank-and-file.[21]

Gorbachev was lucky that month to have been outside Moscow when a Russian general ordered a brutal crackdown on Georgians holding an unauthorized rally in Tbilisi. The Georgian party leader had consulted with Ligachev about how to deal with the crowd and told to expect the army to intervene. Soldiers killed 19 persons with entrenching tools and hundreds were injured by the use of poison gas. Gorbachev later told Defense Minister Yazov at a Politburo meeting that the army was not to suppress demonstrations without a decision of the top civilian leadership. Chebrikov, however, warned that if the party command retreated further in its dealings with the nationalities "the empire will collapse" (*imperiya raspadayetsya*)." This was hardly a sign of one man's panic as Yeltsin was on the verge of telling the Central Committee that nothing less than a "revolutionary situation" existed in the Soviet Union.[22]

The barons still counted for something and the Central Committee met to approve of personnel appointments on the eve of the CPD opening in May. Gorbachev was confirmed as future chairman of the Supreme Soviet, or standing parliament, and Lukyanov would serve as his deputy. The maverick Yeltsin failed to win approval for a new state post.[23]

Unlike the First Duma under Nicholas II, fewer peasants and Bohemian types were present, but the CPD proceedings were just as tumultuous. Politburo members were seated in the audience instead of the platform and subjected to rude catcalls. Speakers blamed Ligachev for the Tbilisi massacre and accused him of shoddy oversight of agriculture, as well as taking bribes. Deputies queried Gorbachev about his perks of office and the supposed political meddling of his spouse. Once above reproach, the CPSU, KGB and Lenin tomb were trashed as worthless relics of a shameful age. Historian Yuri Afanasiev ridiculed the new legislative setup as "Stalinist-Brezhnevist" with an "aggressive-obedient majority." Conservatives struck back with an Afghan war veteran questioning the patriotism of human-rights campaigner Sakharov and shouting the watchwords "Authority, Homeland, Communism!" Gorbachev was elected chairman of the still-collective presidency, which the Supreme Soviet would turn into a personalized office almost a year later.

After the parliamentary crossfire retired Moscow party leader V. I. Konotop in June 1989 sent a letter to the Politburo. He was frozen in time and agonized over recent attacks on Lenin — "the holy of holies" — army, police and KGB. The miscreants were identified as Zionists, nationalists, Bukharinists and Trotskyites. Konotop saw as premature the dismantling of central planning and party hegemony. He dismissed voluntary people's power as absolutely no substitute for strict public order.[24] Subsequent events would leave no doubt that this craving for authoritarian governance was not the attitude of a small minority.

In July Yeltsin and Sakharov cochaired the parliamentary faction Inter-Regional Deputies Group. Their manifesto rejected Article 6 of the USSR Constitution, which exalted the CPSU as "core" of the political system. The right to private ownership was recognized and strong farmers and industrial managers seen as backbone of the future polity. The document also upheld the economic independence of nationality republics. The overall effect was to bring to mind the program of the Constitutional Democrats (Party of the People's Freedom) at century's start. Yeltsin later adopted his faction's platform in an electoral campaign to gain the Russian presidency. His neocapitalist movement attracted to its rallies throngs of up to a half-million persons.

The outer empire in eastern and central Europe crumbled under the weight of fallout from the Soviet tumult. U.S. officials grossly underrated the extent to which Gorbachev's statements presaged a drastic modification of Kremlin foreign policy. Deserving of more serious attention than it got in Washington was Gorbachev's December 1988 announcement of a unilateral reduction of 500,000 Soviet troops, nearly half coming from eastern Europe and the western military districts of the Soviet Union. Gorbachev rejected the use or threat of force as an instrument of statecraft. He was going out on a limb and had to answer to Politburo critics of a speech he made to the United Nations General Assembly pledging steep reduction of Soviet military spending:

> Vitaly Ivanovich [Vorotnikov] has said that in the country and even at home people are asking how is it that we are, so to speak "undressing" all by ourselves? And Yegor Kuzmich [Ligachev] has approached this topic differently — the party must know [about the defense budget cuts]. We are keeping this secret for now, to tell the truth... . [ellipses in text] Now even the party cannot be told about this, we must first put things in order. If we now disclose our defense outlay from the national income this could undercut our United Nations speech. That's because nowhere else in the world is there a country with a situation like ours. It happens only in poverty-stricken countries that devote half of their budgets to military affairs.[25]

Unexpectedly, democratic revolutions shook eastern Europe. A Polish roundtable agreement reached in April 1989 between the Solidarity free trade union and ruling Communists called for genuine parliamentary elections. Two months later elections in Poland resulted in the defeat of the Communist party and formation of a democratic government. The Hungarian border was opened and many East Germans left their homes for the West German embassy in Budapest. From there an exodus flowed to the Berlin Wall and it was pierced in November 1989. With Soviet acquiescence a Hungarian roundtable agreed on a multiparty system and free parliamentary elections. Bulgaria, Czechoslovakia and Romania in turn experienced the end of Communist control. Gorbachev renounced the Brezhnev Doctrine, or the Soviet right to defend shaky foreign Communist regimes. He did so in a July 1989 speech to the Council of Europe that stamped as inadmissible "any interference in internal affairs and any attempts to restrict the sovereignty of states — either friends and allies or anyone else."[26]

Diplomatic talks with the Western powers for a reworking of security accords in Europe were indicated. Anatoli Dobrynin was Soviet ambassador to Washington from 1962 to 1986 and later CPSU secretary for international affairs. He was released from Moscow duties in 1989 and in memoirs regrets that Gorbachev as top diplomat "moved forward without seriously contemplating the consequences. Here lay his weakness. He was either unable or in too much of a hurry to think about the prospective turn of events. Very often, he did not have a detailed plan for implementing his designs, only a fascinating outline. At Politburo meetings, when someone expressed cautious concern about his rapid innovations, Gorbachev would cut him off for 'contradicting the spirit of the new thinking and perestroika.'"

Dobrynin praises Gorbachev for cooperating with the United States and reducing armaments. But he is critical of sudden agreements to the Germans' reunification and their admission to NATO as one nation. Dobrynin attributes this to Gorbachev's expectation of Western economic aid that would help him out of his domestic difficulties.[27] At the time, Soviet journalist Feliks Chuyev openly criticized Gorbachev for agreeing to German unification and hinted at his ultimate political demise: "We have become hostages of today's politics," he said, "for we have lost allies and even betrayed our onetime friends. In the spring of 1953 Beria at a Politburo meeting actually proposed letting the German Democratic Republic go down the capitalist road. That action was the start of his political demise, his being called an agent of foreign imperialism. What Beria failed to do has come to pass after 37 years. But won't the Kremlin Wall come crashing down after the Berlin Wall?"[28]

A bleak view of the Soviet internal situation was taken at a Politburo meeting in September 1989. Chebrikov deplored strikes in 46 provinces and that angry workers were ousting managers from their factories. The shortages of household items had spread from matches to soap. Highway robberies were staged near Moscow, and inside the city burglaries were rising. Ethnic clashes had produced an estimated 700,000 refugees. Inside the Russian Federation the nationality areas seeking to break away included resource-rich Tataria, Bashkiria and Yakutia.[29]

Non-Russian bigwigs were allowed to blow off steam at the September 1989 Central Committee Plenum devoted to nationality affairs. Yakut party secretary Prokopev complained that his region got only 3 percent of the profit from diamonds and gold mined there. He demanded a right to trade with foreign countries for locally produced coal and oil. Prokopev claimed that Yakuts deserved no less than an exclusive right to manage their territory, which covered as much as one-sixth of the Soviet land mass. Kazakhstan party head Nazarbayev minced no words and described his republic as a vast concentration camp (gulag). He criticized the USSR Defense

Ministry for seizing huge tracts of land for conducting missile tests and mining uranium. Nazarbayev groused too that laws were enacted as "in an empire" (*v imperii*).

Others wanted the Center to focus on the evils of Stalinism. The Lithuanian party head reminded that each tenth of his people were arrested in Stalinist times. The party leader of the Jewish Autonomist Region in Siberia recalled the flight of local Jews in connection with the Doctors' Case on the eve of Stalin's death and pinpointed anti–Semitism as the reason for current Jewish emigration from the USSR. These expressions of local nationalism moved the Russian apparatchiks to demand special rights for themselves. Russia parliamentary speaker Vorotnikov urged for his republic its own police ministry, science academy, and radio and television services. The party boss from Smolensk looked toward the formation of a Central Committee to lead the nascent Russian Communist Party, which was a haven for reactionaries.[30]

Demands for stricter law enforcement and higher military preparedness were made at the September 1989 Plenum. Interior Minister Bakatin pointed up the latest crime wave. He said that in the last 8 months there were 1.5 million crimes and 240,000 of them serious. That amounted to a 40 percent jump in the time frame and was unprecedented. This disclosure elicited calls for curfews or martial law in disturbed towns. Defense Minister Yazov objected to Gorbachev seeking arms control pacts with the United States. He warned that as in 1941 a danger of war loomed and was underrated. President George H. W. Bush was said to be modernizing his nuclear arsenal and building a Reaganesque shield to guard against Soviet missiles. Yazov instructed that pacifism was unacceptable in the face of an American strategy of intimidation. Splitting hairs to challenge Gorbachev, the Marshal advised that a sufficiency of armaments was no substitute for an absolutely reliable defense force. The lone fault in nationality relations that Yazov cited was that in 1988, 120,000 conscripts knew no Russian while 20 years earlier that was true of only 10,000. It is noteworthy that in November 1989 party secretary for defense industry Oleg Baklanov told the Politburo that social discipline was the key issue and people awaited "extraordinary measures" to bolster it.[31] Yazov and Baklanov would conspire to overthrow Gorbachev in 1991.

The nationalities problem remained insoluble but Gorbachev was able to advance toward his goal of consolidating power. The September 1989 Plenum assented to a number of high-level personnel changes that seemed to go in that direction. The cautious Shcherbitsky, Chebrikov and Nikonov were dropped from the Politburo. The possibly more cooperative new KGB chief Kryuchkov and state planner Maslyukov replaced them.

Underscoring Gorbachev's failure to reach unanimity in the Kremlin leadership was the crossfire at the January 1990 Politburo meeting devoted to the review of a Draft Platform for adoption at a Central Committee Plenum. The terminal crisis of Communism in eastern Europe had obviously frightened Ligachev and he opposed both the introduction of a multiparty system inside the USSR and detente with the United States. He flatly rejected Gorbachev's New Thinking about foreign affairs and reasserted belief in the antagonistic-class nature of world politics. Ligachev had allies: KGB chief Kryuchkov, who urged firming up the language in the entire Draft; Russian parliamentary speaker Vorotnikov, who wanted to ban talk about "crisis"; Politburo member Zaykov, who resuscitated the forgotten danger of U.S.–Soviet war; and party Secretary Slyunkov, irritated that the Draft failed to mention Marxism-Leninism.[32]

The historic rift of Russian Social-Democracy into hard Bolsheviks and soft Mensheviks was papered over in Gorbachev's directives for the celebration of Lenin's 120th birth anniversary. He told the Politburo in March 1990 that Lenin had to be portrayed as eclectic and pragmatic. Gorbachev explained that when Lenin saw that bookish positions about world revolution were unworkable he took another view and went so far as to reject the existing view of socialism. Lenin was acclaimed for having his own, Social-Democratic outlook, which virtually made him a Menshevik. Yakovlev agreed and emphasized Lenin's ability rapidly to change course in light of new circumstances. The main thing in Marxism as Lenin understood it was to proceed from life rather than dogma, according to Yakovlev.

Later that month Gorbachev caught up with Yeltsin and persuaded the CPSU Central Committee to rescind Article 6 of the USSR Constitution, which legalized the party's monopoly of power. He also gained from barons the party's consent to nominate him for the post of USSR president.[33] Ligachev inwardly would have nothing to do with this latest and most drastic reevaluation of values (more below about this).

Yeltsin was hardly caught napping and his March 1990 platform for elections to the Russian CPD urged transition to a market economy. He was unafraid of the KGB and demanded both reduction of its size and abolition of its Ninth Directorate, which protected and satisfied the material needs of higher elites. Yeltsin took a cue from Lithuania's declaration of independence and said he was ready to sign international treaties for economic and scientific cooperation and offer self-governing status to border areas of the Russian Federation. Running on this platform, Yeltsin's "Democratic Russia" movement won 60–90 percent of the Russian CPD seats in Moscow and Leningrad.[34] The effect of these developments was to compel Gorbachev to focus on means to reverse a trend of nationwide disunion.

The politicized intellectuals were divided over what should be Gorbachev's next move. Some implored him to leave the CPSU, marketize and privatize. Others told him to stick with the Socialist Choice of the Bolshevik Revolution. These rival schools prompted a raucous internal debate like none seen in Moscow since the 1920s.

Aleksandr Tsipko was a philosopher who worked as a consultant of the Central Committee's International Affairs Department in 1986–1980. He wrote anti-orthodox articles in the magazine *Nauka i zhizn* (Science and Life) in 1988–1989. The articles traced the origins of Stalinism to Russian revolutionary extremism and Marxism. Their author saw no substantial difference between Stalin and Trotsky. Now Tsipko examined the lows of perestroika and prescribed drastic remedies. He opined that Gorbachev's Social-Democratic ideas would fail to win the hearts of Soviet Communists and attention had to be paid to the crises in eastern Europe. There, many embraced Liberal values of family, private property, religion and nationalism. "Yeltsin must be given his due," Tsipko said,

> he has grasped the necessity of rapidly decommunizing and deideologizing society, and sensed that the people are tired of the manipulations of the word "socialism" that have gone on for many years. The people don't fear private property or capitalism, just not getting their hands on private property. Give all of them an equal share of private property and they will become ardent defenders of private property. The more that glasnost uncovers our lag of development behind the capitalist countries and the bolder that perestroika reveals the depth of the collapse and crisis of our life, the stronger will be the people's protest against everything connected with the Bolshevik Revolution. Millions are convinced that the Bolshevik Revolution was a tragic mistake and the civil war the beginning of the fatherland's descent and spiral downward.

Tsipko assured that if Gorbachev repudiated socialism he would be able to check national separatism in the borderlands. The pull of material self-interest was implied to outweigh that of nationalism: "We have lost the Baltics largely because of ideological conservatism. Instead of condemning Estonia in 1988 for having adopted a law on private use of land and swearing allegiance to public ownership of the means of production our leaders should have taken an initiative to re-establish the market and traditional mode of life in the Baltics. The benefit from such action would have been twofold — we could have emotionally 'tied' the Baltics to Russia and at the same time begun the revival of a sensible system of economics inside the USSR."

Tsipko advised Gorbachev to keep his presidency and resign from the CPSU, which he expected to produce mass defections. The removal of party cells from the army, KGB and police would ensure the observance of democratic methods within the party and forestall a reactionary coup. Tsipko doubted that Gorbachev's kitchen cabinet was able to devise solutions to social conflicts. He proposed that nonaligned intellectuals be enlisted to serve as consultants to the Presidential Council.[35]

The Kremlin was fragmented over political strategy. Yakovlev offered a radical program to redesign governing structures:

- private land ownership;
- "worker control" of state-owned factories, which harked back to a 1917 Bolshevik decree granting to elected factory committees the right to monitor enterprises;
- freedom for private entrepreneurs;
- abolishing industrial ministries;
- the CPSU relinquishing its monopoly of political power;
- further cutbacks of the party apparatus;
- renewal of the military leadership;
- genuine independence for the republics (Union of Sovereign States);
- start of a military pullout from eastern Europe; and
- acceptance of large loans from the West.[36]

On the other side of the house, Ligachev sent a letter to Gorbachev that disavowed Stalin but restated his worst fear — restoration of capitalism. Ligachev saw threats to Soviet and party unity. Social discipline and living standards had fallen. The Politburo was guilty of having allowed the weakening of the party. Radicals sought to change the CPSU into a parliamentary party and some went so far as to lead nationalistic organizations. The Soviet Army and KGB were defamed. Hostile forces abroad aimed at returning the USSR to the path of capitalist development. The mass media were blackening Soviet history and realities. The Warsaw Pact alliance was disintegrating and NATO growing stronger. East Germany was in urgent need of consolidation.[37]

Gorbachev's college classmate, Lukyanov, was in line for the post of parliamentary speaker after the general secretary became USSR president.

As a senior party official in April 1990 he sent to the Politburo a selection of citizens' letters that resembled Nina Andreyeva's anti-perestroika manifesto. The compilation suggested public disapproval of trends unfavorable to the CPSU, socialism and patriotic education. Reformers were attacked for distorting Soviet history and the national mood was surmised to be explosively dangerous. with hopelessness more prevalent than at any time since World War II.[38]

By May Day 1990 the country was reeling from a goods famine and nationality unrest. Gorbachev was embarrassed while standing atop the Lenin tomb to review the holiday parade of Muscovites. The placards of marchers bore inscriptions such as "Politburo — Resign," "Down with the CPSU" and "Down with Marxism-Leninism." Chants of "Gorbachev resign" were heard and flags of Old Russia waved. Gorbachev left the reviewing stand in gloom.[39]

The USSR CPD met two weeks later and elected Gorbachev USSR president with virtually autocratic powers. An unexpected by-product was the cropping up of presidencies in the national republics and demands for genuine sovereignty. Gorbachev and the Politburo were sure that Communists in the Russian parliament would elect their man, Russian premier Vlasov, to the post of Russian president. This wishful thinking was at odds with a warning from party sociologists that Communists in the Russian parliament voted independent of Kremlin desires.

Yeltsin rose to Russian parliament speaker and accused the Center of pursuing an imperial policy toward the republics. He urged treaties to regulate Russia's relations with the Union and other republics. Yeltsin was ready to accept the sovereignty of 22 ethnic-based republics inside the Russian Federation. He also envisaged a Russian state bank, foreign trade agency and national anthem. A countermove was the rise of a hard-line Russian Communist Party that recruited fired CPSU bureaucrats.[40]

Ligachev fired off a second letter to Gorbachev and the Central Committee on May 28. This raised the twin dangers of Soviet balkanization and isolation. Events in the Baltics, Ukraine and Caucasus indicated that the USSR might soon cease to exist and be replaced by many nonsocialist states. The internal Soviet trends added up to political instability that excluded the possibility of implementing reforms Ligachev requested a Central Committee Plenum to draft and carry out specific measures to rebuff subversive forces.[41]

On New Year's Day 1991, Yeltsin legalized private property — land, capital, machinery and entire factories — in Russia. This *de facto* act of sovereignty was a prelude to Yeltsin six months later winning a popular election for the Russian presidency. He would stage an inauguration that resembled a tsar's coronation. The patriarch of the Russian Orthodox Church blessed the new ruler and a new anthem was based on tsarist composer Glinka's "Patriotic Song."[42] These rituals set the tone for Putin later to designate as Russia's national day the 1612 expulsion of Polish invaders from Moscow.

Gorbachev's determination to keep playing the political game and avoid bloodshed is clear from his rejection of some generals' proposal to crush the Lithuanian separatists and the final decision to impose an oil blockade.[43] Counsels were divided over whether the Soviet president and Communist party general secretary should rule through the party or state executive offices. Ligachev, before retiring in disgust at the July party congress, told Gorbachev to devote himself fully to party affairs.[44] Yeltsin left the party and fenced with Gorbachev over the rights of nationalities. Yeltsin told counterparts in local ethnic republic to "Take as much sovereignty as you can swallow!" But when Chechen president Dudayev announced the independence of his republic, Yeltsin ordered a state of emergency there. The USSR legislature nullified that edict and Gorbachev too shunned violent countermeasures. A "war of laws" started between the USSR and Russian Federation when Yeltsin decreed that Russian acts took precedence over those enacted by the Soviet parliament.

The breakdown of social controls augured a poor harvest, and grain stocks were at 22 million tons when 53 million were required and the Kremlin's foreign currency reserves meager.[45] A Canadian journalist who visited the Soviet Union in summer 1990 observed the despair of the man on the street. He recalls talks in Marx township of the hinterland that pointed to Yeltsin's stardust, Gorbachev's eclipse and perestroika still an empty slogan.[46] The traveler got a look at blackshirts of the Pamyat Society and heard in Moscow that Communist hardliners egged them on. Pamyat members blasted Jews, many of whom fearfully rushed to apply for exit visas. A belief was current that Pamyat had high backing in the party to warn of what might happen if perestroika got out of hand.[47]

The public was unaware that Gorbachev and Yeltsin met in July 1990 and agreed to transform the USSR into a Union of Sovereign States. The presidents created a commission of 13 economists to map a free market reform in one month's time. Representatives of the borderlands were to be invited to enter the commission. In August the USSR Presidential Council and parliamentary Federation Council endorsed the commission's work, a

"500 Days" program crafted by reform economists Shatalin and Yavlinsky. If adopted, the 500 Days meant big price hikes, job losses and welfare cuts.

Gorbachev was fearful of a Kremlin upheaval if he resigned the general secretaryship as a token of commitment to the free market reform. Privately he was repelled at the apparatchiks as "self-interested scum" who "don't want anything except a feeding-trough and power." But, he explained to a confidant, "I can't let this lousy, rabid dog off the leash. If I do that, all this huge structure will be turned against me."[48] The "huge structure" clearly was the party, KGB and military mechanisms.

There were grounds for apprehension since in July 1990 the CPSU Secretariat discussed and endorsed an excited memorandum from a secretary of the Russian Communist Party, V. A. Kuptsov, who warned that democrats in league with foreign enemies were fomenting labor unrest and preparing a coup. In the autumn a congress of democratic forces would supposedly be held and USSR legislatures be forcibly dissolved. The ultimate objective was an east Europe–type roundtable to compel the Soviet President to resign under threat of a general strike.[49]

A month later Gorbachev received from his chief of staff, Boldin, a survey of letters cautioning that a new market had to be socialist and dosed out for several years. New forms of ownership had to exclude "direct or indirect exploitation of the work of others." The survey advised that the public needed an essential minimum of food products with firm state prices. Many were said to believe that sabotage was obstructing the sale of rationed goods and fulfillment of orders that consumers placed months in advance.[50]

Convinced that trouble was brewing, Gorbachev in a September 21 parliamentary speech did an about-face on economic reform. He demanded extraordinary powers to introduce presidential rule and dissolve state bodies in republics. By way of contrast, Yeltsin stuck with the 500 Days and opposed resistance to it. Still obscure was a flurry of troop movements that preceded Gorbachev's tough speech. Communist leaders in the Russian region of Ryazan discussed a KGB report that democrats planned to seize Moscow television, radio, train stations and airports. As a precaution the airborne division stationed in Ryazan was sent to Moscow with its weapons. Another crack military unit headed to the Soviet capital from a peace-keeping mission in Central Asia. A third based at Vitebsk in Russia was also shunted to Moscow. These developments caused such concern that Colonel General V. Achalov, commander of Airborne Forces, stated in *Izvestia* that newly arrived troops in Moscow were routinely preparing for a parade and to harvest potatoes.[51]

What is certain is that many leading Communists were nervous about the food shortages and riots over lack of tobacco and vodka. Leningrad party chief Boris Gidaspov went to the Politburo and declared, "In the morning, going to work, I look at the lines for products that are 100 or 1,000 persons long. I think that if someone breaks a store window a counter-revolution will start in Leningrad. And we won't save the country." The ghosts of 1917 assuredly drove a resolution of the October 1990 Plenum complaining that bread and rolls were missing from bakeries in Leningrad.[52]

The Presidential Council and Politburo met jointly in November and criticism hurled at boat-rocker Yakovlev. Gorbachev agreed with diehards and formed a new Security Council without Yakovlev and other perestroika stalwarts Medvedev and Shatalin. Gorbachev's new team would prove to be decidedly cautious: the power men (*siloviki*) Kryuchkov (KGB), Bakatin (MVD) and Yazov (Defense), Bessmertnykh (Foreign Affairs Ministry), Pavlov (Finance Minister), Pugo (former Latvian KGB head), Primakov (economist) and Gennady Yanayev, a trade union official whom Gorbachev would nominate as his vice-president. Waiting in the wings to replace the centrist premier Ryzhkov, who suffered a heart attack, was Pavlov. He was a conservative about to attack Western bankers for allegedly conspiring against Soviet interests. The maneuvers to regain stability depressed Gorbachev, who consoled an aide that their revolution on behalf of "humane democratic socialism" had "started a global perestroika."[53]

Gorbachev's friends were dispirited that he made a pact with devils. Foreign Minister Shevardnadze resigned and warned of dictatorship. Russian analysts viewed Yanayev as a Stalinist and feared his promotion might bring Yeltsin closer to separatists in Ukraine and Kazakhstan.[54] A liberal proposed suspending the constitution and creating a special committee to prepare for the formation of a national unity government.[55]

A furor arose over the January 1991 killing of 14 Lithuanians who were defending a television center in Vilnyus. Gorbachev distributed the blame evenly between authorities and nationalists who harassed troops in the Baltics. Yeltsin termed Gorbachev's policies criminal and demanded that he step down from the USSR presidency. Gorbachev privately told aides that Yeltsin was innately destructive and an Oppositionist by nature who lately caused strikes.[56] The helpers found Gorbachev irritable during their infrequent meetings. They were sure that KGB and military chiefs met with Gorbachev regularly and ensured that the content of his daily intelligence brief was slanted to sow alarm and distrust. Party and KGB circulars reported that Yeltsin might use the armed forces to seize total power.[57]

Hardliners were running the CPSU Secretariat and in February 1991 it issued an alarmist decree. It claimed that

> so-called "independent" media are waging a systematic campaign of slander against the party, Armed Forces, USSR KGB and MVD organs and forces and defamation of the country's history. Every day we see the pseudo-democrats try under the cover of pluralism of opinions to sow lack of public confidence in the army, drive a wedge between the commanders and subordinates, junior and senior officers and degrade the Motherland's defender. Lofty ideals are subjected to doubt — the soldier's duty, honor and loyalty to his oath. Attempts are made to deploy the army according to nationality areas, and interfere with conscription.

KGB chief Kryuchkov wrote a letter to Gorbachev that detected a new internal bourgeoisie in the operations of underground business persons. Kryuchkov looked forward to the creation of "temporary structures for the implementation of extraordinary measures."[58]

Yeltsin's vendetta with the Communists reached its apogee with a Russian law adopted in April 1991 prohibiting the activity of political parties inside the police and an edict ordering party-free higher schools. By way of contrast Gorbachev urged tighter control of television during a week-long conference at CPSU headquarters. He wanted the party to "Fill the airwaves with our viewpoints!" But hardliners thought this ephemeral and sent letters to the main party office accusing Gorbachev, Yakovlev and Medvedev of petty-bourgeois *reformizm* and demanded their punishment. Clarity failed to result from a Gorbachev-sponsored referendum on whether to keep intact the USSR. Over three-quarters of the voters were affirmative but in Moscow and Leningrad half opposed the idea of a unitary state. Majorities boycotted the referendum in Georgia, Moldavia and the Baltics. Over 70 percent of the Russian ballots approved of Yeltsin's bid for popular election of the Russian head of state.[59]

Hardliners converged on Smolensk in April and demanded action to "save the Motherland." Yakovlev wrote to Gorbachev and warned of an imminent fascist coup. He advised Gorbachev to create a movement for democratic reforms and fight for a single Union state of voluntary members. The appeal had an effect and Gorbachev on April 23 met with Yeltsin and eight other republic leaders. They signed a statement of intent to conclude a new treaty of sovereign states, adopt a revised constitution and reelect Union bodies. Yeltsin was able to keep out of the statement any mention of socialism. At a CPSU Plenum the next day Gorbachev proposed his resignation from the post of general secretary, perhaps to satisfy the Yeltsin camp. But the Politburo failed to see a worthy replacement and refused to allow the Central Committee to examine the proposal.

A dilemma was the sequence to be followed in signing economic and political treaties between Moscow and border republics. Some favored signing the economic treaty first, binding the republics to take on obligations essential for keeping the common economic market intact. Others convinced Gorbachev to reject that approach as an obstacle to republics getting on board for the Union treaty, which offered extensive rights to them. In hindsight, Gorbachev's slogan, "First split up, then integrate," has been criticized for bringing closer "the disintegration not only of the Union but also of a common economic area ... tearing apart thousands of well-established industrial ties."[60] In any event, the socialist dream was gone. In June 1990 Gorbachev had looked forward to a "Union of Sovereign Socialist States." At a May 1991 session with advisors he imagined only a "Union of Sovereign States."[61]

The prospect of independence for republics distressed the *siloviki*. They addressed a June 17 closed meeting of the USSR legislature. Defense Minister Yazov worried about cohesion of the armed forces as republics were opposed to the Union conscription law. He questioned the rightfulness of Soviet troops returning from duty in Europe lacking housing and that many of 100,000 recently discharged officers were unable to claim pensions. MVD chief Pugo reported that since last August his officers had confiscated 50,000 firearms and tons of explosives. In the Caucasus, he said, warring sides were using armored vehicles and machine guns. KGB chief Kryuchkov read a 1977 letter that Andropov sent to the Politburo, "On CIA plans to acquire agents of influence among Soviet citizens." Premier Pavlov laid claim to Gorbachev's right to issue key decrees, and deputy Sukhov shouted, "Down with Gorbachev and the mafia group that surrounds him!" Gorbachev brought a hammer down on the critics.

The economic crisis worsened and drove Gorbachev to a policy shift. Suddenly he was prepared to begin a new era of free markets. In July 1991 Gorbachev told the West's Group of Seven leaders that Soviet military spending since 1988 had declined almost 30 percent. The output of tanks halted and cutbacks were made in the production of combat aircraft, artillery and infantry fighting vehicles. In hope of securing financial assistance from the United States, Gorbachev told the American President that once the Union treaty was signed he would begin a program to privatize state assets Not long after this development Academician Yu. V. Yaremenko foresaw an imminent decline of Soviet industrial output by one-third and the food supply by one-quarter, with unemployment reaching 10 million.[62]

Signing of the new Union Treaty was due on August 20, in line with an accord reached at a July 23 meeting of Gorbachev and republic leaders. That same day an ultrapatriotic article was featured in the newspaper *Sovetskaya Rossiya*. "Word to the People" was run above the signatures of hardliners General V. Varennikov, chief of Ground Forces, V. Starodubtsev of the Peasant Union, and military industrialist A. Tizyakov. "Destroyers and usurpers" were attacked for failing to understand that "the Soviet Union is our home and fortress, built by the great efforts of all peoples and nations, which saved us from disgrace and slavery in times of invasion!" A few days later a CPSU Plenum censured Gorbachev and deprecated a draft party Program that ignored collective farms and deemphasized militant atheism.

The imminence of high-level personnel changes lit a fuse to a powder keg. Yeltsin, Gorbachev and Kazakhstan president Nazarbayev met July 29 and looked forward to joint leadership of the Union of Soviet Sovereign Republics. Due to be fired were USSR vice-president Yanayev, KGB chief Kryuchkov, MVD chief Pugo, Defense Minister Yazov and State Television and Radio chief Kravchenko. Nazarbayev would be the new premier and Gorbachev president of a regenerated Soviet confederation. Yeltsin at the time suspected KGB spying on the talks and later claimed that was the case and may have hurried conspirators to strike for power.[63]

Gorbachev appeared on Soviet television August 2 and reported that a draft Union treaty was ready and would be signed on August 20. Two days later he went south for a vacation at Foros in the Crimea. KGB chief Kryuchkov summoned an aide of his first deputy on August 14 and told him that Gorbachev was suffering from a mental disorder and documents had to be readied for announcing a state of emergency. Gorbachev was supplied with daily intelligence briefs asserting that the domestic situation had sharply deteriorated and the country was ungovernable. A statement was inserted into the press that an old-style patriotic movement would soon hold a nationwide convention.

The coup plotters met on August 17 at a KGB residence near Moscow and decided to send envoys to see Gorbachev and persuade him to approve a state of emergency. If Gorbachev kept silent he was to be declared ill and vice-president Yanayev be named acting USSR president; if Gorbachev protested he was to be restrained, forcibly if necessary. Defense Minister Yazov conferred with generals on August 18 to prepare for the entry of three army divisions into Moscow. The KGB chief ordered a unit of his special forces to be sent to the Baltics.

Gorbachev received the envoys and refused to sign an ukaz for clamping down. When the visitors left it became noticeable that telephones were no longer working. Next Yanayev assumed the presidency and a "Statement of Soviet Leadership" trumpeted a state of emergency in certain areas of the country for six months. USSR laws were declared supreme and the highest governing authority was identified as the State Committee for the USSR State of Emergency (SCSE). A press release was issued to the effect that the draft Union treaty ran counter to the USSR Constitution, the popular will and the March referendum to keep the existing federal structures.

Yeltsin was determined to fight the reactionaries. From the Russian Government building known as the White House, he made an appeal "to the citizens of Russia" that opposed the "state coup aimed at restoring Communist institutions." Yeltsin signed an ukaz nullifying SCSE decisions and declaring the coup a state crime. He once met Generals Lebed and Grachev, whose troops were now in Moscow, and requested their support. A crowd of thousands gathered around the White House and erected barricades to safeguard the building. Yeltsin climbed atop a tank to read his defiant appeal and ukaz. In Leningrad too the SCSE was opposed. Mayor Sobchak told a rally that orders of the putschists would not be obeyed.

The CPSU Politburo and Secretariat sent out coded telegrams to regional bosses urging them to support the SCSE. But the coup fell apart when army and KGB generals decided to avoid a bloodbath to enthrone second fiddlers like Yanayev and other conspirators. The lone casualties of "Operation Thunder" were three civilians killed during a mishap involving army personnel carriers. The vanquished flew to Foros to beg forgiveness and Gorbachev responded with epithets. Russia's vice-president, Yeltsin bodyguards and police officers arrived in Foros to arrest the conspirators and escort the rescued Gorbachevs back to Moscow.

Why did the public and security forces turn their backs on the insurrectionists? The conventional wisdom that army and KGB troop commanders lost their nerve when ordered to arrest Yeltsin is superficial. The centralized Soviet system that the conspirators wished to rebuild on the ruins of perestroika was inextricably tied to the regime's failure to meet popular expectations that Communist party leaders had raised since 1917. Lenin-Stalin-Khrushchev socialism was supposed to ensure for ordinary citizens lives that were easier, freer, cleaner and more dignified than those of people who worked in a market-driven economy. Instead the historical path that Soviets had traveled was filled with chronic shortages, official lawlessness and humiliating subservience to overprivileged bosses. There was every reason to believe that the ultras who sought to reverse perestroika would be no more successful at dealing with systemic inefficiency, waste and administrative chaos than their Kremlin predecessors. The alternative course that Russian nationalist and anti–Communist Yeltsin represented was too attractive as a solution to the USSR's terminal crisis. In sum, Soviet citizens appear to have kept a mental ledger of the historical performance of their government and with populist Yeltsin as a great hope found the 74-year-old regime to be no longer tolerable.

After the coup plotters were defeated Gorbachev resigned his post of general secretary and advised the CPSU Central Committee to disband in view of party leaders having failed to oppose the conspiracy. Gorbachev went to the Russian parliament and met with shouted insults. Yeltsin shamed Gorbachev for having entrusted high office to scoundrels. The Russian president signed an ukaz banning the CPSU and suspended the Russian Communist Party. He nationalized CPSU properties that included buildings, clinics, hotels, consumer and banking services worth billions. The Russian Constitutional Court was unable to reach a decision on the lawfulness of Yeltsin's measures to extinguish the last vestiges of Communist rule.

Yeltsin men were named to the posts of USSR defense minister and KGB chief, who disposed of 500,000 employees and a budget of over 6 billion rubles, according to Shakhnazarov. The downside for Yeltsin was friction between three disjointed branches of power — Supreme Soviet, State Council and presidency, which set the stage for a violent clash that Yeltsin won with the use of tank cannons two years later.

Divisiveness was rife when Gorbachev met on September 1 with the leaders of border republics to resume work on a constitution for his projected Union of Sovereign States. From August through October independence was declared by Ukraine, Belorussia, Moldavia, Azerbaijan, Uzbekistan, Kirgiziya, Tadzhikistan, Armenia and Turkmenia. Yeltsin lifted price controls and privatized firms and banks in Russia. Gorbachev objected to this unilateral move at a November meeting of a new USSR State Council that he chaired. Yeltsin rejected the protest and said Russia would sharply cut its funding of Union agencies. At a second such meeting debate erupted over whether to form a Union confederate state or confederation of Union states. Gorbachev wanted the Union and threatened to leave when he failed to prevail. Yeltsin led those in favor of a confederacy, but with joint armed forces.

Gorbachev may have won half a loaf when Ukrainian President Kravchuk told the Moscow newspaper *Trud* (November 19) that he preferred that Ukraine, Russia and Belorussia remain one state without a political center. But a December 1 referendum in Ukraine strongly backed independence and Kravchuk a few days later renounced the 1922 Union treaty. Out of sight, leaders of Russia, Ukraine and Belorussia met near Minsk and proclaimed that the USSR was replaced by a new Commonwealth of Independent States. The founders explained their action on December 8 in terms of an utter failure of perestroika, which was decried as "the myopic policy of the center [that] led to a deep economic and political crisis, the collapse of production, a catastrophic lowering of the living standard of practically all strata of society ... the growth of social tension in many regions of the former USSR, which led to the inter-ethnic conflicts with great loss of life."

Conceivably Gorbachev thought of surprising the breakaway republics with a show of force. Soviet Defense Minister Shaposhnikov later wrote in memoirs that Gorbachev spoke to him in mid–November and suggested a military takeover: "You, the military people, should take power in your hands, 'impose' a convenient government, stabilize the situation and then leave," Gorbachev reportedly said.[64] We know for certain that Gorbachev appeared at the USSR Defense Ministry on December 10 for a meeting with the commanders of Military Districts. The reception was hostile and notetakers relate that to Shaposhnikov having earlier agreed to transfer command of the armed forces to the three main republic leaders. Unknown to Gorbachev an order was given to transfer the instruments of government communications to Yeltsin. Talking later to Shevardnadze, Gorbachev said he had no animosity. "They've taken power and that's all there is to it," Gorbachev remarked. His Georgian friend observed, "It's a coup!"[65]

At a press conference two days later, Gorbachev denied rumors of a military coup. Yeltsin was faulted for taking advantage of the Ukrainian declaration of independence and made to appear antipatriotic: "We are starting to divide up what was formed over the course of ten centuries." Gorbachev saw more crises in the offing and said he would resign if the Union center was doomed. Eager to play the happy warrior, Gorbachev aired confidence that extreme conservatives would be kept at bay.[66]

Bowing out, Gorbachev signed a December 25 ukaz relinquishing the powers of the USSR president. He took leave from the public in a televised speech that highlighted both progress and torment during his reign. Gorbachev took pride in the demise of the totalitarian system and introduction of freedoms of elections, press and religion. Overrating change in the still-destitute countryside, he hailed the rise of private farmers. Gorbachev took credit for the end of the Cold War and regretted that the Soviet order collapsed before a new one was created. He also seemed to claim the honor of liberating east Europe from Soviet-style socialism by alleging that perestroika had become a universal phenomenon. In general, the self-criticism was minimal and onus put on the defective political culture of Soviet citizens and the August coup for having brought matters to a head.

The hammer and sickle flag of the USSR was lowered from a Kremlin tower and the tricolor of tsardom raised. Differences of opinion would persist on the triggering event of the Soviet break-up. Some thought the power struggle between Gorbachev and Yeltsin made the disintegration inevitable. Others felt that the tipping point was the demand of republic leaders for complete autonomy in the management of finances in their areas. About the underlying trends of the meltdown, Russian analysts agreed that these were

- rising ethnic tensions due in part to a significant reduction of Kremlin subsidies to constituent republics during the 1980s economic crisis;
- blanket state ownership of land, firms and banks severely diminished the supplies of food and consumer goods;
- mass discontent evoked by the governing elites' self-isolation, nearly unlimited terms of office and lack of accountability;
- social-psychological depression over the gap between Khrushchev's 1961 declaration that prosperity would be reached by 1980 and the low living standard of the general populace under Brezhnev during the 1970s;
- overspending of 1970–1980 energy profits on defense and food imports;
- loss of Soviet prestige resulting from the military setback in Afghanistan and fall of Communism in eastern Europe;
- Gorbachev's sweeping one-sided concessions to NATO over German unification;
- Gorbachev's multicandidate elections to party and soviet posts enabled the assertion of local, nationality, professional and regional interests; the party apparatus was demoralized and the CPSU fragmented into national-separatist parties and movements;
- resurgence of the 1917 Duality of Power (Soviet and Governmental) as the USSR Congress of People's Deputies removed the CPSU from state administration and soviets at various levels clashed;
- the USSR parliament tried to subjugate counterparts in Russia, the Baltics and Moldavia; the Russian parliament pushed back.[67]

The leadership failure to anticipate events cannot be underrated. Gorbachev writes in memoirs that he did not expect the leaders of constituent republics to follow his example and create their own presidencies. Those acts heightened the chances of republics seeking to move further away from the growing confusion in Moscow.

* * *

Later, Gorbachev wrote books on the failed coup and Soviet dissolution. He created his own foundation in Moscow and lectured on global issues. With former U.S. President Bill Clinton he co-narrated a performance of "Peter and the Wolf." Clinton paid tribute to Gorbachev at a Washington banquet which both attended to mark the 20th anniversary of the Stavropolian's advent to power. He played a leading role in forming the Union of Social Democrats in 2007 to counter negative tendencies such as corruption. The Union served as base for a new Independent Democratic Party, which aimed at a strong parliament and "less state capitalism." In Russian opinion polls, Gorbachev's ratings were far below those of autocrats Nicholas II, Stalin and Lenin.

Yeltsin suppressed a neo–Bolshevik coup in 1993, ordering artillery to shell the Russian parliament building. He revised the federal constitution to establish firmer presidential authority. Market reforms led to the creation of a class of super-rich amidst impoverished millions. Yeltsin led a chaotic administration but won an electoral victory for a second term. In failing health, he handed over authority in 1999 and died in April 2007, aged 76. There were few displays of public mourning.

Yakovlev became president of the International "Democracy" Foundation in Moscow and chairman of Russia's Presidential Commission for the Rehabilitation of Victims of Political Repression. He did valuable research on Soviet-era documents, and wrote critiques of Marxist theory and Communist oppression. Yakovlev was honored in lengthy obituaries which the Western press ran after his death in 2005 at age 81.

Epilogue

An inspection of Russian newspapers and web forums for the year 2007 reveals lively public interest in Gorbachev's reforms. A glowing press review was that "a special place has to be awarded to perestroika, which must officially and forever be recognized as one of the very great periods of Russian history."

One posting was melancholy: "Young people do not know that perestroika left untouched the foundations of Russian life. What indeed was perestroika? Today people in their twenties do not know its origins nor why it was undertaken." The eternal underpinnings apparently were age-old Russian vices such as abuse of office, bribery, poverty, drunkenness, laziness and stealing.

A third opinion of perestroika on websites was strikingly leftist; "I don't think Gorbachev originally intended to destroy the USSR. He was just an illiterate Marxist and regarded as weightier than textbooks the opinion of stylish liberals, including his spouse Raisa Maksimovna. He was unaware of what might result from rejection of the class approach and shift to a shapeless and unscientific 'democracy' under which vile demagogues such as [Leningrad leader] Sobchak, [Russian leader] Yeltsin, [Lithuanian leader] Landsbergis and other enemies of the people might take charge."

A conspiracy theorist said, "The CIA put Gorbachev in the chair of general secretary and of course after his arrival his opponents at the Politburo soon died. Evidently many inconvenient people were poisoned."

Gorbachev himself was the topic of debate on a Russian Web site in 2009 after he urged the creation of a new liberal party. Some argued that a new Gorbachev would be needed in a generation's time, when the number of enlightened persons had grown and transition from pre–1861 serfdom to a free society was restarted. Indeed, centuries might have to pass before this stage of perestroika was completed. Others countered that Gorbachev should be put on trial for high treason in view of his catastrophic policies that led to disintegration of the Soviet Union. The fallen ruler was accused of contempt for Russian culture and values. These were said to have justified a readiness to have jailed maverick Yeltsin and sent tanks to crush anti–Soviet rebellions in Poland and Ukraine. Due to Gorbachev's errors, Russia was supposedly humbled to the status of appendage of the West and lacking its own idealogy, military and foreign policy.

These attitudes were reminiscent of those current in Russia at the start of the last millennium. Under tsarism only small islands of liberal democratic thought existed on the political map of Eurasia. Among the 150 million inhabitants of the Russian Empire a few thousand were supportive of a law-governed parliamentary system. Absolute monarchy was convenient to influential landowners, merchants and industrialists who prized social stability. A narrowly based center of liberal democrats aimed at rolling back the government by pedigree and its high-flying supporters. The populist left was sharply divided and on its wildly radical edge stood no more than 20,000 Bolsheviks whose mastermind was abroad and disciples banished to the tundras in Siberia. A question mark remains over the future behavior of restive peasants, workers and ethnic groups. If the tsar had kept out of World War I, which entailed a breakdown of social cohesion, perhaps a cataclysmic upheaval like that of 1918–1921 could have been averted. The rise of an unusually repressive autocracy like that of Lenin and Stalin was hardly inevitable. Its seedbed was sown prior to 1917 by thoughtless royals and their adoring elites.

From Lenin to Gorbachev censorship was a mainstay of Soviet rule and exercised so rigorously that many Americans saw the USSR as a country of the blind. The belief that Kremlin subjects were thoroughly brainwashed helped to generate the myth that external influences triggered Gorbachev's westward-looking reforms known as perestroika. But it is mistaken to think that Ronald Reagan or Pope John Paul II were behind the dismantling of totalitarianism in the USSR during 1987–1991. The history of perestroika is the history of Russian and Soviet dissensions. Debate was usual among conservatives, liberals and socialists prior to the downfall of tsarism. After his coup Lenin fought with literalist colleagues over the definition of proletarian dictatorship. The belief of Georgian Bolsheviks in the necessity of inner-party freedom led them to participate in an armed rebellion against Moscow in 1924. The Trotskyites waged a similar campaign and Gorbachev was later convinced that Stalin was opposed in secret voting for top leaders at the 1934 party congress. During the next decade intellectuals sought to convince policy makers to loosen the censorship and introduce multicandidate elections to state posts. The survival of democratic thought in Stalin's police state is remarkable and without it the unfolding of perestroika is almost inconceivable.

After Stalin the building of consensus in the political class was again vital for the framers of policy. Glasnost had to be revived to garner the support of bureaucratic elites for the special agendas of rival leaders. Beria initiated this development with exclusives about Stalinist illegalities. Malenkov put specifics into decrees to enhance the chances for officials' compliance. Khrushchev disclosed alarming statistics about food production to address an issue on which the reputations of top leaders most depended. Years of backstage politicking helped to set the stage for Gorbachev to press for civil liberties and military cutbacks.

American laymen and leaders were remarkably unprepared for the transformation of the USSR. To some extent this was true because apocalyptic scenarios about the imminent demise of Bolshevism were habitual. They dated to 1919 and the Russian Civil War, the 1941 Nazi invasion of the USSR and *1984*, a Soviet dissident intellectual's vision of a riot in a Moscow butcher shop that grew into a nationwide uprising. On the other hand, too many were deceived by the Kremlin facade of tight internal unity and assumption that the Politburo would always manage to "muddle through."

The complacency stemmed in part from the excessive attention that social scientists paid to Soviet ideology and fondness of conceptual acrobatics. A simplistic RAND book, *Operational Code of the Politburo* (1950), drew far-reaching conclusions about Kremlin motives from selected Lenin quotations. It was usual for scholars to picture the Soviet system as faction-free and resistant to domestic pressures for long-term relaxation of central controls. A 1953 textbook cited the case of Nazi Germany, prototypical totalitarian state, and held that only a foreign invasion might serve to alter basically the Soviet regime. One hawkish researcher later refused to see the death of Stalin as a turning point and saw in Moscow's future a "permanent purge" or constant series of witch hunts since instigators were able to hide behind a screen of collective leadership. No more instructive was academic theorizing about whether Soviet history was one coherent or mixed process.

Western specialists on Soviet foreign policy often assumed that Stalin's heirs would relentlessly pursue his course of domestic self-isolation and foreign expansionism. Khrushchev's rhetoric was menacing enough, plugging "wars of national liberation" in a famous 1961 speech to party intellectuals. Only seasoned observers read that verbiage as cover for a broader disputed effort to allocate more resources to consumer branches of industry. A British scholar indeed warned that study of Soviet factionalism was likely to encourage appeasement of the USSR. Supposedly, an emphasis on differences among Nazi leaders before World War II prompted concessions to Hitler that whetted his appetite for more conquests. Actually there was a military-civilian opposition to Hitler in 1938 and the British government wrongly believed that this opposition's foreign policies were not really different from those of Hitler. An opportunity to exploit the discord among German elites was lost and that worked to the benefit of Hitler, who might otherwise have been stripped of his power.

U.S. intelligence services were rarely endowed with the brainpower needed to perform strategic analysis. A confidant of President Franklin Roosevelt recalled that in 1941, "We had terribly underestimated the power of Russia. When she was attacked by Hitler, I heard the highest military authority say, and the common expression around Washington was, that the German armies would move through Russia like a hot knife through butter, I heard [Army Chief of Staff] General Marshall express the most doubtful views of the power of the Russians to resist. The conquest of Russia was expected to be a very short matter."[1] Incidentally, Japanese forecasters concluded as early as August 1941 that the Nazi-Soviet conflict would be long-term.[2]

President Dwight Eisenhower in his 1953 inaugural strongly declaimed against World Communism and that had a chilling effect on U.S. intelligence analysts. Their superiors as good bureaucrats tacked to winds from the White House. An apolitical and Manichean image of the Soviet Union was standard fare in CIA reporting. The Beria purge, however, created a stir and CIA managers in July 1953 started Project CAESAR, a series of papers that were postmortems on Kremlin infighting. Covert operatives were the heart and soul of the CIA and they deprecated this effort as "library research." CAESAR documents released in 2007 show initial reluctance to examine foreign policy implications of the Stalin succession and unfounded belief that the Soviet military was a passive institution in crises. Eventually, confidence in the analysts grew and "working papers" rose to the level of "Intelligence Reports." Llewellyn Thompson, U.S. Ambassador to Moscow in the Khrushchev years, read these studies and this helped to make him a valuable adviser of President Kennedy during the 1962 Cuban Missile Crisis.

The quality of this CIA work was far superior to the day-by-day reporting on Soviet affairs of the Agency's Office of Current Intelligence (OCI). Groupthink was usual and management bereft of intellectual firepower.

OCI made simplistic contributions to the glitzy National Intelligence Digest and a boiled-down version of that daily was served to U.S. Presidents. Equally remiss as a rule was leadership of the Soviet affairs office of the State Department's Bureau of Intelligence and Research (INR). Its stock in trade was the paraphrasing of wire service ticker for the insertion of squibs in The Secretary's Morning Summary. There, too, persons lacking ability often set the tone and their displays of favoritism were reprehensible. Office directors were often recruited from Foreign Service officers out of a job and proved to be amateurs. How mistrustful of original thought bureaucrats must be!

The highest officials of U.S. and British intelligence were sometimes unfit to judge the credibility of their Soviet analysts. A CIA head in the 1960s thought that the Supreme Soviet, rubber-stamp legislature in Moscow, was the real locus of Kremlin decision making. His counterpart in London followed in the footsteps of British officials who in 1948 shrugged off the Stalin-Tito rift as deception. The MI6 director in 1956 wondered if Khrushchev's anti–Stalin speech at the latest party congress might be a hoax. He also took seriously a view that the Sino-Soviet schism was a misinformation gambit made to weaken the West's resistance to Communism.

U.S. assessments of Soviet military capacity were overblown. The defense secretary under Presidents Kennedy and Johnson recognizes that during the Cold War the Atlantic powers often exaggerated Soviet military power and expeditionary capability.[3] The last word about intelligence input to the making of American foreign policy rightfully belongs to Robert L. Hutchings, who during the 1980s formulated strategic options at the U.S. National Security Council. In the midst of the death throes of Communism in eastern Europe he was struck by the unhelpfulness of policy analysts in Washington. In *American Diplomacy and the End of the Cold War*, Hutchings regrets that he found the intelligence community pessimistic and fatalistic about the crises in Soviet orbit states.

A cautionary note is essential. Intelligence research specialists cannot be expected to command predictive powers that surpass those of on-site foreign elites. Bolshevik insiders during the 1920s misjudged Stalin as "safe" and Trotsky dangerously unpredictable. Khrushchev later conceded that his victory in battles for Stalin's mantle was unexpected. Brezhnev's colleagues at first thought him to be an interim leading figure but as master of intrigue he kept the top party job for more than four U.S. presidential terms. A hardened apparatchik, Dmitri Shepilov chose to be on the wrong side in the faction war of June 1957 and paid dearly for betting against Khrushchev.

The rapid crumbling of the Soviet Union came as a surprise to many Russians.

While deploring the tardiness of U.S. intelligence services in recognizing the extraordinary qualities of Gorbachev, it should be remembered that false dawns of relaxation broke on the darkened Russian and Soviet scenes. One short-lived spring occurred after the 1905 Revolution and experiment with a parliament that all too quickly was shelved. A second fleeting breakthrough to modernity was the March 1917 Revolution that laid low tsarism, only to be replaced by a feeble Provisional Government that Bolsheviks overturned. A third mirage of liberalization was the 1936 Stalin constitution, which may have been designed for currying favor with anti-fascists abroad. A fourth reason to reserve judgment about Soviet change was the post–Stalin fight over Kremlin succession that began with the advance of reformers and ended with the triumph of bureaucratic absolutists. All this history may help to account for, but not wholly validate, the usual procrastination of Western intelligence officials.

A few students of Soviet leadership politics regularly delivered the most that could reasonably be expected of professional observers. They kept in mind the fractious nature of Bolshevism and reasoned from monarchical tradition that once Stalin gained primacy a web of court politics would be spun in Moscow. These Kremlin watchers regarded the post–Stalin power structure as indefinite and likely to remain so. Neo-Stalinists (Molotov), Reformists (Malenkov) and Centrists (Khrushchev) were thought to be bidding for a working majority to steer the Presidium. The conflicts over power and policy would endure in the absence of a clear separation of functions at the top and law for the transfer of authority. Expediency and temperament were regarded as more important than fixed principles in decision making. Avoidance of exaggeration about the weight of ideology was in line with historical experience that the further a revolutionary society moves away from its origins the more do national traditions grow assertive.

The most astute Kremlinologists included Franz Borkenau, Robert Conquest, Isaac Deutscher, Ernst Kux, Wolfgang Leonhard, Boris Meissner, Boris Nicolaevsky, Michel Tatu and Victor Zorza. Their findings were ignored by right-wing politicians who never lost sight of Communist beliefs as the ultimate source of undesirable world events. Statesmen of this school reasoned that since the Kremlin's ideology excluded real policy change it was futile to try to do business with it. The chronic summiteer Churchill disagreed, as did his protégé, Harold Macmillan, and the realpolitiker Charles de Gaulle.

Ultimately American leaders welcomed the Soviet turn from peace propaganda to peace diplomacy. Presidents Kennedy and Johnson sensed that a mood shift in the Kremlin was important for White House planning about relations with the USSR. If divisions existed among Soviet leaders an invitation to talk with them and avoidance of hard language might help to strengthen the forces inclined to compromise. U.S. Secretary of State Warren Christopher, who negotiated with Iran about U.S. hostages in 1979–1981, found that diplomacy, to be effective, requires study of the vectors of power on the other side and looking for seams in the cloak of power.

The cracks in the Kremlin wall were large enough for serious investigators to detect. History-based arguments long suspected to exist from circumstantial evidence came to a head with perestroika and revolved around:

1. *Personal leadership.* The right to set USSR policy hinged on winning over the Communist party's Central Committee and then its Politburo or Presidium. Stalin achieved that objective as a unifying figure who enjoyed the trust of local dignitaries. The barons wanted to preserve Lenin's truce between town and countryside and ensure a steadier hand on the tiller than was thought conceivable with the polarizing Trotsky in command.

An emergency in the form of the grain-marketing strike of 1927–1928 made Stalin a rallying point for party members. The existential threat made acceptable a unilateral decision to impose state feudalism in villages and resume the tsarist policy of rapid industrialization. Stalin navigated through intrigues until able to exploit the Kirov murder and establish an unassailable tyranny. No successor was faced with a domestic crisis of the magnitude that Stalin tackled in 1929. None gained the right to conduct blood purges that could shield him from challenge. The post–Stalin leaders of policy ordinarily had to negotiate in order to govern, and deadlocks in the Presidium can be assumed to have occurred and required mediation of the Central Committee.

Yeltsin was a brilliant practitioner of the well-known Soviet art of the politics of revenge. After his ouster from the Kremlin leadership for reformist exuberance, he used the new freedoms to build a vast constituency of ordinary people on a foundation of anti–Communism, won huge electoral victories, aborted a hardliner coup attempt and struck a deal with other republic leaders to bust up the USSR. That opened the gates to the creation of a free-market economy in a truly sovereign Russia and made conceivable a stable democracy emerging there at some future time.

But Yeltsin for the moment effectively restored monarchy. Disgruntled lawmakers staged an armed uprising that Yeltsin quelled with military force. Heir Putin showed that he too would brook no challenge and his United Russia party resembled the defunct CPSU with its youth auxiliary of power-hungry careerists. Putin may not have been involved in the sensational poisonings of foreign critics but with a power base that included many former Chekists he created a regime that allowed such barbarities to go unpunished.

Was luck important in determining the fortunes of political personalities? If the attempt on Lenin's life in 1918 was successful and Trotsky replaced him the intellectuals may have been hounded less than was the case under Stalin. The credentials of Malenkov might have been burnished and Khrushchev held at bay if Eisenhower had approved of Churchill's 1953 bid for an East-West summit. The recovery of Stalinist Frol Kozlov from a 1963 stroke could have resulted in his replacement of Khrushchev and a stronger tightening of the screws than with Brezhnev in the saddle. Defense Minister Ustinov is rumored to have blocked the advance of Gorbachev before 1965 and if he had lived longer the Gorbachev phenomenon may have been avoided. All this tends to give an affirmative reply to the rhetorical question that Israeli premier David Ben-Gurion put to his foreign minister, Abba Eban: "Isn't Marxism stupid?"

The memoirs of former Soviet officials tend to represent Gorbachev as the gravedigger of the Soviet system. There is room for doubt that his incompetence was as breathtaking as that of Nicholas II. On Brezhnev's watch bureaucratic corruption was unparalleled and socialist values fully discredited. Along with Russia-based party racketeers like Medunov, cliques of businessmen and criminals thrived in the borderlands. The Afghan insurgency and Polish standoff dealt heavy blows to Kremlin prestige. It is to Gorbachev's credit that in Russian discourse there is no follow-up epithet to *brezhnevshchina*, last in a long line of figures linked to dark times.

The personal characteristics of Soviet leaders were in one respect similar to their Western counterparts. They practiced deception in war and peace. Lenin imaginatively attributed to French agents the 1921 rebellion of disenchanted radicals at the Kronshtadt naval base outside Petrograd. Stalin was wildly optimistic about the chances for a swift victory over Nazi invaders in a November 1941 speech and admitted to an aide that he lied to boost morale. Khrushchev absurdly denied bureaucratic privilege in the homeland during a polemic with hosts during his U.S. tour in 1959. Gorbachev, in his climb to the top rung, played the good Communist despite great misgivings about the system and in power is believed to have hidden his intention to introduce major economic reforms lest that offend influential party men.

Personal differences on the critical nationalities issue were politically meaningful. Lenin and Stalin were aware of the historical consciousness of the Great Russians. The first Soviet leader dwelt on his people's pride in an essay and his successor exploited their long-standing patriotism and admiration of strongmen. Gorbachev was blind to the depth of the grievances of non–Russians. And Yeltsin recognized a feeling among Russian elites that their area's riches were unfairly redistributed to distant ethnic groups.

2. *Party role*. Lenin and Trotsky were clueless about the functions that their ruling party should perform after it seized state power. Lenin's insistence that generalist party officials be administrators was in keeping with his conviction that experts were too vulnerable to liberal influences. The party-firsters later may have feared that curtailment of apparatchik power would bring a downturn of privilege and openings for bribery. Stalin, who long personified the "specialist-eating" *apparat*, ultimately had misgivings about the party functionalists. Unlike Khrushchev and Brezhnev, Beria, Malenkov, Kosygin and Gorbachev looked upon the professionals as most capable of surmounting the hurdles of national backwardness. Anyone seeking an explanation for the tendency of Khrushchev and Brezhnev to maximize party intervention into economic activity must take account of the older man's poor education, influence of Stalinist "cavalry charges" on his political style, and the protégé's imitation of his capo.

3. *Economics*. Battle lines were drawn in the 1920s between those pressing for crash industrialization through squeezing of the villages and others wishing to cement the strained relations between town and countryside. It was the bungling of state economists and peasant greed that provoked a food shortage. That led to Stalin making a fateful choice to introduce central planning with a forcing of heavy industry. The year-long struggle that raged over this issue suggests that a real alternative existed to what Stalin called his revolution from above.

The straitjacket of central planning became a root cause of vast waste and corruption. A burden of armaments that the people had to bear after World War II worsened the dire shortages of basic consumer goods. During the 1950s and 1960s vain efforts were made to force the development of consumer industries to spur labor productivity. Each failed because of resistance from vested interests, either Stalin himself or alliances of party and top brass. The Brezhnev regime seems to have been heavily mortgaged to the defense establishment. A new constellation of forces in the Kremlin enabled Gorbachev to loosen the grip of central planners and cut defense outlays. But unraveling resulted from the absence of self-discipline and marketing skills among unchained managers. Yeltsin turned his back on Gorbachev's Socialist Option of 1917 and championed the Western practice of minimal government direction of economic affairs. With some variation to the benefit of political clients, Putin would abide by the rules of laissez faire.

4. *History.* We cannot be sure of the source of Soviet leaders' habitual use of the past as factional weapon. They were familiar with Historical Materialism, a pseudo-scientific component of Marxism, and originally imagined that the 1789 French Revolution opened a window of understanding on their own experiment. Or the traumas of Soviet politics were so severe as to prompt the classic Russian question, "Who is guilty?" In any case, the cabinet meetings of Western governments rarely if ever resembled the Politburo as scenes of arguments over old national dramas. From Stalin to Gorbachev bitter exchanges occurred over the courage of individual leaders during the Civil War, rightfulness of compelling peasants to join collective farms and wisdom of decapitating the military command when global storms were looming. Ironically, Trotsky and Bukharin were among the first to manipulate the past to discredit rivals, and eventually Stalin demonized them as lifelong spies and terrorists.

With the post–Stalin downgrading of the secret police, Khrushchev substituted for Stalinist melodrama a depersonalized version of party history. Brezhnev was more forgiving of Stalinist outrages and Gorbachev asked for a rewriting of his party history manual. Putin had Stalin acclaimed in school textbooks as a great state manager and Stalin was voted Russia's third most popular historical figure in a nationwide poll. It can be assumed that circumstance had something to do with this: like the glamorous Churchill and Eisenhower, Stalin was on the winning side in World War II. But a significant minority of Russians obviously despise Stalin as heartless tyrant.

5. *Foreign Relations.* Gorbachev's New Thinking magnified a strand of party opinion favoring cooperation with the West to boost security and commerce. The partisans of this moderate course included foreign commissars of the 1920s and 1930s, Grigori Chicherin and Maxim Litvinov. Litvinov appears to have been skeptical of Stalin's optimism about the chances for improving relations with Nazi Germany, stressing the Hitler movement's ideological hatred of the Soviet Union, anti–Semitism and intention to incorporate Austria into the Reich. The Machiavellian Stalin in May 1939 sacked Litvinov and sought a deal with Hitler through Molotov as foreign commissar. Stalin probably got conflicting advice on world affairs from Zhdanov, seeming advocate of resolute measures, and Malenkov, a less decisive figure. Khrushchev later practiced limited coexistence in relations

with the West and quarreled with steadfast America-hating Maoists. "Internal Chinese" inside the USSR included Molotov under Khrushchev and Shelepin under Brezhnev. Gorbachev-era hawks were deputy party leader Ligachev and military planners Sokolov and Yazov. The hardliners were rebuffed with relative ease and failed to thwart sweeping internal reforms or the making of substantial concessions to the Western powers.

The Yeltsin years (1992–1999) were good for a thin stratum of super-wealthy industrialists created in fire sales of state-owned properties. With the market reforms and lifting of price controls, ordinary citizens who had cheered Yeltsin's campaigns against bureaucratic perks reviled him for their loss of life savings. Russian national income fell by half and life expectancies by more than what was the case during World War II. The ethnic-based regions amended their constitutions in response to Yeltsin's encouragement to "take all the sovereignty you can swallow." Criminal gangs went on rampages in public. NATO expansion was pushed eastward in spite of the assurances of Western statesmen to Gorbachev that caution would be exercised. The humiliations endured under Yeltsin left bad feelings and the turnout for his funeral in April 2007 was sparse.

Putin as Yeltsin's successor viewed internal politics in the conventional manner of *Kto kovo* or Who [will destroy] whom? He was born in 1952 and it is unknown if any of his kin were Stalin victims. A Leningrader from a poor family, Putin is reputed to have grown up as a brawler, which may explain his passion for the martial arts. Obviously intelligent, he was educated in the Law Department at Leningrad State University. As a KGB recruit Putin reportedly helped to curb dissident activities in Leningrad and later served in East Germany. In the Gorbachev years Putin worked at the Leningrad city hall as chief aide to mayor Sobchak and there came to the attention of Yeltsin's coterie. In 1998 he was named director of the Federal Security Service, a KGB successor for monitoring internal affairs. Secretary of Yeltsin's Security Council, Putin weekly briefed the Russian president. When Yeltsin's health failed in summer 1999, Putin became prime minister and that December was named acting president. Yeltsin extolled Putin as a "strong man" (*silnyy chelovek*) in his televised farewell to the nation. The tribute hinted that firm action was essential to bolster national stability.

After mysterious explosions at Russian apartment buildings, Putin initiated a new war against Chechen separatists in the Caucasus. He led a "Unity" bloc in parliamentary elections and rallied voters tired of internal bickering. After election to Russia's presidency in March 2000 Putin enacted a law allowing him to remove any regional official whom he thought to be violating the federal Constitution.

A speech that Putin made to the Russian Federal Assembly in April 2005 was nostalgic of the bygone inner empire:

> The collapse of the Soviet Union was the greatest geopolitical disaster of the century. Tens of millions of our citizens and countrymen found themselves outside Russian territory. The epidemic of disintegration spread to Russia: savings were devalued, the old ideas destroyed, institutions broken up or hastily reformed. The country's integrity was violated by terrorist action and the subsequent capitulation at Khasavyurt [the 1996 ceasefire confirming the victory of Chechen rebels]. Groups of oligarchs, which controlled the flow of information, served only their own corporate interests. Widespread poverty was accepted as normal. All this against a background of economic collapse, financial instability and social paralysis.[4]

The primacy of state over private interests may have been one of the Soviet values that Putin wished to restore.

Gorbachev on the sidelines disapproved of Putin's methods to bring to heel maverick regions. The election of regional governors was replaced with a system whereby they would be nominated by the president and approved by their legislatures. Russian nationalists drove the policy debate over federal relations with warnings like one posted on a Moscow web site in August 2007: "Putin and company know that ethnic policy in Russia is a really dangerous matter. It could mean the 100 per-cent separation of Chechnya and the entire North Caucasus, and serious probability of that happening in Tatarstan, as well as Bashkiria and the Siberian regions."

A highlight of the reassertion of centralism and personalized leadership was a speech that presidential aide Vladislav Surkov made at the Russian Academy of Sciences in June 2007. He faulted as too conciliatory the posture of Gorbachev and Yeltsin when dealing with the Atlantic powers: "Perestroika and the period of the first reforms showed that *one-sided concessions in international affairs have a zero chance of capitalization and have even a negative effect.* They not only fail to soften up rigid positions but on the contrary provoke still greater pressure and desire for still more concessions" (italics in text).[5] United Russia spokesman Ilya Konstantinov brashly claimed that under Gorbachev and Yeltsin "the authorities willfully destroyed the state and its institutions."[6]

Putin handed over the Russian presidency to Dmitri Medvedev in 2008 and kept for himself the premiership. The rise of Medvedev typifies the

shefstvo or patron-client relationship in Soviet and Russian politics. The
Putin-led St. Petersburgers (*piterskiye*) were in effect a new ruling dynasty.
Medvedev was born in September 1965 into a family of professors at Leningrad State University. The starkly different social backgrounds of the eventual duumvirs Putin and Medvedev were sure to bring differences of style
to the conduct of public affairs. Medvedev was a sportsman and rock-band
enthusiast, graduated from the Law Department of LSU and in 1990 earned
a doctorate in private law. Medvedev grew close to future Leningrad mayor
Sobchak and worked under Putin in the Leningrad City Administration.
Putin, in 1999, elevated Medevedev to deputy head of the presidential staff.
During the 2000 elections Medvedev headed the presidential campaign
headquarters. After serving as an executive in the powerful and reputedly
corrupt Gazprom concern, he was named presidential chief of staff in 2003,
and from there vaulted to the first deputy premiership in 2005.

The Russian military incursion into Georgia during August 2008 was
overblown in foreign commentary as a Kremlin neo-imperialist thrust. A
later consensus of experts was that Moscow responded to a Georgian attempt
to regain by military means the breakaway region of South Ossetia that was
in the grasp of pro–Russian clans. After a cease-fire in the Georgia conflict
Medvedev indicated that he would remain faithful to liberal causes such as
"economic development, the expansion of business, creative and personal
freedom," without "any reference to whether the country is in a particular
situation surrounded by enemies."

Putin was conciliatory when he keynoted the Davos world forum in
January 2009. The global financial crisis had severely impacted Russia: production was down 20 percent, unemployment had risen to 6 million and
foreign currency reserves plunged. Putin solicited foreign investment and
warned against excessive state meddling in domestic economic activities.
Unpredictability increased once the decline of world oil prices threatened
to cut Moscow's payments to the regional treasuries, which in some cases
amounted to half of an area's yearly budget.

In broader perspective, the Russian and Soviet regimes traveled at a
rhythm familiar to other world powers. The British Sinologist Guy Wint
spoke of a "clearly marked cyclical course of Chinese history" that he thought
was caused by pressures of population. Arthur Schlesinger Sr. defined U.S.
historical swings in the domestic terms of the 19th and early 20th centuries.
They oscillated every 16 years, he wrote, "between periods of concern for
the rights of the few and periods of concern for the wrongs of the many."
Russian imperial historian Vasili Klyuchevsky discerned his country's peri-

odic "binding" (*kreposhcheniye*) followed by "unbinding" (*raskreposhcheniye*). This overview is certainly applicable to the Soviet experience. The urban centers were Bolshevized in 1917–1921 and in the early 1930s rural areas brought under single party control. A post–Stalin "thaw" was striking but a crackdown soon followed. Gorbachev and Yeltsin did a liberalizing turnabout while Putin reconcentrated political power in Moscow. All this hints that the chances for a rebirth of political pluralism in Russia are not so slim as might be imagined from some punditry. It can be expected that constraints such as legal nihilism, local patriotism and inveterate bad habits will slow the rate of Russia's progress to European standards of living and civil society. So far neither Putin nor Medvedev has shown any sign of wanting to restore the central planning or stifling political controls that were emblematic of the Soviet party-state. Still newer circumstances and mind-sets will determine what comes after them.

Appendix 1:
Kremlin Political Signals

Harry Truman once quipped, "The only thing really new in the world is the history that you don't know." That applies to the art that Sovietologist Myron Rush has called "esoteric communication," or writing between the lines. The father of that arcane practice seems to have been Aesop, who in ancient Greece penned morality fables and often used animals as the characters. Over the following centuries nonconformists resorted to Aesopian or veiled language to compose messages offensive to the high and mighty. Shakespearean studies inform that in the England of Queen Elizabeth I, aristocratic feuds were conducted through literary indirection and stage symbolism. Polonius in *Hamlet* is thought to have been a spoof of William Cecil, counselor of Elizabeth.

Under the Tsars politics and imaginative literature with subterranean texts were inextricable. A man of letters notes that "Political and social criticism, pursued and driven underground by the censorship, was forced to incorporate itself in the dramatic imagery of fiction. This was certainly one of the principal reasons for the greatness during the nineteenth century of the Russian theater and novel, for the mastery by the Russian writers — from Pushkin's to Tolstoy's — of the art of implication. In the fifties and sixties, the stories of Turgenev, which seem mild enough to us today, were capable of exciting the most passionate controversies — and even, in the case of *A Sportsman's Sketches*, causing the dismissal of the censor who had passed it — because each was regarded as a political message" (Edmund Wilson, *Literary Essays and Reviews of the 1930s & 40s*. The Library of America, New York: 2007).

Russian revolutionaries in the tsarist period got around the official censorship by using camouflage language. The practice was so well-developed that Imperial police chief Pleve said to the socialist N. K. Mikhailovsky, "Why do you want freedom of the press when even without it you are such a master of saying between the lines all that you wish to say?"[1] Strides were made toward freedom of expression after the 1905 revolution, and Bernard Pares has commented on the media situation from 1907 to 1914. He informs that the censorship was criticized in the Duma, and only in the provinces were there arbitrary fines imposed by local governors. In the capital, serious monthlies could be published freely although an order was circulated forbidding any mention of Rasputin.[2] Wallace seconded this opinion in the 1912 edition of his vivid *Russia*. He notes that the press carried arguments opposed to recent ministers of foreign affairs, who were deemed too subservient to foreign states, and against Count Witte, who, as minister of finance, sacrificed landowner interests to those of industrialists.

During the First World War the Russian press was subjected to military and political censorship. The Kadet organ *Rech* responded with an article, "How to read the newspaper?" (August 15, 1915), which told readers to follow and draw inferences from Duma speeches on what was happening in the British and French legislatures with reference to those bodies' relations with government executives. The relevant materials could "be used as supplements for understanding the secret white rectangles" or blank spaces in Russian papers where the censors had ordered the deletion of text grating on the authorities. Historian I.V. Alekseyeva tells us that Russian archives hold a police report on a lecture about France in 1870 that the Kadet F. I. Rodichev delivered shortly before the 1917 collapse of tsarism: "The speaker laid stress on shortcomings in the political structure of France that are also to be found in Russia. He did not utter the word 'Russia' but left no doubt in anyone's mind that while talking about France he was thinking of Russia."

Veiled discourse recurred after Lenin seized power and restored press censorship. The new rulers manipulated standard formulas and used allegory to stake out different visions in quarrels over policy, gain personal popularity and smear rivals. Party members scrutinized the press to learn from vague hints what was expected of them in thought and action. The importance of cryptic language is explained in a gifted analyst's account of the Stalin-Trotsky debate on Socialism in One Country, or whether the successful building of socialism in Russia depended on the outcome of world revolution:

> As sometimes happens in important disputes, where both sides are strongly committed to certain common principles, so in this controversy, too, its explanation cannot be found in the literal meaning of the disputants' words,

certainly not in their zealous reiteration of 'common' principles, but must rather be sought in the subtle, often imperceptible, shifts in the emphasis of their arguments.... The audience that listens to the disputants is left unmoved by their professions of common principle; it treats these as part of a customary ritual. But it pricks up its ears at the different hints and allusions thrown out by either side; and it avidly absorbs all their undertones and unspoken conclusions, It quickly learns to tell the operative part of any formula from the reservations and escape clauses that seem to contradict it.[3]

Interestingly, it was during the Stalin-Trotsky power conflict that *Pravda* (November 2, 1924) rebuked Trotsky for using "semi–Aesopian language" and "code" in a recent literary fight with Kremlin foes.

The size of prize audiences for codified texts can be estimated from a speech that Stalin made in March 1937. He put the party's "general staff" at 3,000 to 4,000; its "officer corps" at 30,000 to 40,000; and "non-commissioned officers" at 100,000 to 150,000.[4] Swiss analyst Ernst Kux in 1958 estimated that the CPSU had about 1,000 members who belonged to the Central Committee, were the first secretaries of republics, provinces and districts, and leading administrators of the Central Committee; and about 300,000 were local party secretaries, the secretaries of party organizations in enterprises, agencies, troop units and party instructors.[5] Evidently, a Stalin heir had to gain a consensus among those officials in the drafting of policies if those actions were to be implemented. An example of partisan text aimed at obstructing reform was the pamphlet written by Khrushchev ally Shepilov in 1953 undercutting Malenkov's policy of encouraging work in the private farm plots.

Soviet officials openly recognized the technique of veiled texts as a political tactic. A British historian recounts how Politburo member Zinoviev used parable to attack his colleague, Bukharin, in 1925. Zinoviev published an article in *Pravda* that was ostensibly a critique of essays by the émigré economist N. V. Ustryalov. Zinoviev said that Ustryalov's work constituted a harmful "canonization of the kulak," a position illustrative of the "danger of degeneration," which Lenin had regarded as inherent in the prolongation of peaceful evolution at home and delay of revolution abroad. Ustryalov, according to Zinoviev, was "the ideologue of the bourgeoisie." When Stalin entrusted his henchmen to discredit Zinoviev, Kaganovich charged that Zinoviev's *Pravda* article "professed to be about Ustryalov, but the real target was comrade Bukharin."[6]

Solzhenitsyn wrote of the role of disguised political messages. In a novel set in the mid–1950s, he describes the eagerness with which admin-

istrator Rusanov awaited delivery of his newspapers. He was jealous if someone else opened a fresh newspaper before him. Others could not understand
a newspaper as he did. Rusanov understood newspapers as a coded instruc-
tion that someone who knew the ropes could interpret. A true picture of
Soviet life could be gotten from small hints, the arrangement of articles,
and things that were played down or omitted.[7] Similarly, onetime Soviet
philosophy professor Alexander Zinoviev, in a 1976 novel about life in a
Soviet-type state called Ibansk—led by a Brezhnev-like figure—writes:
"Here's the leading article of the Newspaper. For you it's twaddle and demagogy. But for an expert it's a world of information. Here one finds lots of
visible and invisible assessments. The first business of an Ibansk careerist is
to learn to read such texts, which mean nothing for outsiders. For you and
me these texts are a hollow sound. But they are a guide to action for those
people."[8]

Under Gorbachev, Stalin's name was linked to "the emergence of a special political language which requires one to 'read between the lines,' follow indirect signs which have an almost ritualistic importance, in order to
understand the real sense of what is said and done."[9] Stalin-era officials were
said to be "able to read *Pravda*'s lead article between the lines," and asked,
when the dictator was dead and quoted less frequently in the press, "What
does this mean? Where is the pendulum swinging?"[10]

Stalin legatees carried on the tradition of disguised news items, and
Khrushchev's son, Sergei, recalls an example from the columns of *Pravda*
in April 1956. A "chronicle" notice printed at page two announced in heavy
type that deputy premier (for agriculture) Lobanov was replaced and chief
biologist Lysenko had resigned from the presidency of the Lenin Agricultural Sciences Academy. "The unusual place chosen for this information and
the type size," explains Sergei Khrushchev, "meant that special importance
should be given to the announcements. They were to be read as a change
of policy and not merely an ordinary shifting of personnel."[11]

The authority of individual leaders was registered in an elaborate system of status symbols. A master of ceremonies clearly arranged the proto-
col for the location of Politburo members on occasions such as the parades
on Red Square and meetings of the quasi-parliament. The same was true
of recording the proper volume of applause—"stormy, prolonged" or "prolonged"—for leadership speeches at public gatherings. And the number of
lines devoted to each of the top leaders in the biographical directory *Deputies
of the USSR Supreme Soviet* was obviously reflective of political weight.

Malenkov and Khrushchev experienced the full gamut of kudos and taunts. In December 1949 *Pravda* ran the articles of Politburo members dedicated to Stalin's 70th birthday and Malenkov's was published first. "To those who understand such things," Roy Medvedev comments, "this was a clear sign of special trust."[12] Similarly, Malenkov, on his 50th birthday in January 1952, was more acclaimed than any other of Stalin's underlings on such occasions. At the other end, *Pravda*, on October 11, 1964, heralded the removal of Khrushchev by unusually spelling his title "first" rather than "First" secretary of the CPSU. A savvy party member would have excluded the possibility of happenstance, to judge from word about a seminar at CPSU headquarters: "still another question was raised. Why are posts in the party such as that of General secretary and party Chairman written with capital letters in the Draft [CPSU Rules] while the party congress is written with a small one? Isn't this a sign of all-powerful hierarchy in the party? Under Lenin it was the other way round. Party congresses were written in capitals and posts in small letters. Only a brush-stroke, but it gives rich food for thought."[13]

One of the classics of abstruse signaling was reported in the diary entry of the American ambassador to Tokyo for May 2, 1941. Foreign Minister Matsuoka spoke to a public meeting and made several veiled barbs at cabinet colleagues. He implied treasonable action on their part by linking their actions to the name of the one man in Japanese history who in the Middle Ages sought to usurp the throne.[14]

Appendix 2: Identifications of Essential Figures

Andropov, Yuri V. (1914–1984). General secretary and KGB chief. Party operative mentored by veteran Finnish Communist Otto Kuusinen. Urged genuine policy debates inside the party and wanted Gorbachev to be his successor.

Beria, Lavrenti P. (1899–1953). Georgia party head, USSR NKVD chief and first deputy premier. The original post–Stalin reformer. Arrested in June 1953 and shot that December.

Brezhnev, Leonid I. (1907–1982). General secretary and president. The most corrupt party chief, who ousted his patron Khrushchev in 1964 and set a course of pragmatic conservatism.

Bukharin, Nikolai I. (1888–1938). Economist and publicist. Opposed Stalin's plan for rapid industrialization and farm collectivization. Arrested in 1937 and shot after a show trial. Rehabilitated under Gorbachev.

Bulganin, Nikolai A. (1895–1975). Worked in the Soviet secret police on railroads during the Civil War. Factory director and mayor of Moscow. Defense minister and premier. Ousted in 1958 for involvement in a plot to overthrow Khrushchev.

Chebrikov, Viktor M. (1923–1999). Politburo member and KGB chief. An internal affairs specialist, critical of *glasnost* and replaced by Gorbachev.

Chernenko, Konstantin U. (1911–1985). A longtime aide of Brezhnev who replaced Andropov as general secretary in 1984 and soon died.

Dzerzhinsky, Felix E. (1877–1926). First secret police chief. Worked closely with Stalin to isolate non–Russian nationalists and Trotskyites.

Furtseva, Yekaterina A. (1910–1974). Politburo member and culture minister. A Khrushchev favorite until suddenly dropped from the highest leadership in 1960.

Gorbachev, Mikhail S. (b. 1931). General secretary and president. Adopted reforms in the spirit of Russian and European Social-Democracy,

Grechko, Andrei A. (1903–1976). Politburo member and defense minister. A Brezhnev friend who played an important role in the March 1970 political crisis.

Grishin, Viktor V. (1914–1992). Politburo member and Moscow party head. Ultraconservative of the Brezhnev era.

Gromyko, Andrei A. (1909–1989). Politburo member, foreign minister and president. A traditionalist deceived into sponsoring Gorbachev for the top party post.

Kaganovich, Lazar M. (1893–1991). Politburo member, party secretary and deputy premier. Stalinist troubleshooter and onetime patron of Khrushchev, who ousted him in 1957.

Kamenev, Lev B. (1883–1936). Politburo member and Moscow Soviet head. Attacked Stalin at the 1925 party congress. Shot on a charge of treason after the August 1936 show trial. Rehabilitated under Gorbachev.

Khrushchev, Nikita S. (1894–1971). Party first secretary and premier. Won the battle for succession to Stalin. Ended criminal penalties for party factionalism and agitated for higher living standards. Endlessly tinkered with bureaucratic structures and was ousted in 1964 for creating administrative confusion.

Kirichenko, Aleksei I. (1908–1975). Politburo member and party secretary. Abrasive Khrushchev deputy suddenly demoted to a regional post in 1960.

Kirov, Sergei M. (1886–1934). Politburo member and party secretary. Popular boss of Leningrad thought to have urged a liberalizing course prior to his murder, probably committed on Stalin's order.

Kosygin, Aleksei N. (1904–1980). Politburo member and premier. Industrialist and Stalin favorite. Later opposed Khrushchev's feud with China, party micromanagement of the economy and overspending on defense.

Kozlov, Frol R. (1908–1965). Politburo member and party secretary. Enforcer of postwar purges in Leningrad, Great Russian conservative and briefly Khrushchev's deputy.

Kunayev, Dinmukhamed A. (1912–1993). Politburo member and Kazakhstan party head. Corrupt Brezhnevist ousted by Gorbachev. Riots in Alma-Ata followed his replacement by a Russian.

Lenin, Vladimir I. (1870–1924). Founder of the Bolshevik Party and Soviet State. An authoritarian personality who loathed intellectuals and had a flair for political maneuver. Committed a grave error naming Stalin to the post of party general secretary and was mortally stricken before he could rectify this misstep.

Ligachev, Yegor K. (b. 1920). Politburo member and party secretary. Andropov appointee from Siberia. Demoted by Gorbachev for obstructing reform. He warned against unraveling of the USSR before his 1990 retirement.

Malenkov, Georgi M. (1902–1988). Politburo member, party secretary and premier. Started his political career as clerical secretary of the Politburo and advanced on the coattails of Stalin. After Stalin he led a reformist government that Khrushchev toppled in a fierce dispute over investment policy. Sent into internal exile in 1957 and expelled from the party in 1962.

Martov, Yuli O. (1873–1923). A Lenin associate in St. Petersburg worker night schools in the 1890s. Led left-wing Mensheviks since 1903. Allowed to emigrate and died in Germany.

Mazurov, Kirill P. (1914–1989). Politburo member and Byelorussia party head. Refused to obey a Khrushchev order to socialize private livestock and evaded punishment.

Mikoyan, Anastas I. (1895–1978). Politburo member, first deputy premier and president. He was a foreign trade and policy expert. A mediator in leadership squabbles of the 1920s. Stuck with Khrushchev to the end and soon joined him in retirement.

Molotov, Vyacheslav M. (1890–1986). Politburo member, party secretary, premier and foreign minister. A dyed-in-the-wool Stalinist expelled from the party command in 1957 and from the CPSU in 1962. Chernenko restored him to party membership.

Nicholas II, Tsar (1868–1918). Resisted constitutionalism and courted disaster by mobilizing his inferior army against Germany in 1914. Russian generals advised him to abdicate in 1917. On Lenin's order the Bolsheviks shot the entire royal family.

Podgorny, Nikolai V. (1903–1983). Politburo member, party secretary and president. Innately conservative protégé of Khrushchev. Espoused hawkish views during the Middle East War of 1973.

Poskrobyshev, Aleksandr N. (1891–1965). Stalin's personal secretary and chief of the Secret Department, later Special Sector, CPSU Central Committee, which controlled informants that gathered information about Soviet dignitaries. Believed to have organized the great purge of 1937–1938. Secretary of the Presidium and Bureau of the Presidium, CPSU Central Committee from 1952 to 1953.

Rashidov, Sharif R. (1917–1993). Brezhnev's party head in Uzbekistan and notorious for ties with embezzlers and gangsters.

Rykov, Aleksei I. (1881–1938). Politburo member and premier. Warned against a Bolshevik power monopoly in 1917. Joined the Bukharin faction defending NEP in 1928 and was later shot. Rehabilitated under Gorbachev.

Ryutin, Martemyan N. (1890–1937). Moscow party official. Wrote a "platform" in 1932 urging the removal of Stalin and disbanding of collective farms. Sentenced to ten years imprisonment and later shot.

Ryzhkov, Nikolai I. (b. 1929). Politburo member and premier. Industrialist of the Gorbachev era who resisted market reforms and large-scale purchases of Western consumer goods.

Semichastny, Vladimir E. (1924–2001). KGB chief. A friend of neo-Stalinist Shelepin who helped to organize the ouster of Khrushchev. Removed on the pretext of allowing the defection of Stalin's daughter to the United States.

Serov, Ivan A. (1905–1990). KGB chief and military intelligence chief. Rallied Khrushchev's supporters in June 1957 to keep him in power.

Shcherbitsky, Vlodymyr V. (1918–1990). Politburo member and Ukraine party head. Brezhnev loyalist who forced Russification and deposed by Gorbachev.

Shelepin, Aleksandr N. (1918–1994). Politburo member, party secretary and KGB chief. Khrushchev protégé who helped organize his ouster. A hardliner sidetracked in 1967 and dropped from the leadership in 1975.

Shelest, Petro Ye. (1908–1996). Politburo member and Ukraine party head. Rumored to have pressed for the 1968 invasion of Czechoslovakia and opposed the Nixon-Brezhnev summit in 1972.

Shepilov, Dmitri T. (1905–1995). Politburo candidate, party secretary and foreign minister. A Khrushchev ally who joined the Molotov-Malenkov group in 1957 and was exiled to Kirgiziya, expelled from the party in 1962 and regained membership in 1976.

Shevardnadze, Eduard A. (b. 1928). Politburo member and foreign minister. Gorbachev's choice for Foreign Minister; resigned in 1990 with a warning of imminent dictatorship.

Stalin, Iosif V. (1878–1953). General secretary and premier. Ruled for nearly 30 years and gave to Bolshevism the facade of a religion. Renowned for the policies of farm socialization, rapid development of heavy industries and party purges.

Suslov, Mikhail A. (1902–1982). Politburo member and party secretary. Chief censor and believer in Stalin; chaired Central Committee meetings that deposed Malenkov, Molotov, Kaganovich, Zhukov and Khrushchev.

Tikhonov, Nikolai A. (1905–1997). Politburo member and premier. Brezhnevist who succeeded Kosygin as head of government and was retired under Gorbachev.

Trotsky, Leon D. (1879–1940). Politburo member, foreign and war commissar. The most capable of Lenin's associates but a polarizing figure who alarmed new

Soviet elites. Exiled from the USSR in 1929 and killed in 1940 by a Stalinist agent in Mexico.

Ustinov, Dmitri F. (1908–1984). Politburo member and defense minister. A technologist who reportedly pressed for the 1979 invasion of Afghanistan.

Voroshilov, Kliment Ye. (1881–1969). Politburo member and defense commissar. Stalin crony since the Civil War. Opposed Khrushchev's innovations but was kept at the top to disguise the breadth of neo-Stalinist resistance.

Voznesensky, Nikolai A. (1903–1950). Politburo member and deputy premier. Rumored to have been Stalin's choice for successor as premier and assumed to have clashed with Beria over investment policy. Repressed under Stalin and rehabilitated under Khrushchev.

Yakovlev, Aleksandr N. (1923–2005). Politburo member and party secretary. In Brezhnev's time was downgraded for criticism of Great Russian nationalism and later acclaimed as "godfather of glasnost."

Yeltsin, Boris N. (1931–2007). Party secretary and Russian president. Campaigned against bureaucratic privilege during perestroika. Conspired with the leaders of Ukraine and Belorussia to terminate the USSR.

Yezhov, Nikolai I. (1895–1940). Party secretary and NKVD chief. Originally a member of Stalin's personal cabinet, he orchestrated the worst purge in Russian history during 1937. Secretly tried and shot.

Zhdanov, Andrei A. (1896–1948). Politburo member and party secretary. Early advocate of the Hitler-Stalin pact and scourge of free-thinking intellectuals. Reportedly suffered heart failure after losing the special trust of Stalin.

Zhukov, Georgi K. (1896–1974). Politburo member and defense minister. Designed the greatest victories of the Red Army in World War II. Downgraded by Stalin and later allied with Khrushchev. Dismissed from all high posts in 1957.

Zinoviev, Grigori Ye. (1883–1936). Politburo member and Leningrad party head. One of Lenin's closest aides and a left-wing rival of Stalin in the 1920s. Tried for anti–Soviet activity and shot. Rehabilitated under Gorbachev.

Chapter Notes

Preface

1. William G. Hyland, "Brezhnev and Beyond," *Foreign Affairs*, Fall 1979. Reprinted by permission of FOREIGN AFFAIRS (Fall 1979). Copyright (1979) by the Council on Foreign Relations, Inc., www.Foreign Affairs.org.

2. Paul Kennedy, *The Rise and Fall of the Great Power: Economic Change and Military Conflict from 1500 to 2000* (New York: Random House, 1987).

3. Michael Ellman and Vladimir Kontorovich, eds., *The Destruction of the Soviet Economic System: An Insiders' History* (Armonk, NY: M. E. Sharpe, 1998).

Chapter 1

1. John Lewis Gaddis, *The Cold War: A New History* (New York: Penguin, 2005).

2. Good accounts of the tsarist order are Part One, "The Agony of the Old Regime," in Richard Pipes, *The Russian Revolution* (New York: Knopf, 1990); and Part One, "Russia Under the Old Regime," and Part Two, "The Crisis of Authority (1891–1917)," in Orlando Figes, *A People's Tragedy: A History of the Russian Revolution* (New York: Viking, 1997). An admirable scholarly work is Hugh Seton-Watson, *The Russian Empire 1801–1917* (New York: Oxford University Press, 1990). An original study of the Westernizing *zemstvo*, or provincial self-government, movement is Roberta T. Manning, *The Crisis of the Old Order in Russia: Gentry and Government* (Princeton, NJ: Princeton University Press, 1982). Valuable analytical essays are in Anna Geifman, ed., *Russia under the Last Tsar: Opposition and Subversion 1894–1917* (Oxford: Blackwell, 1999). A vivid account of the interplay of Russian domestic and foreign politics during the First World War is I. V. Alekseyeva, *Agoniya serdechnogo soglasiya: Tsarizm, burzhuaziya i ikh soyuzniki po Antante 1914–1917* [The Agony of the Entente Cordiale. Tsarism, Bourgeoisie and their Entente allies 1914–1917] (Leningrad: Lenizdat, 1990). The essentials of eastern front warfare 1914–1918 are in Martin Gilbert, *The First World War: A Complete History* (New York: Henry Holt, 1994); and Hew Strachan, *The First World War* (New York: Viking, 2004). Useful translations of Russian documents are on the website of the School of History of the University of East Anglia, Norwich: uea.ac.uk/his/webcours/russia/.

3. Yuri Got'e, *Time of Troubles: The Diary of Iurii Vladimirovich Got'e. Moscow. July 8, 1917 to July 23, 1922*, trans., ed. and Introduced by Terence Emmons (Princeton, NJ: Princeton University Press, 1988)

4. Geifman, 1999.

5. Michael Hughes, *Inside the Enigma. British Officials in Russia, 1900–1939* (London: Hambledon, 1997).

6. Donald Mackenzie Wallace, *Russia on the Eve of War and Revolution* (New York: Vintage, 1961).

7. Hughes, 1997.

8. Biographical information from Dmitri Volkogonov, *Trotsky: The Eternal Revolutionary*, trans. Harold Shukman (New York: Free Press, 1996).

9. Joseph C. Grew, *Turbulent Era: A Diplomatic Record of Forty Years: 1904–1945*, Vol. I, ed. Walter Johnson, assisted by Nancy Harrison Hooker (Boston: Houghton Mifflin, 1952).

10. Document posted at uea.ac.uk/his/webcours/russia/.

11. The following biographical sketch of

Lenin and early Bolshevism is based on Robert V. Daniels, *The Conscience of the Revolution: Communist Opposition in Soviet Russia* (Cambridge, MA: Harvard University Press, 1965), Richard Pipes, *Russia Under the Old Regime* (Harmondsworth: Penguin, 1990); and Dmitri Volkogonov, *Lenin: A New Biography*, trans. and ed. Harold Shukman (New York: Free Press, 1994).

12. Informative on Stalin's pre-revolutionary years are Anton Antonov-Ovseyenko, *The Time of Stalin: Portrait of a Tyranny*, trans. George Saunders with an Introduction by Stephen F. Cohen (New York: Harper and Row, 1981); and Volkogonov, 1991.

13. Fitzroy Maclean, *Eastern Approaches* (Oxford: Jonathon Cape and the Book Society, 1949).

14. The report is posted on the website of the International "Democracy" Foundation in Moscow: www.idf.ru.

15. Hughes, 1997.

16. *Ibid.*

17. Got'e, 1988.

18. Edward Acton and Tom Stableford, *The Soviet Union: A Documentary History*, Vol. I, 1917–1940 (Exeter: University of Exeter, 2005).

19. John W. Wheeler-Bennett, *Brest-Litovsk: The Forgotten Peace: March 1918* (New York: Macmillan, 1963).

20. Document posted at uea.ac.uk/his/webcours/russia/.

Chapter 2

1. The views of both schools are examined in Giuseppe Boffa, *The Stalin Phenomenon*, trans. Nicholas Fersen (Ithaca and London: Cornell University Press, 1992).

2. Arsen B. Martirosyan, *Stalin posle voyny, 1945–1953 gody* [Stalin after the War, 1945–1953] (Moscow: "Veche," 2007).

3. S. V. Volkov, "Kakiye lyudi pravili SSSR?" [What Kind of People Ruled the USSR?] (2007), available at www.contr-tv.ru.

4. Richard Pipes, *Russia Under the Bolshevik Regime* (New York: Knopf, 1993).

5. Acton and Stableford, 2005.

6. Documents on the Georgian controversy are in Acton and Stableford, 2005.

7. Daniels, 1965, and Figes, 1997.

8. V. I. Lenin, *Polnoye sobraniya sochineniy: Tom 45: Mart 1922–Mart 1923* (Moscow: Politizdat, 1964).

9. Daniels, 1965.

10. Sergei Khruschev, ed., *Memoirs of Nikita Khrushchev: Commissar*, Vol. 1, trans. George Shriver, supplementary material trans. Stephen Shenfield (University Park, PA: Pennsylvania State University Press, 2004).

11. Daniels, 1965.

12. Zhirnov, 1989.

13. Nikolai I. Bukharin, *Izbrannye proizvedeniya* [Selected Works] (Moscow: Politizdat, 1988).

14. *Stenogrammy zasedaniy Politbyuro TsK RKP (b)-VKP (b). 1923–1939 gg. V trekh tomakh* [Stenograms of the TsK RKP (b)-VKP (b) Politburo Meetings. 1923–1938. In three volumes], advisory Board: K. M. Anderson, P. Gregory, O. V. Khlevniuk, A. K. Sorokin, R. Sousa, A. Yu. Vatlin (Moscow: Rosspen, 2007). Hereafter referred to as *SZP*.

15. Daniels 1965 and Acton and Stableford 2005.

16. *SZP* 2007.

17. *Ibid.*

18. *Ibid.*

19. *Kommunist*, No. 5, 1990.

20. Yuri Yemelyanov, *Stalin: Put k vlasti* [Stalin: The Road to Power] (Moscow: "Veche," 2007).

21. *SZP*, 2007.

22. Acton and Stableford, 2005.

23. See Martin Malia, *The Soviet Tragedy: A History of Socialism in Russia, 1917–1991* (New York: Free Press, 1994).

24. www.echo.msk.ru.

25. Daniels, 1965.

26. Stephen F. Cohen's *Bukharin and the Bolshevik Revolution* (London: Wildwood House, 1974) is the best account of the subject.

27. Daniels, 1965.

Chapter 3

1. *SZP*, 2007.

2. Cf. Andrei Sorokin at www.echo.msk.ru/557577 and Robert Conquest, *The Harvest of Sorrow: Soviet Collectivization and The Terror Famine* (New York: Oxford University Press, 1986).

3. Valentin M. Berezhkov, *At Stalin's Side: His Interpreter's Memoirs From the October Revolution to the Fall of the Dictator's Empire*, trans. Sergei V. Mikheyev (New York: Carol, 1994).

4. *SZP*, 2007.

5. Lars T. Lin et al., *Stalin's Letters to Molo-*

tou, 1925–1936 (New Haven and London: Yale University Press, 1995); and *SZP,* 2007.

6. Boris Nicolaevsky, *Power and the Soviet Elite: "The Letter of an Old Bolshevik" and Other Essays,* ed. Janet D. Zagoria (New York: Praeger, 1965); and Acton and Stableford, 2005.

7. Volkogonov, 1991.

8. Antonov-Ovseyenko, 1981, and Nicolaevsky, 1965.

9. Antonov-Ovseyenko, 1981, Daniels, 1965, and *SZP,* 2007.

10. *SZP,* 2007.

11. Nicolaevsky, 1965, and Yuri Zhukov, *Inoy Stalin. Politicheskiye reformy v SSSR v 1933–1937* [A Different Stalin. Political Reforms in the USSR in 1933–1937] (Moscow: Vagrius, 2003).

12. Anastas I. Mikoyan, *Tak bylo. Razmyshleniya o menuvshem* [So It Was. Reflections about the Past] (Moscow: Vagrius, 1999).

13. Khrushchev, 2004.

14. Zhukov, 2003.

15. *Rossiyskaya gazeta,* October 27, 1995.

16. Zhukov, 2003.

17. Leonid A. Naumov, *Stalin i NKVD* [Stalin and the NKVD] (Moscow: "Eksmo," 2007).

18. David Mayers, *The Ambassadors and America's Soviet Policy* (New York: Oxford University Press, 1995).

19. Hughes, 1997.

20. Maclean, 1949.

21. *Voyenno-istoricheskii zhurnal,* No. 1, 1993.

22. Mikoyan, 1999.

23. *Ibid.*

24. See the interview with Zemskov at www.contr-tv.ru.

25. Unusual biographical information on Beria is in Zhukov, *Stalin: tayny vlasti* [Stalin: Secrets of Power] (Moscow: Vagrius, 2005); and Mikoyan, 1999.

26. Volkov, 2007.

27. Medvedev, 1983, and Zhukov, 2005.

28. Biographical material on Khrushchev is in *Bolshaya sovetskaya entsiklopediya,* Vol. 46, Moscow: Politizdat, 1957; *SZP,* 2007; and the posting at www.x-libri.ru.

29. John Erickson, *The Road to Berlin: Stalin's War with Germany, Volume Two* (New Haven and London: Yale University Press, 1999).

30. Zhukov, 2005.

31. This report is posted on the Moscow website of the International "Democracy" Foundation: www.idf.ru.

32. Edward Acton and Tom Stableford, eds., *The Soviet Union: A Documentary History,* Vol. II, 1939–1991 (Exeter: University of Exeter, 2007).

33. *Ibid.*

34. Cf. Herbert P. Bix's *Hirohito and the Making of Modern Japan* (New York: HarperCollins, 2000); and Gaddis' *The Cold War: A New History.*

35. Yelena Zubkova, *Russia After the War: Hopes, Illusions, and Disappointments, 1945–1957,* trans. and ed. Hugh Ragsdale (New York: M. E. Sharpe, 1998).

36. *Ibid.*

37. Yuri Aksenov and Yelena Zubkova, "Predvestiye peremen. Letopis Desyatiletiy: 1947–1956" [Herald of Changes. Annals of a Decade: 1947–1956], *Literaturnaya gazeta,* June 14, 1989.

38. Zubkova, 1998.

39. The Varga controversy is discussed in the works of Robert Conquest and Leonard Schapiro.

40. Anton Antonov-Ovseyenko, "Beria," *Yunost,* No. 12, 1988.

41. See the "Caesar Papers" posted at www.foia.cia.gov.cpe.

42. Amir Weiner, *Making Sense of War: The Second World War and the Fate of the Bolshevik Revolution* (Princeton, NJ: Princeton University Press, 2001).

43. Pikhoya, (1995[a]) and Nikolai Krementsov, *Stalinist Science* (Princeton, NJ: Princeton University Press, 1997).

44. *Kommunist,* No. 13, 1990.

45. *Moskovskaya pravda,* August 15, 1990.

46. Zhukov, 2005.

47. Volkogonov, 1994.

48. Zhukov, 2005.

49. *Voprosy istorii KPSS,* No. 7, 1990.

50. *Prezidium TsK KPSS, 1954–1964. Osnovnye protokolnye zapisi zasedaniy. Stenogrammy. Postanovleniya. T. 1: Chernoviye protokolnye zapisi. Stenogrammy/ Gl. Red. A. A. Fursenko — 2-e isp. i dop* [CC CPSU Presidium. 1954–1964. Rough Notes of the Sessions, Minutes, Decrees, Vol. 1: Rough Notes. Stemographic Records. ed.-in- chief A. A. Fursenko — 2nd ed., corrected and supplemented] (Moscow: Rosspen, 2004).

51. V. A. Kutuzov, "Tak nazyvayemoye 'Leningradskoye delo'" [The So-Called "Len-

ingrad Case"], *Voprosy istorii KPSS*, No. 3 (1989); and Zhukov, 2005.

52. Zhukov, 2005

53. *Ibid.*

54. *Ibid.*

55. Crankshaw, 1948.

56. Weiner, 2001, and Aleksandr N. Yakovlev, *A Century of Violence in Soviet Russia*, foreword by Paul Hollander and trans. Anthony Austin (New Haven and London: Yale University Press, 2002).

57. Anatoli Ponomarev, *N. S, Khrushchev: Put' k Liderstvu* [N. S. Khrushchev: The Path to Highest Leadership] (Moscow: "Znaniye," 1990).

58. Mikoyan, 1999.

59. *Ibid.*

60. Rudolf K. Balandin, *Malenkov. Tretiy vozhd strany Sovetov* [Malenkov. Third Leader of the Land of Soviets] (Moscow: "Veche," 2007).

61. *Pravda*, January 30, 1953.

62. Zhukov, 2005.

63. See the citation of a book by former central party official K. N. Brutents in Martirosyan, 2007.

64. Moscow website APN.ru, May 5, 2007.

Chapter 4

1. G. W. Breslauer mistakenly saw "a post–Stalin consensus within the political establishment ... a broadly shared elite consensus to manage ... conflicting imperatives and ... to keep conflict within bounds by removing the most divisive items from the policy agenda," according to John L. H. Keep, *Last of the Empires: A History of the Soviet Union 1945–1991* (New York: Oxford University Press, 1995).

2. Zhukov, 2005.

3. *Ibid.*

4. *Ogonyok*, No. 33, 1993.

5. Zhirnov, 1989.

6. The CPSU Central Committee decree of April 3, 1953, "On Falsification of the So-Called Doctor-Wreckers Case," is posted on the Moscow website of the International "Democracy" Foundation: www.idf.ru.

7. Boris Starkov, "Koye-chto novenkoye o Berii" [Something New About Beria], *Argumenty i fakty*, No. 46 (683) (November 1993); and D. M. Stickle, ed., *The Beria Affair: The Secret Transcripts of the Meetings Signalling the End of Stalinism*, trans. Jeanne Farrow (Commack, NY: Nova Science, 1992).

8. Zhukov, 2005.

9. Starkov, 1993 and Pikhoya, (1995).

10. *Molotov, Malenkov, Kaganovich. 1957. Stenogramma iyunskogo plenuma TsK KPSS i drugiye dokumenty* [Molotov, Malenkov, Kaganovich. 1957. Minutes of the June Plenum CC CPSU and Other Documents] (Moscow: "Demokratiya," 1998).

11. Zhirnov, 1989.

12. *Stenogramma VII zakrytogo plenuma Tsentral'nogo Komiteta KP Latvii ot 7–8 iyulya 1959 goda* [Transcript of the 7th Closed Plenum of the Central Committee CP Latvia, July 7–8, 1959], *Kommunist sovetskoy Latvii*, No. 2 (1989).

13. *Partiynoye slovo* (Tbilisi), No. 17–18, 1990.

14. Mikoyan, 1999.

15. *Molotov, Malenkov, Kaganvich*, 1998.

16. Pavel and Anatoli Sudoplatov, *Special Tasks: The Memoirs of an Unwanted Witness, A Soviet Spymaster* (Boston: Little, Brown, 1994).

17. Victor Baras, "Beria's Fall and Ulbricht's Survival," *Soviet Studies*, Vol. 27, No. 3 (July 1975).

18. Fyodor Burlatsky, "Khrushchev: Sketches for a Political Portrait," *Literaturnaya gazeta*, February 24, 1988 (FBIS-SOV-88-037).

19. Antonov-Ovseyenko, 1988, N. A. Barsukov, "Stranitsy istorii KPSS. Na puti k XX s"ezdu" (On the road to the 20th Congress) [Pages of CPSU History], *Pravda*, November 10, 1989; and Roy Medvedev, *Nikita Khrushchev* (Moscow: "Eksmo," 2006).

20. Antonov-Ovseyenko, 1988, Andrei Sakharov in *Znamya*, No. 12, 1990; and N. A. Barsukov, "Stranitsy istorii KPSS. Yeshcho vperedi XX s"ezd" [Pages of CPSU History. The 20th Congress Lay Ahead], *Pravda*, November 17, 1989.

21. Stickle, 1992.

22. Zhukov, 2005.

23. Stickle, 1992.

24. *Ibid.*

25. *Ibid.*

26. Burlatsky, 1988.

27. Pikhoya, (1995).

28. Boffa, *Inside the Khrushchev Era*, trans. Carl Marzani (London: George Allen and Unwin, 1960).

29. Balandin, 2007.

30. Zhukov, 2005.

31. *Ibid.*

32. A good account of this development is found in Mary McCauley, *Khrushchev and the*

Development of Soviet Agriculture: The Virgin Lands Programme 1954–1964, London: Macmillan, 1976.

33. Zhukov, 2005.

34. Barsukov, November 17, 1989.

35. *Prezidium TsK KPSS, Tom 2. Postanovleniya. 1954–1958. Glavnyy redaktor A. A. Fursenko* [Vol. 2. Decrees: 1954–1958. Editor-in-chief A. A Fursenko] (Moscow: Rosspen, 2006).

36. *Ibid.*

37. *Prezidium TsK KPSS*, 2004, and Mikoyan, 1999.

38. *Prezidium TsK KPSS*, 2004.

39. Medvedev, 1983; Nicolaevsky, 1965; and Barsukov, November 17, 1989.

40. *Prezidium TsK KPSS*, 2004.

41. N. A. Barsukov, "Khrushchevskiye vremena: Neprinuzhdennye besedy s politicheskimi deyatelyami 'velikogo desyatiletiya'" [The Khrushchev Times: Informal Chats with Political Figures of "The Great Decade"], *Neizvestnaya Rossiya, XX vek* (Moscow, 1992).

42. *Prezidium TsK KPSS*, 2004.

43. *Ibid.*

44. Zarya Serebryakova, "Ottepel, zamorozki, ottepel ..." [Thaw, Frost, Thaw], *Nezavisimaya gazeta*, February 24, 1996.

45. RFE/RL Newsline, February 15, 2006, posted to the website: www.rfel.org.

46. Veliko Micunovic, *Moscow Diary*, trans. David Floyd, Introduction by George Kennan (New York: Doubleday, 1980).

47. *Ibid.*

48. *Prezidium TsK KPSS*, 2004.

49. *Ibid.*

50. *Ibid.*

51. *Prezidium TsK KPSS*, 2004.

52. Myron Rush, *The Rise of Khrushchev* (Washington, DC: Public Affairs Press, 1958).

53. *Prezidium TsK KPSS*, 2004.

54. *Ibid.*

55. *Ibid.*

56. Mikhailov's reports are posted to the Moscow website of the International "Democracy" Foundation: www.idf.ru.

57. *Litraturnaya gazeta*, June 14, 1989.

58. Micunovic, 1980.

59. *Ibid.*

60. *Prezidium TsK KPSS*, 2004.

61. Micunovic, 1980.

62. *Prezidium TsK KPSS*, 2004.

63. *Ibid.*

64. *Ibid.*

65. An unedited verbatim record of the June Plenum is *Molotov, Malenkov, Kaganovich*, 1998. Unverified reports and highlights are in Barsukov, "Proval 'Antipartiynoy Gruppy.' Iyunskiy plenum TsK KPSS" [Collapse of the "Anti-Party Group." CPSU Central Committee Plenum of June 1957], *Kommunist*, No. 8. (1990); Dmitri Kosyrev, "... i primkhnuvshiy k nim Shepilov" [... and Shepilov Who Joined Them], *Rossiyskaya gazata*, September 1, 1995; Pikhoya, (1995); P. A. Rodionov, "Kak nachinalsya zastoy?: Zametki istorika partii" [How Did the Stagnation Begin? Notes of a Party Historian], *Znamya*, No. 8 (1989); Volkogonov, 1994; Yakovlev, 2002; and Balandin, 2007.

66. Oleg Troyanovsky, *Cherez gody i rasstoyaniya. Istoriya odnoi semi* [Across Time and Space: The Story of One Family] (Moscow: Vagrius, 1997).

67. Keep *op cit.* relies on an article by Canadian scholar T. J. Colton.

68. *Memoirs of Nikita Khrushchev. Reformer*, Vol. 2, ed. Sergei Khrushchev, trans. George Shriver, supplementary material trans. Stephen Shenfield (University Park, PA: Pennsylvania State University Press, 2006).

69. Pikhoya, (1995).

70. *Prezidium TsK KPSS*, 2004.

71. *Ibid.*

72. *Ibid.*

73. Micunovic, 1980, and *Prezidium TsK KPSS*, 2004.

74. *Prezidium TsK KPSS*, 2004.

75. Micunovic, 1980.

76. *Stenogramma*, 1989.

77. *Prezidium TsK KPSS*, 2004.

78. *Ibid.* and *Prezidium TsK KPSS, Tom 3. Postanovleniya 1959–1964. Glavnyy redaktor A. A. Fursenko* [Vol. 3. Decrees. 1959–1964. editor-in-chief A. A. Fursenko] (Moscow: Rosspen, 2008).

79. *Ibid.*

80. *Ibid.*

81. See CIA Staff Study. "Unorthodox Ideas in the USSR," June 27, 1963, available at www.foia.cia.gov/cpe.

82. *Prezidium TsK KPSS*, 2004.

83. *Prezidium TsK KPSS*, 2008.

84. *Ibid.*

85. izvestia.com/history.

86. Yu Aksyutin, "Khrushchev, god 1964-y" [Khrushchev and 1964], *Trud*, November 26, 1989; Aleksey Osipov, *Krakh administrativno-*

komandnoy sistemy [Crash of the Administrative-Command System] (Moscow: "Znaniye," 1990); and Rodionov, 1989.

87. Osipov, 1990.

88. *Pravda*, August 11, 1964; M. Lemeshev, *Ekonomicheskaya gazeta*, September 26, 1964; and A. Goltsev, *Kommunist*, No. 14, 1964.

89. Sergey Khrushchev, "Pensioner of All-Union Importance," *Ogonyok*, No. 40 (October 1–8, 1988), No. 41 (October 8–15, 1988), No. 42 (October 15–22, 1988), and No. 43 (October 22–29, 1988) (FBIS- SOV- 8- 236, 237, 238 and 240); A. Druzensko, "Oktyabr, Oktyabr, perevorotnyi mesyats. Ob odnom iz 'istoricheskikh' Plenumov TsK, sluzhivshikhsya 30 let nazad, s Radey Nikitichnoy Adzhubey beseduyet Anatoly Druzenko" [October, October, a Month of Turning Points. Anatoly Druzenko Talks with Rada Nikitichna Adzhubey about One of the "Historic" Central Committee Plenums], *Izvestiya*, October 13, 1994; and Mikoyan, 1999.

90. Barsukov, 1992.

91. Osipov, 1990.

92. Ponomarev, "Intrigi i repressii po pravilam igry" [Intrigues and Repressions According to Rules of the Game], *Rossiyskaya gazeta*, July 29, 1995.

93. V. Ye. Semichastny, Interview conducted by *Argumenty i fakty*, No. 20 (May 20–26, 1989) (FBIS-SOV- 89–100); Mikoyan, 1999; and *Prezidium TsK KPSS*, 2008.

94. Medvedev, 1983.

Chapter 5

1. *Pravda*, October 20, 1964.

2. See the annual publication of the U.S. Defense Department: *Soviet Military Power*.

3. V. Stepanov, *Izvestiya*, December 19, 1962.

4. *Pravda*, October 25 and 29, November 1 and 5, and December 2, 1964; and *Izvestiya*, November 19, 1964.

5. *Pravda*, November 17 and 18, December 6 and 23, 1964; and *Partiynaya zhizn*, No. 24, 1964.

6. Georgi Arbatov, *The System: An Insider's Life in Soviet Politics* (New York: Times Books, 1992); and Anatoli Dobrynin, *In Confidence: Moscow's Ambassador to America's Six Cold War Presidents* (New York: Times Books, 1995).

7. Troyanovsky, 1997.

8. *Ekonomicheskaya gazeta*, April 21, 1965.

9. Osipov, 1990.

10. *Pravda*, September 28, 1965.

11. P. T. Vasilenkov, *Organy sovetskogo gosudarstva i ikh sistema na sovremennom etape* (Moscow: Politizdat, 1967). The all-union type of ministry operated enterprises from a single agency in Moscow. The union-republic type had a USSR-level ministry in Moscow and like-named subordinate ministries in several or all of the 15 union republics.

12. Yevgeni Primakov, *Russian Crossroads: Toward the New Millennium*, trans. Felix Rosenthal (New Haven and London: Yale University Press, 2004).

13. *Pravda*, November 6 and 7, 1964; and *Sovetskaya Rossiya*, November 14, 1964.

14. *Plenum TsK KPSS, 24–26 marta 1965 goda, Stenograficheskii otchyot* (Moscow: Politizdat, 1965).

15. See party-state decree of May 16, 1966, in *Spravochnik partiynogo rabotnika* (7th ed.) (Moscow: Politizdat, 1967).

16. *XXIII s"ezd KPSS 29 marta-8 aprelya 1966 goda, stenograficheskii otchyot*, Vols. I and II (Moscow: Politizdat, 1966).

17. *Pravda*, June 25, 1967.

18. *Frankfurter Allgemeine Zeitung*, July 8, 1967.

19. *Pravda*, December 21, 1969.

20. *Memoirs of Nikita Khrushchev. Statesman*, Vol. 3, ed. Sergei Khrushchev, trans. George Shriver, supplementary material trans. Stephen Shenfield (University Park, PA: Pennsylvania State University Press, 2007).

21. *Pravda*, July 29, 1966.

22. *Kommunist*, No. 15, 1967.

23. Medvedev, 1983.

24. Leonid Pleshakov, "Appointed Ambassador ..." (interview with Nikolay Grigoryevich Yegorychev), *Ogonyok*, No. 6 (February 4–11, 1989) (JPRS-UPA-89–023).

25. *Ibid.*

26. *Ibid.*

27. Rudolf G. Pikhoya, *Moskva. Kreml. Vlast. Dve istorii odnoy strany. Rossiya na izlome tysyacheletiy, 1985–2005* [Moscow. Kremlin. Power. Two Histories of One Country. Russia at the Turn of a Century, 1985–2005]. (Moscow: Rus-Olimp, AST, Astrel, 2007).

28. Mayers, 1995.

29. Intelligence Report, "Brezhnev's Struggle for Dominance," December 5, 1969, available at www.foia.cia.gov/cpe/asp.

30. Robert A. D. Ford, *Our Man in Moscow:*

A Diplomat's Reflections on the Soviet Union
(Toronto: University of Toronto, 1989).

31. Rodionov, 1989, and Ford, 1989.

32. Arbatov, 1992.

33. Dobrynin, 1995.

34. Roy Medvedev, "L. I. Brezhnev: Nabrosok politicheskogo portreta" [L. I. Brezhnev: Sketch for a Political Portrait], *Rabochiy klass i sovremennyy mir*, No. 6 (1988).

35. *Ibid.*

36. *Pravda*, April 14, 15, 17 and 22, 1970.

37. Volkogonov 1994.

38. R. Lynev, "Ot ottepeli do zastoia. Beseda s personal'nym pensionerom, byvshim chlenom Politbyuro Ts KPSS" [From Thaw to Stagnation. Talk with Special Pensioner, Former Member of the CPSU CC Politburo (G. I. Voronov)], *Izvestiya*, November 18, 1988; and G. I. Voronov, "Nemnogo vospominaniy" [A Few Recollections], *Druzhba narodov*, No. 1 (1988). See, too, the article by *Izvestiya* observer Anatoly Ivashchenko in *Chelovek i zakon*, No. 3 (1978).

39. Voronov, 1988.

40. *Ibid.*

41. Dobrynin, 1995.

42. *Ibid.*

43. Yakovlev, 2002.

44. V. Golovachev, "What Is to Be Done About Prices?" (interview with USSR Finance Minister V. Pavlov), *Trud*, July 26, 1990 (FBIS-SOV-90-149); and V. Romanenko and A. Binev, "An Unknown Prime Minister" (interview with Academician D. Gvishiani), *Argumenty i fakty*, No. 46 (1990) (FBIS-SOV-90-227).

45. Ye. I. Chazov, *Klinicheskiye razbory po kardiologii* (Clinical Battles Over Cardiology). (Moskva: Medicina, 1995).

46. T. Zamyatina, "So mnoy sovetovalis chetyre genseka" [Four General Secretaries Consulted Me), *Argumenty i fakty*, No. 20 (657) (May 1993).

47. Boris Yeltsin, *Against the Grain: An Autobiography*, trans. Michael Glenny (New York: Summit, 1990).

48. *Encounter*, London, November 1980. A different view, holding that Communist ideology was powerful until Gorbachev's policy of openness, is in David Satter, *Age of Delirium: The Decline and Fall of the Soviet Union* (New Haven: Yale University Press, 2001).

49. Anatoli S. Chernyaev, *My Six Years with Gorbachev*, trans. and ed. Robert D. English and Elizabeth Tucker (University Park, PA: Pennsylvania State University Press, 2000).

50. Abel Aganbegyan, *Inside Perestroika: The Future of the Soviet Economy* (New York: Harper and Row, 1989).

51. Rodionov, 1989.

52. See "2 Scandals Have All Moscow Abuzz," *New York Times*, February 27, 1982; and "Soviets Said to Arrest, Fire Officials in Scandal," *Washington Post*, February 27, 1982.

53. *Pravda*, March 13, May 12 and 28, and June 3 and 16, 1982.

54. *Kommunist*, No. 6, 1982.

55. *Voprosy istorii KPSS*, No. 2, 1982.

56. Osipov, 1990.

57. *Ibid.*

58. Dobrynin, 1995.

59. Rodionov, 1989.

60. Chernyaev, 2000.

61. *Pravda*, November 13, 1982.

62. Roy Medvedev and Giuletto Chiesa, *Time of Change: An Insider's View of Russia's Transformation*, trans. Michael Moore (New York: Pantheon, 1989).

63. V. Pechenev, "Tretya Programma KPSS: uroki nedavney istorii. Iz vospominaniy byvshego pomoshchnika Generalnogo sekretarya TsK KPSS" [Third CPSU Program: Lessons of Recent History. From the Reminiscences of a Former Assistant of the CC CPSU General Secretary], *Ogonyok*, No. 23 (1990).

64. Moshe Lewin, *The Soviet Century*, ed. Gregory Elliott (New York: Verso, 2005).

65. Volkogonov, 1994.

66. *Ibid.*

67. V. Pechenev, *Gorbachev: k vershinam vlasti. Iz teoretiko-memornykh razmyshlenii* [Gorbachev: To the Heights of Power. Reflections of a Theoretical and Memoir Character] (Moscow: Vagrius, 1991).

68. Chernyaev, 2000.

69. Osipov, 1990.

70. "At the Level of Demands of Developed Socialism. Some Topical Problems of CPSU Theory, Strategy and Tactics," *Kommunist*, No. 13 (1984).

71. Deutscher, 1965.

72. Medvedev and Chiesa, 1989.

73. Pechenev, 1991.

74. Chernyayev, 2000, and Pikhoya, 2007.

Chapter 6

1. Keep, *op. cit.*

2. Mayers, 1995.

3. Arbatov, 1992.

4. Ford, 1989.
5. Pikhoya, 2007.
6. Volkhov, 2007.
7. Pikhoya, 2007.
8. Chernyaev, 2000.
9. Pikhoya, 2007
10. *V Politbyuro TsK KPSS. Po zapisyam Anatoliya Chernyayeva, Vadima Medvedeva, Georgiya Shakhnazarova (1985–1991). Sost. A. Chernyayeva (ruk. proyekta). A. Veber, V. Medvedeva. Izdaniye 2-e, ispravleniye i dopolnennoye* [At the CPSU Central Committee Politburo. Based on the Notes of Anatoli Chernyayev, Vadim Medvedev and Georgi Shakhnazarov (1985–1991). Compilers A. Chernyayev (Project Leader). A. Veber, V. Medvedev. Second Edition. Revised and Supplemented] (Moscow: Gorbachev-Fond, 2008). From this point on cited as *VPB*, 2008.
11. Medvedev and Chiesa, 1989.
12. Rodionov, 1989.
13. Pikhoya, 2007.
14. Yeltsin, 1990. Recollections of Ardayev about Yeltsin in Sverdlovsk were posted on the website BBCRussian.com (April 24, 2007).
15. Chernyaev, 2000.
16. Geoffrey Hosking, *The First Socialist Society: A History of the Soviet Union From Within* (Cambridge, MA: Harvard University Press, 1993).
17. Pikhoya, 2007.
18. Chernyaev, 2000.
19. *VPB*, 2008.
20. *Ibid.*
21. *Pravda*, February 26, 1986.
22. *VPB*, 2008.
23. Medvedev and Chiesa, 1989.
24. *VPB*, 2008.
25. Pikhoya, 2007 and *VPB*, 2008.
26. Chernyaev, 2000.
27. *Ibid.*
28. *VPB*, 2008.
29. *Ibid.*
30. *Ibid.*
31. Chernyaev, 2000.
32. *VPB*, 2008.
33. Chiesa and Medvedev, 1989.
34. *VPB*, 2008.
35. Leon A. Onikov, *KPSS: anatomiya raspada. Vzglyad iznutri apparata TsK* [CPSU: Anatomy of Collapse. View from Inside the Central Committee Machinery] (Moscow: "Respublika," 1996).
36. *VPB*, 2008.

37. *Ibid.*
38. *Ibid.*
39. Eduard Glezin, "Yanvarskaya vesna. Perestroika yest glasnost plyus demokratizatsiya vsyei strany" [Springtime in January. Perestroika Is Openness Plus Democratization of the Whole Country], *Izvestiya*, April 28, 2007.
40. Medvedev and Chiesa, 1989.
41. *Ibid.*
42. *VPB*, 2008.
43. *Ibid.*
44. *Ibid.*
45. Pikhoya, 2007.
46. *Ibid.*
47. Medvedev and Chiesa, 1989.
48. Chernyaev, 2000.
49. *Ibid.*
50. Medvedev and Chiesa, 1989.
51. *VPB*, 2008.
52. Chernyaev, 2000.
53. *VPB*, 2008.
54. *Ibid.*
55. Pikhoya, 2007.
56. *Izvestiya TsK KPSS*, No. 2, 1988.
57. *VPB*, 2008.
58. *Ibid.*
59. *Izvestiya TsK KPSS*, No. 2, 1988.
60. *VPB*, 2008.
61. Pikhoya, 2007.
62. *Ibid.*
63. Chiesa and Medvedev, 1989.
64. Karyakin, 1988.
65. Chernyaev, 2000.
66. Ligachev, 1993.
67. *VPB*, 2008.
68. *Ibid.*
69. *Ibid.*
70. *Ibid.*
71. *Ibid.*
72. Our account of the Kremlin crisis in March–April 1988 is based on Medvedev and Chiesa, 1989; Chernyaev, 2000; and Pikhoya, 2007.

Chapter 7

1. Sergey Khrushchev's memoir is in *Ogonyok*, Nos. 40, 41, 42 and 43 (1988).
2. I. Virabov, "Zemlyak" [Fellow Villager], *Komsomolskaya pravda*, February 17, 1989; and I. Lukin and Ye. Ukhov, "Bronzovye mify" [Bronze Myths], *Trud*, April 5, 1989.
3. Fyodor Burlatsky, "Stalin-Khrushchev-Brezhnev: The Problem of Political Leadership

in Soviet Society," *Obshchestvennyye nauki*, No. 1 (January–February 1989) (FBIS- SOV- 89-041).

4. Aganbegyan, 1989.
5. *VPB*, 2008.
6. *Ibid.*
7. Ligachev, 1993.
8. Yeltsin, 1990.
9. Pikhoya, 2007.
10. Chernyaev, 2000.
11. Yeltsin, 1990.
12. *VPB*, 2008.
13. *Ibid.*
14. *Ibid.*
15. Chernyaev, 2000.
16. Pikhoya, 2007.
17. *Tokyo Shimbun*, March 25, 1989 (FBIS-SOV-89-062).
18. Chernyaev, 2000.
19. Yeltsin, 1990.
20. Chernyaev, 2000, and *VPB*, 2008.
21. Pikhoya, 2007, and *VPB*, 2008.
22. *Ibid.*
23. *Ibid.*
24. *Ibid.*
25. Pikhoya, 2007.
26. A concise overview is Robert L. Hutchings, *American Diplomacy and the End of the Cold War: An Insider's Account of U.S. Policy in Europe, 1989–1992* (Baltimore: Woodrow Wilson Center and Johns Hopkins, 1997).
27. Dobrynin, 1995.
28. *Literaturnaya Rossiya*, December 21, 1990.
29. *VPB*, 2008.
30. *Ibid.*
31. *Ibid.*
32. *Ibid.*
33. *Ibid.*
34. Pikhoya, 2007.
35. Valeri Vyzhutovich, "Sudba idei: O tom, chto oznachayet 'sotsialisticheskiy vybor' v teorii i na praktike" [Fate of an Idea: What the 'Socialist Choice' Means in Theory and Practice] (interview with Dr. of Philosophical Sciences Aleksandr Tsipko), *Moskovskiye novosti*, No. 24 (June 17, 1990). Tsipko's advice came as no surprise to Gorbachev, who met with economists on October 23 and November 1, 1989, and heard proposals for allowing free price-formation, unrestricted sales of housing and the creation of small businesses for conducting internal and foreign trade. Gorbachev concluded that the presentations offered useful "food for thought" (*VPB*, 2008).

36. Chernyaev, 2000.
37. Ligachev, 1993.
38. Pikhoya, 2007.
39. Chernyaev, 2000.
40. Pikhoya, 2007.
41. Ligachev, 1993.
42. Pikhoya, 2007.
43. Chernyaev, 2000, and Hosking, 1993.
44. Chernyaev, 2000.
45. Economist Yegor Gaidar recalls these hard times on the website BBCRussian.com (April 24, 2007).
46. Marq de Villiers, *Down the Volga In a Time of Troubles* (Toronto: HarperCollins, 1991). This vivid work affords unusual insights into popular views of Gorbachev and his reforms.
47. *Ibid.*
48. Chernyaev, 2000.
49. Pikhoya, 2007.
50. *Ibid.*
51. Pikhoya, 2007.
52. *Ibid.*
53. *VPB*, 2008.
54. TASS International Service in Russian, December 28, 1990 (FBIS-SOV-90-250).
55. Yuri Afanasiev, "When the Russian People Wake," *Berlingske Tidende*, December 21, 1990 (FBIS-SOV-90-250).
56. *VPB*, 2008.
57. Chernyaev, 2000.
58. Pikhoya, 2007.
59. *Ibid.*
60. Primakov, 2004.
61. *VPB*, 2008.
62. *Ibid.*
63. The ensuing account of the August 1991 coup and its sequel is based on Gorbachev's *Memoirs* and Russian press accounts.
64. Pikhoya, 2007.
65. *VPB*, 2008.
66. *Ibid.*
67. See, e.g., Pikhoya, 2007.

Epilogue

1. Robert H. Jackson, *That Man: An Insider's Portrait of Franklin D: Roosevelt*, edited and introduced by John Q. Barrett, with a foreword by William E. Leuchtenburg (New York: Oxford University Press, 2003).
2. Nobutaka Ike, *Japan's Decision for War: Records of the 1941 Policy Conferences*, translated, edited, and introduced by Nobutaka Ike (Stanford: Stanford University Press, 1967).

3. Robert S. McNamara with Brian VanDe-Mark, *In Retrospect: The Tragedy and Lessons of Vietnam* (New York; Times Books, 1995).

4. See posting to the website www.kremlin.ru/eng.

5. "Russkaya politicheskaya kultura. Vzglyad na utopia" [Russian Political Culture. A Look at Utopia], June 21, 2007, available at www.edinrus.ru/news.

6. "Ideologiya novoy Rossii" [Ideology of the New Russia], December 20, 2006, available at the Nizhny Novgorod website: www.apn-nn.ru.

Appendix 1

1. Seton-Watson, *op. cit.*

2. *The Fall of the Russian Monarchy, A Study of the Evidence.* New York: Vintage, 1961.

3. Isaac Deutscher, *Stalin: A Political Biography.* New York: Oxford University Press, 1949.

4. Volkogonov, 1991.

5. Politische Studien, January–May 1958.

6. Edward Hallett Carr, *A History of Soviet Russia: Socialism in One Country,* Vol. 1. New York: Penguin, 1996.

7. Alexander Solzhenitsyn, *Cancer Ward.* trans. by Nicholas Bethell and David Burg. New York: Farrar, Straus and Giroux, 1969.

8. Alexander Zinoviev, *Zyyayushchiye vysoty* (The Yawning Heights). Lausanne: L'Age d'homme, 1976.

9. *Voprosy filosofii,* No. 1, 1988

10. *Izvestiya,* Jan. 3, 1991.

11. *Druzhba narodov,* No. 5, 1990.

12. Medvedev, 1983.

13. *Partiynaya zhizn,* No. 10, 1990.

14. *Ten Years in Japan: A Contemporary Record Drawn from the Diaries and Private and Official Papers of Joseph C. Grew, United States Ambassador to Japan 1932–1942.* New York: Simon and Schuster, 1944.

Bibliography

Acton, Edward, and Tom Stableford, eds. (2005). *The Soviet Union: A Documentary History.* Volume I, 1917–1940. Exeter: University of Exeter.

_____ and _____, eds. (2007). *The Soviet Union: A Documentary History.* Volume II, 1939–1991. Exeter: University of Exeter.

Afanasiev, Yuri (1990). "When the Russian People Wake." *Berlingske Tidende,* December 21 (FBIS-SOV-90-250).

Aganbegyan, Abel (1989). *Inside Perestroika: The Future of the Soviet Economy.* Trans. Helen Szamuely. New York: Harper and Row.

Aksenov, Yuri, and Yelena Zubkova (1989). "Predvestiye peremen. Letopis Desyatiletiy: 1947–1956" [Herald of Changes. Annals of a Decade: 1947–1956]. *Literaturnaya gazeta,* June 14.

Aksyutin, Yu (1989). "Khrushchev, god 1964-y" [Khrushchev and 1964]. *Trud,* November 26.

Antonov-Ovseyenko, Anton (1981). *The Time of Stalin: Portrait of a Tyranny,* Trans. George Saunders with an Introduction by Stephen F. Cohen. New York: Harper and Row.

_____. (1988). "Beria." *Yunost,* No. 12.

Arbatov, Georgi (1990). "Iz nedavnogo proshlogo" [From the Recent Past]. *Znamya,* No. 9.

_____. (1992). *The System: An Insider's Life in Soviet Politics.* New York: Times Books.

Babich, Dmitri (September 27, 1995). "An Entire Epoch Died in his Arms. Yevgeni Chazov Set Back the Beginning of *Perestroika* by a Minimum of Five Years" (interview with Yevgeni Chazov, former USSR Minister of Health), *Komsomolskaya pravda* (FBIS- SOV-95).

Balandin, Rudolf K. (2007). *Malenkov. Tretiy vozhd strany Sovetov* [Malenkov. Third Leader of the Land of Soviets]. Moscow: "Veche."

Baras, Victor (1975). "Beria's Fall and Ulbricht's Survival." *Soviet Studies,* Vol. 27, No. 3 (July).

Barsukov, N. A. (1989a). "Stranitsy istorii KPSS. Mart 1953-go" [Pages of CPSU History. March 1953]. *Pravda,* October 27.

_____. (1989b). "Stranitsy istorii KPSS. Yeshcho vperedi XX s"ezd" [Pages of CPSU History. The 20th Congress Lay Ahead]. *Pravda,* November 17.

_____. (1990). "Proval 'Antipartiynoy Gruppy.' Iyunskiy plenum TsK KPSS" [Collapse of the "Anti-Party Group." CPSU Central Committee Plenum of June 1957]. *Kommunist,* No. 8.

_____. (1992). "Khrushchevskiye vremena: Neprinuzhdennye besedy s politicheskimi deyatelyami 'velikogo desyatiletiya'" [The Khrushchev Times: Informal Chats with Political Figures of "The Great Decade"]. *Neizvestnaya Rossiya, XX vek* (Moscow).

_____. (1996). "'Ya byl prichasten k dokladu o kulte lichnosti...' Beseda s D.T. Shepilovym" ["I Had a Hand in the Report on the Personality Cult..." Talk with D.T. Shepilov]. *Ogonyok,* No. 7, Feb.

Bayalinov, K. (1989). "Shtrikhi k politicheskomu portretu. Mayatnik nadezhdy. Pyatnadtsat mesyatsyev Yu. V. Andropova" [Brush-Strokes for a Political Portrait. Pendulum of Hope. The Fifteen Months of Yu. V. Andropov]. *Komsomolskaya pravda*, August 23.

Bazhanov, Boris (1992). *Vospominaniya byvshego sekretarya Stalina* [Memoirs of a Former Secretary of Stalin]. St. Petersburg: Vsemirnoye slovo.

Berezhkov, Valentin M. (1994). *At Stalin's Side: His Interpreter's Memoirs From the October Revolution to the Fall of the Dictator's Empire*. Trans. Sergei V. Mikheyev. New York: Carol.

Bix, Herbert P. (2000). *Hirohito and the Making of Modern Japan*. New York: HarperCollins.

Boffa, Giuseppe (1960). *Inside the Khrushchev Era*. Trans. Carl Marzani. London: George Allen and Unwin.

_____. (1992). *The Stalin Phenomenon*. Trans. Nicholas Fersen. Ithaca and London: Cornell University Press.

Bogoslavskiy, S. (1991). "Kremlevskiye tayny. Verkh po lesnitse, vedushchey vniz" [Kremlin Secrets. Up a Ladder Which Leads Downward]. *Literaturnaya gazeta*, January 30.

Bolshaya sovetskaya entsiklopediya. Vol. 46. Moscow: Politizdat, 1957.

Bukharin, Nikolai I. (1926). *Partiya i oppozitsionnyy blok* [The Party and the Opposition Bloc]. Moscow-Leningrad: Gosudarstvennoye Izdatelstvo.

_____. (1988). *Izbrannye proizvedeniya* [Selected Works]. Moscow: Politizdat.

Burlatsky, Fyodor (1988). "Khrushchev: Sketches for a Political Portrait." *Literaturnaya gazeta*, February 24 (FBIS-SOV-88–037).

_____. (1989). "Stalin-Khrushchev-Brezhnev: The Problem of Political Leadership in Soviet Society." *Obshchestvennyye nauki*, No. 1 (January–February) (FBIS- SOV- 89–041).

_____. (1991). *Khrushchev and the First Russian Spring: The Era of Khrushchev through the Eyes of His Advisor*. New York: Macmillan.

Chazov, Ye. I. (1995). *Klinicheskiye razbory po kardiologii* [Clinical Battles Over Cardiology]. Moskva: Medicina.

Chernov, Vladimir (1995). "Posledniy narkom velikoy imperii" [Last People's Commissar of a Great Empire]. *Ogonyok*, No. 48 (November).

Chernyaev, Anatoli S. (2000). *My Six Years with Gorbachev*. Trans. and ed. Robert D. English and Elizabeth Tucker. University Park, PA: Pennsylvania State University Press.

CIA Staff Study (1963). "Unorthodox Ideas in the USSR." June 27. Available at www. foia.cia.gov/cpe.

Crankshaw, Edward (1948). *Russia and the Russians*. New York: Viking.

_____. (1951). *Cracks in the Kremlin Wall*. New York: Viking.

Daniels, Robert V. (1965). *The Conscience of the Revolution: Communist Opposition in Soviet Russia*. Cambridge, MA: Harvard University Press.

Davies, Sarah, and James Harris, eds. (2005). *Stalin. A New History*. New York: Cambridge.

Deutscher, Isaac (1965). "The Failure of Khrushchevism." *The Socialist Register*. Available at socialistregister.com.

_____. (1965). "Moscow: The Quiet Men. 1. Constellations of Lobbies." *The Nation*, April 5.

de Villiers, Marq (1991). *Down the Volga In a Time of Troubles*. Toronto: HarperCollins.

Dmitriyevsky, Sergei I. (2003). *Stalin. Predtecha natsionalnoy revolyutsii* [Stalin. Herald of National Revolution]. Moscow: "Eksmo."

Dobrynin, Anatoli (1995). *In Confidence: Moscow's Ambassador to America's Six Cold War Presidents*. New York: Times Books.

Dolgorukov, Pavel D. (2007). *Velikaya razrukha. Vospominaniya osnovatelya partii kadet. 1916–1926* [The Great Wreck. Memoirs of the Kadet Party Founder, 1916–1926]. Moscow: Tsentrolitgraf.

Druzenko, A. (1994). "Oktyabr, Oktyabr, perevorotnyi mesyats. Ob odnom iz 'istoricheskikh' Plenumov TsK, sluzhivshikhsya 30 let nazad, s Radey Nikitichnoy Adzhubey beseduyet Anatoly Druzenko" [October, October, a Month of Turning Points. Anatoli Druzenko Talks with Rada Nikitichna Adzhubey about One of the "Historic" Central Committee Plenums]. *Izvestiya*, October 13.

Ellman, Michael, and Vladimir Kontorovich, eds. (1998). *The Destruction of the Soviet*

Economic System. An Insiders' History. Armonk, NY: M. E. Sharpe.

Figes, Orlando (1997). *A People's Tragedy: The Russian Revolution, 1891–1924.* New York: Viking.

Ford, Robert A. D. (1989). *Our Man in Moscow: A Diplomat's Reflections on the Soviet Union.* Toronto: University of Toronto.

Gaddis, John Lewis (2005). *The Cold War: A New History.* New York: Penguin.

Gazur, Edward P. (2001). *Secret Assignment: The FBI's KGB General.* London: St. Ermin's.

Geifman, Anna, ed. (1999). *Russia under the Last Tsar: Opposition and Subversion 1894–1917.* Oxford: Blackwell.

Glezin, Eduard (2007). "Yanvarskaya vesna. Perestroika yest glasnost plyus demokratizatsiya vsyei strany" [Springtime in January. Perestroika Is Openness Plus Democratization of the Whole Country]. *Izvestiya,* April 28.

Golovachev, V. (1990). "What Is to Be Done About Prices?" Interview with USSR Finance Minister V. Pavlov. *Trud,* July 26 (FBIS-SOV-90-149).

Goltsev, A. (1964). *Kommunist,* No. 14.

Gorbachev, Mikhail (1996). *Memoirs.* Foreword by Martin McCauley. New York: Doubleday.

Got'e, Yuri (1988). *Time of Troubles: The Diary of Iurii Vladimirovich Got'e. Moscow. July 8, 1917 to July 23, 1922.* Trans., ed. and introduced by Terence Emmons. Princeton, NJ: Princeton University Press.

Gromyko, A. A. (1989). "Karibskiy krizis. O glasnosti teper i skrytnosti togda" [The Caribbean Crisis. Openness Now and Concealment Then]. *Izvestiya,* April 15.

Gusev, O. (1989). "General Strokach protiv Lavrentiya Berii" [General Strokach versus Lavrenty Beria]. *Sovetskaya kultura,* February 7.

Hosking, Geoffrey (1993). *The First Socialist Society: A History of the Soviet Union From Within.* Cambridge, MA: Harvard University Press.

Hughes, Michael (1997). *Inside the Enigma. British Officials in Russia, 1900–1939.* London: Hambledon.

Hutchings, Robert L. (1997). *American Diplomacy and the End of the Cold War: An Insider's Account of U.S. Policy in Europe, 1989–1992.* Baltimore: Woodrow Wilson Center and Johns Hopkins.

Ike, Nobutaka (1967). *Japan's Decision for War: Records of the 1941 Policy Conferences.* Trans., ed., and introduced by Nobutaka Ike. Stanford: Stanford University Press.

Jackson, Robert H. (2003). *That Man: An Insider's Portrait of Franklin D. Roosevelt.* Ed. and introduced by John Q. Barrett. Foreword by William E. Leuchtenburg. New York: Oxford University Press.

Karaulov, Andrey (1989). "Excerpts from Recent Interview with Petro Shelest, Former Member of the CPSU CC Presidium and First Secretary of the Ukrainian CP CC." *Moscow News,* September 10 (FBIS-SOV-89-178).

Karyakin, Yuri (1988). "'Zhdanovskaya zhidkost,' ili protiv ochernitelstva" [The "Zhdanov Liquid" Or Against Slander]. *Ogonyok,* No. 19.

Keep, John L. H. (1995). *Last of the Empires: A History of the Soviet Union 1945–1991.* New York: Oxford University Press.

Khrushchev, Nikita. *Memoirs of Nikita Khrushchev. Commissar* (2004). Vol. 1. Ed. Sergei Khrushchev. Trans. George Shriver. Supplementary material trans. Stephen Shenfield. University Park, PA: Pennsylvania State University Press.

_____. *Memoirs of Nikita Khrushchev. Reformer* (2006). Vol. 2. Ed. Sergei Khrushchev. Trans. George Shriver. Supplementary material trans. Stephen Shenfield. University Park, PA: Pennsylvania State University Press.

_____. *Memoirs of Nikita Khrushchev. Statesman* (2007). Vol. 3. Ed. Sergei Khrushchev. Trans. George Shriver. Supplementary material trans. Stephen Shenfield. University Park, PA: Pennsylvania State University Press.Khrushchev, Sergey (1988). "Pensioner of All-Union Importance." *Ogonyok,* No. 40 (October 1–8), No. 41 (October 8–15), No. 42 (October 15–22), and No. 43 (October 22–29) (FBIS-SOV-8-236, 237, 238 and 240).

Kosyrev, Dmitri (1995). "... i primkhnuvshiy k nim Shepilov" [... and Shepilov Who Joined Them]. *Rossiyskaya gazata,* September 1.

Krementsov, Nikolai (1997). *Stalinist Science.* Princeton, NJ: Princeton University Press.

"Kto stoyal za spinoy ubiytsy Kirova?" [Who Stood Behind Kirov's Murderer?]. *Rossiyskaya gazeta,* October 27, 1995.

Kutuzov, V. A. (1989). "Tak nazyvayemoye 'Leningradskoye delo" [The So-Called "Leningrad Case"]. *Voprosy istorii KPSS,* No. 3.

Lemeshev, M. (1964). *Ekonomicheskaya gazeta,* September 26.

Lewin, Moshe (2005). *The Soviet Century.* Ed. Gregory Elliott. New York: Verso.

Ligachev, Ye. K. (1993). *Inside Gorbachev's Kremlin: The Memoirs of Yegor Ligachev.* Introduction by Stephen F. Cohen. Trans. Catherine A. Fitzpatrick, Michele A. Berdy and Dobrochna Dyrcz-Freeman. New York: Pantheon.

Lin, Lars T., Oleg V. Naumov, and Oleg V. Khlevniuk (1995). *Stalin's Letters to Molotov, 1925–1936.* New Haven and London: Yale University Press.

Lukin, I., and Ye. Ukhov (1989). "Bronzovye mify" [Bronze Myths]. *Trud,* April 5.

Lukyanov, Anatoli (1999). *V vodovorote rossiyskoy smuty. (Razmyshleniya, dialog, dokumenty)* [In the Maelstrom of the Russian Troubles. (Reflections, Dialogues and Documents)]. Moscow: "Kniga i Biznes."

Lynev, R. (1988). "Ot ottepeli do zastoya. Beseda s personal'nym pensionerom, byvshim chlenom Politbyuro Ts KPSS" [From Thaw to Stagnation. Talk with Special Pensioner, Former Member of the CPSU CC Politburo (G. I. Voronov)]. *Izvestiya,* November 18.

Martirosyan, Arsen B. (2007). *Stalin posle voyny, 1945–1953 gody* [Stalin After the War, 1945–1953]. Moscow: "Veche."

Mayers, David (1995). *The Ambassadors and America's Soviet Policy.* New York: Oxford University Press.

McCauley, Mary (1976). *Khrushchev and the Development of Soviet Agriculture: The Virgin Lands Programme 1954–1964.* London: Macmillan.

McNamara, Robert S., with Brian VanDeMark (1995). *In Retrospect: The Tragedy and Lessons of Vietnam.* New York: Times Books.

Medvedev, Roy (1983). *All Stalin's Men.* Trans. Harold Shukman. New York: Anchor Press/Doubleday.

_____. (1988). "L. I. Brezhnev: Nabrosok politicheskogo portreta" [L. I. Brezhnev: Sketch for a Political Portrait]. *Rabochiy klass i sovremennyy mir,* No. 6.

_____. (2006). *Nikita Khrushchev.* Moscow: "Eksmo."

Medvedev, Roy, and Giuletto Chiesa (1989). *Time of Change: An Insider's View of Russia's Transformation.* Trans. Michael Moore. New York: Pantheon.

Medvedev, Roy, and Zhores Medvedev (2004). *The Unknown Stalin. His Life, Death and Legacy.* Trans. Ellen Dahrendorf. New York: Overlook Press.

Micunovic, Veliko (1980). *Moscow Diary.* Trans. David Floyd. Introduced by George Kennan. New York: Doubleday.

Mikoyan, Anastas I. (1999). *Tak bylo. Razmyshleniya o menuvshem* [So It Was. Reflections about the Past]. Moscow: Vagrius.

Mikoyan, Sergo (1989). "Politicheskoye dolgoletiye" [Political Longevity]. *Knizhnoye obozreniye,* No. 1, January 6.

Molotov. Malenkov. Kaganovich. 1957. Stenogramma iyunskogo plenuma TsK KPSS i drugiye dokumenty [Molotov. Malenkov. Kaganovich. 1957. Minutes of the June Plenum CC CPSU and Other Documents]. Moscow: "Demokratiya," 1998.

Naumov, Leonid A. (2007). *Stalin i NKVD* [Stalin and the NKVD]. Moscow: "Eksmo."

Nicolaevsky, Boris (1965). *Power and the Soviet Elite: "The Letter of an Old Bolshevik" and Other Essays.* Ed. Janet D. Zagoria. New York: Praeger.

Novikov, V. N. (1989). "V gody rukovodstva N. S. Khrushcheva" [In the Years of N. S. Khrushchev's Leadership]. *Voprosy istorii,* Nos. 1 and 2.

Onikov, Leon A. (1996). *KPSS: anatomiya raspada. Vzglyad iznutri apparata TsK* [CPSU: Anatomy of Collapse. View from Inside the Central Committee Machinery]. Moscow: "Respublika."

Osipov, Aleksei (1990). *Krakh administrativno-komandnoy sistemy* [Crash of the Administrative-Command System]. Moscow: "Znaniye."

Pechenev, V. (1990). "Tretya Programma KPSS: uroki nedavney istorii. Iz vospominaniy byvshego pomoshchnika Generalnogo sekretarya TsK KPSS" [Third CPSU Program: Lessons of Recent History. From the Reminiscences of a Former Assistant of the CC CPSU General Secretary]. *Ogonyok*, No. 23.

_____. (1991). *Gorbachev: k vershinam vlasti. Iz teoretiko-memornykh razmyshlenii* [Gorbachev: To the Heights of Power. Reflections of a Theoretical and Memoir Character]. Moscow: Vagrius.

Pikhoya, Rudolf G. (1995). "O vnutripoliticheskoy bor'be v sovetskom rukovodstve. 1945–1958" [Internal Political Struggle in Soviet Leadership. 1945–1958]. *Novaya i noveyshaya istoriya*, No. 6.

_____. (1995). "Ternistyi put' k ottepeli" [Winding Path to the Thaw]. *Argumenty i fakty*, No. 46 (787) (November).

_____. (1996). "Bomba pod diktaturu proletariata: Kak TsK KPSS sozdaval politicheskuyu oppozitsiyu samami sebe" [A Bomb Under the Dictatorship of the Proletariat: How the CPSU CC Created a Political Opposition Against Itself]. *Rossiyskaya gazeta*, March 15.

_____. (1996). "Kak gotovilsya 'sekretnyy doklad': Neizvestnye fakty iz taynogo arkhiva Politbyuro TsK KPSS" [How the "Secret Report" Was Prepared. Unknown Facts from the Secret Archive of the CPSU CC]. *Rossiyskiye vesti*, February 21.

_____. (2007). *Moskva. Kreml. Vlast. Dve istorii odnoy strany. Rossiya na izlome tysyacheletiy, 1985–2005* [Moscow. Kremlin. Power. Two Histories of One Country. Russia at the Turn of a Century, 1985–2005). Moscow: Rus-Olimp, AST, Astrel.

Pipes, Richard (1990). *Russia Under the Old Regime*. Harmondsworth: Penguin.

_____. (1993). *Russia Under the Bolshevik Regime*. New York: Knopf.

Pisarenko, Konstantin A. (2006). *Tridtsatiletnyaya voyna v politbyuro, 1923–1953* [The Thirty-Year War at the Politburo, 1923–1953]. Moscow: "Veche."

Plenum TsK KPSS (1965). *24–26 marta 1965 goda, Stenograficheskii otchyot*. Moscow: Politizdat.

Pleshakkov, Leonid (1989). "Appointed Ambassador...." Interview with Nikolay Grigoryevich Yegorychev. *Ogonyok*, No. 6 (February 4–11) (JPRS-UPA-89-023).

Plutnik, Albert (1995). "Lichnyy perevodchik Stalina" [Stalin's Personal Translator]. *Izvestiya*, September 22.

Ponomarev, Anatoli (1990). *N. S. Khrushchev: Put' k Liderstvu* [N. S. Khrushchev: The Path to Highest Leadership]. Moscow: "Znaniye."

_____. (1995). "Intrigi i repressii po pravilam igry" [Intrigues and Repressions According to Rules of the Game]. *Rossiyskaya gazeta*, July 29.

Prezidium TsK KPSS (2004). *1954–1964. Osnovnye protokolnye zapisi zasedaniy. Stenogrammy. Postanovleniya. T. 1: Chernoviye protokolnye zapisi. Stenogrammy/Gl. REd. A. A. Fursenko — 2-e isp. i dop* [CC CPSU Presidium. 1954–1964. Rough Notes of the Sessions, Minutes, Decrees, Vol. 1: Rough Notes. Stenographic Records. Editor-in-chief A. A. Fursenko — 2nd ed., corrected and supplemented]. Moscow: Rosspen.

_____. (2006). *Tom 2. Postanovleniya. 1954–1958. Glavnyy redaktor A. A. Fursenko* [Vol. 2. Decrees. 1954–1958. Editor-in-chief A. A. Fursenko]. Moscow: Rosspen.

_____. (2008). *Tom 3. Postanovleniya 1959–1964. Glavnyy redaktor A. A. Fursenko* [Vol. 3. Decrees. 1959–1964. Editor-in-chief A. A. Fursenko]. Moscow: Rosspen.

Primakov, Yevgeni (2004). *Russian Crossroads: Toward the New Millennium*. Trans. Felix Rosenthal. New Haven and London: Yale University Press.

Rodionov, P. A. (1989). "Kak nachinalsya zastoy?: Zametki istorika partii" [How Did the Stagnation Begin? Notes of a Party Historian]. *Znamya*, No. 8.

Romanenko, V., and A. Binev (1990). "An Unknown Prime Minister." Interview with Academician D. Gvishiani. *Argumenty i fakty*, No. 46 (FBIS-SOV-90-227).

Rush, Myron (1958). *The Rise of Khrushchev*. Washington, DC: Public Affairs Press.

Satter, David (2001). *Age of Delirium: The Decline and Fall of the Soviet Union*. New Haven: Yale University Press.

Semichastny, V. Ye. (1989). Interview with
Argumenty i fakty, No. 20, May 20–26
(FBIS-SOV- 89-100).

Serebryakova, Zarya (1996). "Ottepel,
zamorozki, ottepel ..." [Thaw, Frost, Thaw].
Nezavisimaya gazeta, February 24.

Shakhnazarov, Georgi (2001). *S vozhdyami i
bez nikh* [With the Leaders and Without
Them]. Moscow: Vagrius.

Shatunovskaya, Olga (1990). "Vospominaniya starogo veterana: Falsifikatsiya"
[Recollections of an Old Veteran:
Falsification]. *Argumenty i fakty*, No. 22
(503) (June 2–8).

Shepilov, Dmitri (2001). *Neprimknuvshiy*
[Who Did Not Join Them]. Moscow: Vagrius, 2001.

Shlomin, V. (1995). "'Delo' voyennykh
moryakov" [The Naval Sailors' "Case"].
Rossiyskaya gazeta, July 15.

Starkov, Boris (1993). "Koye-chto novenkoye
o Berii" [Something New about Beria].
Argumenty i fakty, No. 46 (683) (November).

*Stenogramma VII zakrytogo plenuma Tsen-
tral'nogo Komiteta KP Latvii ot 7–8 iyulya
1959 goda* [Transcript of the 7th Closed
Plenum of the Central Committee CP
Latvia, July 7–8, 1959]. *Kommunist sovetskoy Latvii*, No. 2 (1989).

*Stenogrammy zasedaniy Politbyuro TsK RKP
(b)-VKP (b). 1923–1939 gg. V trekh tomakh*
[Stenograms of the TsK RKP (b)-VKP (b)
Politburo Meetings. 1923–1938. In Three
Volumes]. Advisory Board: K. M. Ander-
son, P. Gregory, O. V. Khlevniuk, A. K.
Sorokin, R. Sousa, and A. Yu. Vatlin.
Moscow: Rosspen, 2007.

Stickle, D. M., ed. (1992). *The Beria Affair:
The Secret Transcripts of the Meetings Sig-
nalling the End of Stalinism*. Trans. Jeanne
Farrow. Commack, NY: Nova Science.

Sudoplatov, Pavel, and Anatoli Sudoplatov
(1994). *Special Tasks: The Memoirs of an
Unwanted Witness, A Soviet Spymaster*.
Boston: Little, Brown.

Trotsky, Leon (1936). *The Revolution Betrayed: What Is the Soviet Union and Where
Is It Going?* Trans. Max Eastman. Tran-
scribed for the Internet by Zodiac. Available at www.marxists.org/archive/trot-
sky/1936/revbet/index.htm.

Troyanovsky, Oleg (1997). *Cherez gody i
rasstoyaniya. Istoriya odnoi semi* [Across
Time and Space. The Story of One Fam-
ily]. Moscow: Vagrius.

Tsereteli, Irakli (2007). *Krizis vlasti. Vospominaniya lidera menshevikov, deputata II Go-
sudarstvennoy dumy. 1917–1918* [Crisis of
Power. Reminiscences of the Menshevik
leader and Second Duma Deputy]. Moscow: Tsentrolitgraf.

*V Politbyuro TsK KPSS. Po zapisyam Anatoliya
Chernyayeva, Vadima Medvedeva, Georgiya
Shakhnazarova (1985–1991). Sost. A.
Chernyayeva (ruk proyekta). A. Veber, V.
Medvedeva. Izdaniye 2-e, ispravleniye i
dopolnennoye* [At the CPSU Central Com-
mittee Politburo. Based on the Notes of
Anatoli Chernyayev, Vadim Medvedev
and Georgi Shakhnazarov (1985–1991).
Compilers A. Chernyayev (Project Leader),
A. Veber, V. Medvedev. Second Edition.
Revised and Supplemented]. Moscow:
Gorbachev-Fond, 2008.

Vasilenkov, P. T. (1967). *Organy sovetskogo gosudarstva i ikh sistema na sovremennom
etape*. Moscow: Politizdat.

Vinnikova, L. (1993). "'Spetsparttyurma'"
[The Special Party Prison]. *Argumenty i
fakty*, No. 20 (657) (May).

Virabov, I. (1989). "Zemlyak" [Fellow Vil-
lager]. *Komsomolskaya pravda*, February 17.

Volkogonov, Dmitri (1991). *Stalin: Triumph
and Tragedy*. Ed. and trans. Harold Shukman. New York: Grove Weidenfeld.

_____. (1994). *Lenin: A New Biography*.
Trans. and ed. Harold Shukman. New
York: Free Press.

_____. (1996). *Trotsky: The Eternal Revolu-
tionary*. Trans. Harold Shukman. New
York: Free Press.

Volkov, S. V. (2007). "Kakiye lyudi pravili
SSSR?" [What Kind of People Ruled the
USSR?]. Available at www.contr-tv.ru.

Voronkov, Vladimir (1995). "Nachalo:
Pol'skiye sobytiya 1980 goda skvoz' okna
moskovskoy Staroy ploshchadi" [The Be-
ginning. Polish Events of 1980 through the
Windows of Moscow's Old Square].
Izvestiya, August 26.

Voronov, G. I. (1988). "Nemnogo vospominaniy" [A Few Recollections]. *Druzhba
narodov*, No. 1.

Voslensky, Mikhail (1984). *Nomenklatura: The Soviet Ruling Class*. Preface by Milovan Djilas. Trans. Eric Mosbacher. London: Bodley Head.

Vyzhutovich, Valeri (1990). "Sudba idei: O tom, chto oznachayet 'sotsialisticheskiy vybor' v teorii i na praktike" [Fate of an Idea: What the "Socialist Choice" Means in Theory and Practice]. Interview with Dr. of Philosophical Sciences Aleksandr Tsipko. *Moskovskiye novosti*, No. 24 (June 17).

Wallace, Donald Mackenzie (1961). *Russia on the Eve of War and Revolution*. New York: Vintage.

Weiner, Amir (2001). *Making Sense of War: The Second World War and the Fate of the Bolshevik Revolution*. Princeton, NJ: Princeton University Press.

Yakovlev, Aleksandr N. (2002). *A Century of Violence in Soviet Russia*. Foreword by Paul Hollander. Trans. Anthony Austin. New Haven and London: Yale University Press.

Yeltsin, Boris (1990). *Against the Grain: An Autobiography*. Trans. Michael Glenny. New York: Summit.

Yemelyanov, Yuri (2007). *Stalin: Put k vlasti* [Stalin: The Road to Power]. Moscow: "Veche."

Yevseyev, Aleksandr (1990). "Look with Open Eyes...." Report on Interview with Arkady Volsky, USSR People's Deputy. *Nedelya*, No. 36 (September 3–9) (FBIS-SOV-90-196).

Zamyatina, T. (1993). "So mnoy sovetovalis chetyre genseka" [Four General Secretaries Consulted Me]. *Argumenty i fakty*, No. 20 (657) (May).

Zhirnov, Yevegni. "Desyat 'zheleznykh' narkomov" (Ten "Iron" People's Commissars), *Komsomolskaya pravda* (Moscow), September 29, 1989.

Zhukov, Yuri (1994). "Kremlevskiye tayny: Stalina otstranili ot vlasti v 1951 godu?" [Kremlin Secrets: Was Stalin Disempowered in 1951?]. *Nezavisimaya gazeta*, December 21.

_____. (2003). *Inoy Stalin. Politicheskiye reformy v SSSR v 1933–1937* [A Different Stalin. Political Reforms in the USSR in 1933–1937]. Moscow: Vagrius.

_____. (2005). *Stalin: tayny vlasti* [Stalin: Secrets of Power]. Moscow: Vagrius.

Zubkova, Yelena (1998). *Russia After the War: Hopes, Illusions, and Disappointments, 1945–1957*. Trans. and ed. Hugh Ragsdale. New York: M. E. Sharpe.

Index

239